INTRO
TO F
TERRORISM

INTRODUCTION TO POLITICAL TERRORISM

Leonard Weinberg
University of Nevada, Reno

Paul Davis
University of Nevada, Reno

McGRAW-HILL PUBLISHING COMPANY

New York St. Louis San Francisco Auckland Bogotá Caracas Hamburg
Lisbon London Madrid Mexico Milan Montreal New Delhi Oklahoma City
Paris San Juan São Paulo Singapore Sydney Tokyo Toronto

This book was set in Times Roman by the College Composition Unit.
The editors were James D. Anker and James R. Belser;
the production supervisor was Phil Galea.
The cover was designed by John Hite.
R. R. Donnelley & Sons Company was printer and binder.

INTRODUCTION TO POLITICAL TERRORISM

1 2 3 4 5 6 7 8 9 0   DOC DOC   8 9 4 3 2 1 0 9

ISBN 0-07-068996-2

Library of Congress Cataloging-in-Publication Data

Weinberg, Leonard B.
    Introduction to political terrorism.
    Includes index.
    1. Terrorism. I. Davis, Paul B., (date).
II. Title.
HV6431.W438 1989 363.3'2   88-27213
ISBN 0-07-068996-2

ABOUT
THE AUTHORS

LEONARD WEINBERG is a professor of political science at the University of Nevada, Reno. He is the author of *After Mussolini: Italian Neo-Fascism and the Nature of Fascism* (1979), and coauthor of *The Rise and Fall of Italian Terrorism* (1987), and *Comparing Public Policies* (1977). His articles have appeared in a number of professional journals, including *Terrorism* and *The British Journal of Political Science*. In addition, he has been a Fulbright senior research fellow at the University of Florence and is a member of the Committee on Political Sociology of the International Political Science Association.

PAUL DAVIS received his Ph.D in political science from the University of Utah in 1978. He has taught at various universities and colleges for the past seventeen years. He is currently an associate professor at Truckee Meadows Community College in addition to teaching at the University of Nevada, Reno.

For Herman Rappaport (1912–1988),
a man who loved books and hated violence.

Rebecca Davis

CONTENTS

PREFACE

For almost two decades political terrorism has been a major source of concern for many people in the United States and elsewhere. Among other things, its manifestations have caused scholars, journalists, and government officials to investigate its causes, forms, and consequences. One product of their investigations has been a vast body of literature devoted to various aspects of the terrorist problem. Much of this writing, published in academic journals, scholarly monographs, and government reports, is not easily accessible to university students or others with an interest in the subject. The purpose of *Introduction to Political Terrorism* is to summarize this writing in such a way as to provide students with a clear understanding of contemporary terrorism and the techniques that have been employed to limit its incidence and defeat its practitioners.

A long list of people provided indispensable assistance in the completion of this work. Among those who deserve special mention are James Anker (our editor at McGraw-Hill) and the following reviewers he persuaded to scrutinize the manuscript: Jonathan R. Adelman, University of Denver; Donald Bell, Tufts University; Yaroslav Bilinsky, University of Delaware; Caroline Dinegar, University of New Haven; John Finn, Wesleyan University; George V. Kacewicz, California State University—Long Beach; Andrej Korbonski, University of California—Los Angeles; Vojtech Mastny, Boston University; Peter Merkl, University of California—Santa Barbara; Mark J. Miller, University of Delaware; Vittorfranco Pisano, Defense Intelligence College; David Rapoport, University of California—Los Angeles; Leonas Sabaliunas, Eastern

Michigan University; and Robert A. Wood, North Dakota State University. At the University of Nevada, Reno, we would like to express our appreciation to Michael Richardson, Marilyn Woosley, Gwendi Tecklenburg, Timothy Haller, and the staff at the Getchell Library.

Leonard Weinberg

Paul Davis

INTRODUCTION TO POLITICAL TERRORISM

CHAPTER 1

INTRODUCTION

October 3, 1968—Argentina—A local guard at the U.S. Atoms-in-Action exhibit in Buenos Aires surprises two men placing an object in the USIA exhibit structure. The two flee, and as the guard picks up the object, it explodes and burns his hands, also tearing a large hole in the roof of the structure housing the exhibits.

January 22, 1969—Soviet Union—A lone gunman attempts to assassinate four cosmonauts and Leonid Brezhnev in Moscow by firing shots into their motorcade en route to a Kremlin celebration.

March 19, 1970—Turkey—Turkish students throw three Molotov cocktails at three foreign-owned buildings, causing slight damage.

July 28, 1971—Italy—A male PFLP* member gives a Western woman who believed she was his girlfriend booby-trapped luggage to take on board an El Al plane flying from Rome to Lod Airport. Israeli security men prevent the plot from succeeding.

July 22, 1972—Northern Ireland—On Bloody Friday, twenty-two bombs explode in Belfast in the space of eighty minutes, killing eleven people and wounding 130. The IRA claims credit.

August 29, 1973—Japan—The U.S. embassy annex in Tokyo, which houses the defense attaché office and other embassy facilities, is slightly damaged by a Molotov cocktail. No injuries are reported.

*Popular Front for the Liberation of Palestine.

December 1, 1974—India—A Swissair DC8 flying from Bombay to Karachi is hijacked by Mohammad Aslam, 24, who points a gun at the crew and demands to be flown to Libya or Lebanon. Shortly after the aircraft lands at Karachi to refuel, Aslam is overpowered by the crew and taken into custody.

July 1975—Netherlands—Several Moluccans are given prison sentences of up to five years for plotting to kidnap Queen Juliana and members of her royal family.

April 1976—Lebanon—Radical Palestinian guerrillas are believed responsible for emptying the safe deposit vaults in major Beirut banks, the Banco di Roma and the Bank Misr-Liban.

April 24, 1977—Israel—A bomb explodes on board a bus on its way to Beersheba, injuring twenty-eight, ripping out seats, and smashing windows. Arab passengers going to their jobs who had left the bus ten minutes earlier are suspected in the bombing.

February 13, 1978—Italy—Italian health officials ban the sale of grapefruit in Milan and Bergamo after an Israeli-imported grapefruit in Bergamo is found to be poisoned with mercury. Later, tainted grapefruit is found in Milan.

December 18, 1979—Philippines—Jeremy Ladd Cross, 40, of Lawrence, Massachusetts, a U.S. businessman, is shot in the neck by two men on motorcycles. He and his Filipino wife were leaving their offices in suburban Pasay City.

1980—El Salvador—Roman Catholic Archbishop Oscar Arnulfo Romero is assassinated by a right-wing sniper. Within an hour thirty bombs explode throughout the country. Romero's funeral is interrupted by explosions and gunfire, leaving twenty-six dead.

1981—Thailand—An Indonesian Garunda Airlines jet is hijacked by Jihad Command. Indonesian commandos storm the plane, killing four hijackers.

1982—Turkey—Airport attack in Ankara by the Armenian Secret Army for Liberation of Armenia leaves eight dead.

1983—Lebanon—Islamic Jihad bomb kills 241 U.S. servicemen in suicide mission against Marine barracks. Two minutes later, a bomb kills fifty-eight at nearby French barracks.

1984—Great Britain—The Grand Hotel in Brighton is bombed during the Conservative party convention by the Provisional IRA, killing four, including one member of Parliament. Prime Minister Thatcher escapes injury.

1985—Atlantic Ocean—An Air India jet crashes, killing 329. Sikh extremists are suspected of planting the bomb.

April 5, 1986—West Germany—A bomb wrecks a West Berlin disco full of U.S. troops. Killed: a U.S. serviceman and a Turkish woman.

Wounded: 204, including fifty Americans. Anti-American Arab Liberation Front and West German groups claim responsibility. Evidence implicates Libya.[1]

What do the events just described have in common? Obviously they are all acts of violence, or at least attacks on people or property in which the threat to kill, injure, or destroy is present, if not always carried out. But is there anything else that would lead us to attach a common label to these events? For anyone who watches television or reads the newspapers, the answer to this question is once again apparent. These events are ones to which the term "terrorism" has been applied.

Clearly not all acts of violence or even attacks intended to achieve some political goal should be considered acts of terrorism. The invasion of Normandy by the Western Allies during the Second World War and the Russian Revolution during the First World War involved the massive use of violence and were intended to achieve political purposes: the defeat of the Nazi and czarist regimes. But these events, although they were widely publicized by the mass media and many people were no doubt scared by their occurrence, are rarely thought to be acts of terrorism. What is it then about the first set of events that justifies the label of terrorism and serves to distinguish those events from the Normandy landing and the Russian Revolution?

A DEFINITION

Arriving at a generally accepted definition of terrorism is not an easy task. In fact, one recent study has reported the existence of more than 100 separate definitions whose use has been proposed by different analysts over the years.[2] How is this overabundance of meanings to be explained? Part of the problem surely has to do with the fact the word is a politically charged one. There are few, if any, groups or nations these days who want the label used to characterize their own behavior, because to apply the term is usually sufficient to condemn those whose actions are being scrutinized. Is terrorism then simply a word used by spokespersons for American and other Western nations to condemn their violent domestic opponents, for example, the Provisional IRA (Irish Republican Army) in Northern Ireland, or certain Third World countries, such as Libya and Iran, whose policies have brought them into conflict with their own? What should we make of the counterclaims made by these "terrorist" groups and nations to the effect that they are not the perpetrators but the victims of economic or political terrorism initiated by their "imperialist" or "fascist" accusers?

The word also has taken on an accordianlike quality. Often advocates for governments whose legitimacy has been challenged, such as in South

Africa, have expanded its meaning to apply to nearly all forms of organized protest as a means of discrediting their opponents. On the other
hand, advocates of "national liberation" or revolutionary change frequently wish to squeeze the word terrorism out of our vocabulary: its use
apparently makes them feel uncomfortable. As one such advocate put it:
"'terrorism' as a word is absurd and meaningless on its face except as a
calculated element of propaganda. The word is used by unscrupulous
governments that want people to accept as their personal enemy someone the state has defined as its enemy."[3]

To raise such issues is to point out the current political climate, the
war of words, within which the effort to define the phenomenon must
take place. If we wish to use the word terrorism not as a means to curse
our opponents but as a way to help us study an important form of conflict
in the world, there are available three approaches to defining it.

First, we may treat the term historically, and determine its original us-
age. If we do this we discover that the word was applied first to describe
the behavior of the Jacobins during the French Revolution, in particular
during the years (1793–1794) of Robespierre's ascendancy.[4] Both supporters and enemies of the Jacobins used it to characterize a period, the
Reign of Terror, during which suspected opponents of the revolution
were hunted down and executed, to the apparent glee of the Paris mobs.
All this seems far removed from the events described at the beginning of
this chapter. Nevertheless, there are some things to be learned by viewing terrorism from an etymological perspective. Specifically, the measures pursued by the French revolutionaries had the effect of creating
widespread fear and uncertainty among large numbers of people beyond
the immediate victims of this purge, a fear that they might be next. This
fear was heightened no doubt by the fact that certain segments of the
population—monarchists, would-be émigrés, the nobility—were likely to
fall under suspicion irrespective of whether they supported, opposed, or
remained detached from the revolutionary upheaval. Also, the Jacobins
were a largely self-selected faction of revolutionaries who saw themselves as meeting the authentic revolutionary aspirations of the French
people by acting against those who conspired against them. Using violence to stimulate fear and anxiety among enemies, defined on the basis
of membership in some general category in the population, by a small
group acting in the name of the people and worried that powerful forces
were conspiring against them—these elements present in the Reign of
Terror are ones which shed considerable light on the nature of modern
terrorism.

A second way to define terrorism is by denotation, by simply citing
instances or examples of the phenomenon with which we are concerned.

This approach has been widely used by national governments and international organizations in the present era when they have wanted to impose criminal sanctions or cite certain types of violence and often politically motivated behavior. Particularly at the United Nations and other international bodies when representatives of Western, communist, and Third World nations cannot agree on a definition of the word, the tendency has been to abandon the effort and simply seek to outlaw particular violent acts, without reference to the term.[5] Thus, the skyjacking of commercial airliners and the taking hostage of diplomatic personnel (internationally protected persons) have been criminalized under international law. We can also use this denotative approach, with some benefit, in our attempt to define terrorism. Acts to which the word has been applied include the following: bombings, assassinations, kidnappings and hostage taking, robberies, piracy, and skyjacking. These are all acts that are committed by single individuals or small groups of people. They are also acts that the penal laws of most nations treat, if such acts are committed for reasons of private gain or personal vengeance, as crimes. For example, an important American politician of the 1930s, Louisiana Senator Huey Long, was assassinated in 1935 by an individual who held a personal grudge against him. We do not ordinarily think of this murder as an act of terrorism because his killer did not claim that opposition to Long's politics provided the motive for the deed. On the other hand, when other prominent political leaders, Prime Minister Margaret Thatcher of Great Britain or Italy's former prime minister Aldo Moro, were the victims of either successful or unsuccessful assassination attempts, we refer to these as acts of terrorism. Why? The answer in these and other cases concerns the motivations of those perpetrating the crimes: personal vengeance in the Long case, political for Thatcher's and Moro's attackers. By approaching a definition of terrorism denotatively, through the compilation of a list of acts which seem to fall into a common category, we learn that such acts are almost always acts of criminal violence committed in order to achieve a political purpose.

We may of course abandon our effort to define terrorism at this point, satisfied that we have accomplished our task. Indeed, some writers have maintained that to go any further is hopeless. They have argued that terrorism has taken so many diverse forms, has occurred in so many different social and historical contexts, that any attempt to define it connotatively, by identifying its essential attributes, is a fruitless undertaking.[6] They reason that, like pornography, terrorism is something you simply recognize when you see it. But this view, if accepted, takes us back to the starting point. After all, what is a work of pornography for some has socially redeemable value for others. Or, in other words, one person's terrorist is another person's freedom fighter. Must we throw up our hands and abandon the attempt to stipulate a connotative definition with this dubious proposition?

No; in fact, our effort to define terrorism by noting instances or examples of it provides us with considerable help. The events cited had in common the fact that they were all politically motivated crimes. The only ingredient missing from a connotative definition is the psychological component. The third element that the events described at the beginning of this chapter had in common was that they were all intended to evoke a response in some audience which was wider than that immediately involved in the events. The objective of harming immediate victims, e.g., passersby in a public square or vacation-bound passengers in a railroad station, is subordinate to the purpose of sending a message to some broader target population. Whether or not the act produces the desired effects and what these effects are likely to be are matters that remain to be discussed, but this at least is the aim of those who have committed an act of terrorism. In short, terrorism is politically motivated crime intended to modify the behavior of a target audience.

WHAT TERRORISM IS NOT

Terrorism is not an ideology but a strategy which may be used by individuals, groups, or states for different purposes. It is a strategy, however, that is often confused with other violent political measures, most commonly with guerrilla warfare and various types of state-initiated violence, for example, genocide. Let us see if we can distinguish terrorism from other forms of political violence.

Groups and individuals who use terrorism often refer to themselves as guerrillas, or urban guerrillas, who are waging war against some state or political regime. It is true that terrorism and guerrilla warfare have things in common. As opposed to conventional forms of armed conflict between large standing armies, both terrorism and guerrilla warfare rely on unconventional means with which to attack their opponents. Nevertheless, there are some very striking differences between the two approaches.[7] Guerrilla war, such as that Fidel Castro waged with such success in Cuba during the 1950s, is basically rural in character, with the guerrilla fighters establishing bases in inaccessible locations, such as jungles or mountains, far from major cities and the bastions of state power. Guerrillas typically begin by conducting small-scale hit-and-run operations against vulnerable outposts of state authority, such as local government buildings or small police or military detachments. When government forces counterattack, the guerrillas retreat. The conflict is essentially one between the insurgent guerrillas and the government fought in remote locales. The struggles of the communist New People's Army active in the Philippines today may serve as an example.

Particularly in the early phase of hostilities, guerrilla organizations may attack or kill noncombatants, such as government tax collectors or wealthy landlords, as a means of bringing their cause to the attention of the local population and to show the government's vulnerability. In fact, some analysts have maintained that terrorism represents an initial step in guerrilla insurgencies or internal wars, one to be ascended as the prospects for success improve.[8] Guerrilla organizations aspire to liberate progressively wider areas of a country from government control and in the process form an alternative source of political authority which then serves as a countergovernment in these zones. At the end of this road, if their operations succeed, the guerrillas will recruit and organize a conventional-looking army which, in turn, will seize power when it marches into the country's capital city, as happened not only in Cuba in 1959 but in China, Vietnam, and Cambodia as well.

The strategy of insurgent terrorist groups differs from that of guerrillas waging warfare in a number of ways. First, terrorist bands make a distinction between combatants and noncombatants but in a way precisely the opposite of the way guerrilla organizations define their targets. While the guerrilla organizations wage war against weakly deployed government forces, and either by design or by accident inflict some civilian casualties along the way, terrorist groups usually avoid attacking their armed opponents, preferring instead to commit acts of violence against unarmed civilians.

Indeed, this is what gives terrorism its shock value. Setting off a bomb in a crowded department store, taking hostage children in an elementary school: these are acts which usually generate much publicity. They also call attention to a second way in which the strategy of terrorism differs from that of guerrilla warfare; specifically, terrorism usually is an urban phenomenon, one involving operations in big cities or major metropolitan areas. Its manifestations tend to occur in urban settings—on crowded buses, in public buildings, cafés, and restaurants—where we do not expect to encounter violence. Correlatively, the victims of terrorist attacks usually are not the sort of people—schoolchildren, shoppers, airline passengers—we normally expect to be the objects of politically motivated assaults.

Also, an act of terrorism is not, as is sometimes believed, the same as the assassination of individual political figures or the sabotage of public or private property. Both of these violent activities may be undertaken for terrorist purposes, for example, when the person or property attacked has some broader symbolic meaning for a wider audience, but this need not always be the case. In many instances the object of attack is both victim and target. Thus, terrorists may explode a bomb in front of an airline office in the hope of deterring prospective passengers from flying to or from a particular nation. Saboteurs, on the other hand, may blow up a bridge or railroad line in order to prevent their enemies from resupplying their forces at a remote location. In the latter case, the violence is not terrorism because it is not used to convey a message. Similarly, a commercial airliner may be skyjacked by individuals seeking to escape from one nation by having its pilot fly it to another. But another airliner may be taken over by individuals who demand that newspapers publish their political manifesto in exchange for the lives of its passengers. The latter is an act of terrorism, while the former is not. Or, as one analyst has remarked: "The nature of terrorism is not inherent in the violent act itself. One and the same act...can be terrorist or not, depending on intention and circumstance."[9]

REGIME TERROR

In distinguishing terrorism from guerrilla warfare and other types of politically inspired violence we have focused, of necessity, on terrorism as practiced by groups contending with or in opposition to some state authority. But states themselves may pursue a strategy of terrorism against their own nationals. All states, by definition, seek to exert some degree of control over the inhabitants of territories within their borders. Not uncommonly they will employ coercive means to achieve this end. Yet not all types of state coercion or force constitute terrorism. States have a wide range of coercive strategies available to them. These range from punishing individual lawbreakers, deviants, or troublemakers, variously defined, to the extermination of large segments of the population within their control, as exemplified by the recent attempt at genocide committed against the Cambodian people by the Pol Pot regime. These are certainly instances of state violence but not state terrorism. State or regime terrorism occurs when the violence is used instrumentally, to call attention, that is, when its purpose is to modify the behavior of those not immediately the victims of attack. Thus certain Central American states will sometimes carry out reprisals against noncombatants (e.g., by executing every nth person) in areas they believe to be places of support for their opponents.[10] When states engage in such practices, they are seeking to send messages to others concerning the consequences of aiding their enemies. When they engage in acts of reprisal or related types of audience-attracting violence, states are practicing terrorism. Or, as Adolf Hitler put it:

> I shall spread terror through the surprising application of all means. The sudden shock of a terrible fear of death is what matters. Why should I deal oth-

erwise with all my political opponents? These so-called atrocities save me hundreds of thousands of individual actions against the protestors and discontents. Each one of them will think twice when he learns what is awaiting him.[11]

There is a special problem in considering certain acts of state violence as falling within the definition of terrorism. Since part of our definition included the stipulation of criminal behavior, the question arises: Can acts committed in the name of a state be considered crimes? After all, the judgment of what is or is not a crime is ordinarily determined by the state.

There are several ways of responding to this problem. First, we may accept the premise that the state is the ultimate source of law. But we may also note that government authorities are perfectly capable of violating the law. Thus, during much of the Stalinist era in the Soviet Union capital punishment was formally prohibited by the Russian penal code. Yet this legal provision did not restrain Stalin's secret police from executing many Soviet citizens. Second, agents of a state may circumvent the law by forming covert "death squads" which then proceed to carry out terrorist operations in contexts where the courts or other legal institutions are powerless to prevent them. The recent histories of Argentina and Guatemala offer examples of this type of criminal conduct.

Alternatively, we may reject the premise that the state is the exclusive determinant of law. If we define terrorism as politically motivated crimes committed to achieve a psychological impact on some audience, then governments are all too capable of performing such deeds, whether or not these deeds are recognized as crimes under the domestic law of the state in whose name they are committed. Finally, in thinking about state or regime terrorism we should not assume that all states are necessarily unified entities. To be sure, in some cases the rulers of a state may unleash a campaign of terror against some segment of its population. Yet, in other cases such campaigns may be waged by certain state institutions, such as the secret police, local government authorities, or elements within the military, without the knowledge or consent of a country's nominal rulers.

PURPOSES AND TACTICS

When passengers standing in front of an airport check-in counter in Rome are gunned down or when Christmas shoppers at a London department store are killed or injured as the result of a bomb explosion, it seems natural to refer to these individuals as the victims of senseless violence. Terrorism appears irrational often because its perpetrators seem to have carried out attacks on people so removed from whatever political dispute prompted their violence that it is unlikely to advance their cause. It seems equally implausible that the victims had any particular interest in retarding the cause of the terrorists. Terrorism seems senseless because conventional notions of cause and effect, guilt and innocence, are broken down.

But, as has been stressed, the immediate victims are not the ultimate targets of terrorist operations. The sense behind the violence rests in its impact on the audience that witnesses it. In this regard, one obvious purpose of terrorism is to terrify. Compared with the normal fear that accompanies the awareness that one is confronted by some clear danger, the condition of being terrified refers to a far more general state of anxiety or foreboding: the feeling of dread that anything can happen at any time or place and that there is little one can do to reduce the threat. It is not always clear how and when or even if terrorists succeed in inducing a sense of terror in their audience; other responses are apparently more common. What *is* clear is that there are political advantages to be gained from stimulating this reaction.

Yet, even if its targets do not suffer some uncontrollable sense of anxiety, terrorist violence can have other consequences and be put to other uses. For one, it can play a role in advertising a cause. The nineteenth-century anarchist Kropotkin referred to terrorism as "propaganda of the deed." It is a way of calling attention to a problem or grievance in a far more dramatic way than the distribution of handbills and pamphlets.

Another purpose for which terrorism has been used is that of provocation. By committing particularly horrifying acts of violence, terrorists oftentimes hope to provoke their enemies into carrying out indiscriminate reprisals against a segment of the population believed to sympathize with their cause. When this happens, the terrorists believe the very brutality of the reaction will transform the passive or indifferent into active supporters of their objectives who will come to view the enemy in the same light as the terrorists. Related to this purpose, although conceived more broadly, terrorist activities often are intended to disrupt and disorient opponents and undermine the support they may receive from the population.

Terrorist violence may bring some benefit to its practitioners in other ways as well. It can raise their morale along with that of whatever group in whose name they claim to be acting by disclosing the vulnerability of their enemies. Or, if the victims belong to some disliked group, e.g., foreign businesspeople, a successful terrorist attack may arouse admiration for their deed among the general population. Accordingly, some terrorist groups in Latin America acquired the reputation of being modern-day Robin Hoods by holding the wealthy for ransom and distributing some of the proceeds to the poor.

Terrorism also plays a role in sustaining the group that is responsible for the violence. The killing or maiming of dissidents may serve as a warning to other members of the band concerning the potential consequences of betrayal. Robbing a bank or obtaining ransom in exchange for the freedom of hostages not only attracts attention, it also provides the terrorist group with money to maintain itself. And, well-publicized acts of terrorism may serve to win the group new recruits who find its exploits exciting or its goals noble.[12]

Whatever their purposes, contemporary terrorists have relied on a limited number of means with which to achieve them. According to one estimate 95 percent of all terrorist incidents have involved just six tactics.[13] The repertoire includes assassinations, bombings, kidnappings, barricade and hostage situations, and hijackings. Because of advances in technology, the detonation of a bomb is the easiest task for terrorists to accomplish. Correspondingly, it is also the most frequent type of terrorist-caused event. While acts of air piracy and the seizure of prominent political leaders or other well-known individuals may attract greater attention or cause more disruption, such acts also require greater skill in their execution and pose greater danger to their perpetrators.

As this observation suggests, acts of terrorism exhibit variation in terms of their complexity. Some are relatively simple one-step events, such as shooting a victim from a safe distance or leaving a time bomb in a crowded market. Others involve more complicated operations. Such terrorist acts as skyjacking an airliner or kidnapping individuals and holding them hostage for some time are actions involving two or more stages. As a general rule, a good measure of a terrorist group's capacities is its ability to carry out relatively complicated operations either by moving from one location to another or by extending action over time, or both. Terrorist groups that are able to bring off such multistep attacks typically have more elaborate organizational networks and greater logistical support than those that are only capable of a simple assault.

Terrorist attacks also display variation in the nature of their immediate targets or victims. A fundamental distinction is between attacks on property or people. In regard to the life cycle of such terrorist bands as the West German Red Army Faction and the Italian Red Brigades, it is common for such groups to begin their operations by launching attacks on property, for example, the nocturnal bombing of public buildings or setting fire to parked automobiles, while being relatively careful to avoid harming people. But over time, and for reasons that may be related to the group's growing isolation from the outside world, their violence often escalates into deliberate attacks on human targets.

Furthermore, if people are the victims, there is also variation in the degree of selectivity involved. Some terrorist attacks are directed against specific individuals whose assassination or kidnapping has some symbolic meaning for the terrorists and their audience. Other events are ones in which the victims, either single individuals or groups, belong to a segment of society for which the terrorists feel indiscriminate hostility. And finally, some terrorist attacks are carried out on a random basis, directed against individuals who happen to be in the wrong place at the wrong time when the bomb goes off.

VARIETIES OF TERRORISM

Terrorist activity takes on a variety of different forms. One commonly used distinction is between "terrorism from below" and "terrorism from above," or, in other words, the terrorism of private groups and that of states.[14] However, there are some obvious problems with using this distinction for the analysis of contemporary terrorism. It is not uncommon these days for certain states to provide assistance to private terrorist groups active in other countries as a means to weaken or destabilize their political regimes. Accusations of this state sponsorship of terrorist groups have been directed recently at Iran, Libya, Syria, North Korea, and the Soviet Union, among others. Is this terrorism from below or above? Except in cases where a state can be shown to have sent its own agents abroad to commit terrorist attacks, as in the instance of a North Korean team of assassins which killed several South Korean officials in Burma some years ago, we prefer to regard the phenomenon as a form of terrorism from below. The private terrorist groups receiving assistance usually have lives of their own with goals and objectives distinct from those of the foreign governments which are sponsoring or secretly promoting their operations.

The use of insurgent or terrorism-from-below groups as surrogates for governments that wish to undermine other regimes seems a different form of activity than the terrorism states inflict on their own populations, situations where the state typically has its entire police and military apparatus at its disposal to carry out these violent operations.

A second widely used distinction in analyzing terrorism is that between its domestic and international varieties. Domestic terrorism refers to situations in which all the relevant participants—terrorist groups, victims, and audience—are to be found in the same country. During the 1970s the Italian Red Brigades committed its acts of violence in Italy against other Italians to win support of an audience of working-class Italians for the cause of revolution against the Italian state. In this case we are dealing with a manifestation of domestic terrorism.

International terrorism, on the other hand, refers to situations where there is some national mix in the terrorist group, its victims, the intended audience, and the location of its activities. Thus, recently Italian territory has been the site of terrorist violence perpetrated by groups from the Middle East against American and Israeli targets, ones located on Italian soil or aboard Italian ships and planes. When this kind of national mix is present, we are dealing with instances of international terrorism.

GOALS

Still another way by which terrorism is often classified is by reference to the ultimate goals or aims of the perpetrating groups.[15] As we have mentioned, terrorism is a violent technique, one which may be used by groups or states pursuing diverse objectives.

Today when the word terrorism is used, it is commonly linked to groups whose aims are revolutionary in the sense they wish to bring about a radical redistribution of wealth, power, and status in a society. Such groups usually profess a commitment to Marxism, variously defined, and seek to bring about an end to capitalism and the advent of a dictatorship of the proletariat. The revolutionary goal is intended to bring an end to the exploitation of one segment of society, the working class, and achieve its redemption by pushing that society to a new and more equitable stage of development.

The rhetoric of such groups as the Tupamaros in Uruguay, the Montoneros in Argentina, the Red Brigades and Front Line in Italy, and the Red Army Faction in West Germany are illustrative of these aims. But it also makes some sense to distinguish among such terrorist groups on the basis of their conceptions of revolution. For some the goal has been revolution within one country, while for others, such as the German Red Army Faction and the Japanese Red Army, revolution is conceived in global terms to mean the elimination of Western imperialism in general, and their operations are intended to bring an end to worldwide domination of multinational corporations and related forms of capitalist exploitation.

Terrorism also has been used by groups pursuing ethnic-separatist or nationalist aims. Their objectives are not revolutionary in the sense discussed above, but instead involve the formation of an independent nation out of a region which is currently part of another. It may sometimes involve the desire to replace the control exercised by one state over a territory with that of another. For example, the long-term goal of the Provisional IRA in Northern Ireland is to detach that regional division from the control of Great Britain and reunite it with the Republic of Ireland. Or, the goal of the ETA (Euzkadi Ta Askatasuna) organization in Spain is that of detaching the Basque region from the control of Madrid and the formation of a separate independent Basque nation-state.

It is not uncommon for terrorist groups whose aims are ethnic and/or separatist to justify their behavior in terms of the revolutionary rhetoric of Marxism-Leninism, as has been the case with the Ustasha, a group using terrorist means to create a separate state for Croatia, which is presently a region of Yugoslavia. Yet during the 1930s the same organization, pursuing the same goal, employed the ideology of fascism to rationalize its actions. Although the doctrines are different, the ethnic-separatist goal has remained the same; we should not allow ourselves to confuse the rhetoric of proletarian revolution in this and other cases with the ethnic-separatist reality.

In our time terrorism also has been used by groups which are not seeking to change the status quo but to preserve it, or, frequently, by groups seeking to restore some condition their adherents believe existed in the past. This variety of reactionary terrorism has been employed in the United States by such groups as the Ku Klux Klan and, recently, by affiliates of the Aryan Nations movement as a means to restore white Anglo-Saxon domination of American life. It has been employed by various Protestant groups in Northern Ireland to prevent that region from falling under the control of the Catholic-dominated Republic of Ireland. Neo-fascist and neo-Nazi bands in Italy and West Germany have directed terrorist attacks against "Reds" or foreign guest workers on behalf of analogous objectives. And "death squads" in Latin America have conducted campaigns of terror to inhibit the development of trade union organizations and the initiation of land reform measures.

The kinds of goals of terrorist groups we have identified to this point have in common the fact they are wide in scope, ones aimed at promoting or thwarting far-reaching domestic and international changes. But the strategy of terrorism also may be used in the pursuit of less far-reaching goals. Sometimes single policy issues may spark groups to terrorist activity. Illustratively, the United States recently has been the site of a wave of bombings of abortion clinics. The aim of those bands responsible for the attacks is not revolutionary, ethnic-separatist, or reactionary but simply that of deterring others from either providing or using the services offered by such clinics. Obviously not all public policy issues are likely to evoke terrorist reactions. Those issues that do would seem to engage fundamental religious or ethical concerns.

In discussing the variety of aims to which the strategy of terrorism may be put we have focused on the goals of private groups. But these aims are not necessarily the same as those of states or political regimes that inflict terrorism on their own populations. There appear to be two distinctive goals associated with state terrorism: repression and mobilization. Incumbent political regimes have used terrorism as a means of repressing elements in their populations they view as a threat, real or imagined, to the continuation of their rule. In our time, military regimes in Latin America, Sub-Saharan Africa, and the Middle East have used terrorism to achieve this purpose. It is a common goal of state terrorism.

From time to time, however, regimes have employed terror not to repress dissent but to mobilize support and stimulate effort on behalf of their goals. The industrial development of the Soviet Union in the 1930s under Stalin occurred against a background of such terror. Workers and others could be made to work long hours for very little pay in an atmosphere of fear when some of those who did not meet production quotas or other standards would have to face the violent consequences. The Great Proletarian Cultural Revolution in China under Mao's leadership involved the application of terrorist measures, particularly among members of the state and party apparatus, as a means of mobilizing the revolutionary zeal of millions of Chinese.

The reader should be warned against assuming that the motivation for achieving the ultimate goals of terrorist groups or regimes is necessarily identical to the motivation of individuals who join a terrorist band or commit terrorist acts on behalf of a state. The desire for revenge, the acquisition of money, the enhancement of status, the allure of action are motives, among others, that may come into play (they will be discussed in Chapter 4).

UNANSWERED QUESTIONS

At this point we have developed some understanding of what terrorism is and how it differs from other types of political violence. By now we are also aware of its various purposes, tactics, and goals. But this understanding still leaves us with a list of vital unanswered questions about the phenomenon. Those questions of paramount importance are: Is terrorism a totally new form of violence whose growth is related to the development of modern means of mass communication? Or is terrorism an old strategy with a long history behind it whose impact has been magnified by recent technological advances? What events took place around the world in the period between 1965 and 1970 that seem to have sparked the outbreak of terrorism with which we have become too familiar? How serious a threat is terrorism? Has it caused massive numbers of deaths and injuries? Governments to collapse? And national populations to tremble in fear? Does it work? Do terrorists get what they want?

These are tantalizing questions, but there are still others that are equally intriguing. What sorts of people become terrorists? Where do they come from? Are they mentally ill? If terrorism is a political virus, as some have argued, how does it spread? Is it by conspiracy or some other type of contagion? What are terrorist groups like? Are they small bands whose members are constantly on the run, or are they complex groups comparable to other political organizations? How have the victims of terrorist attacks reacted to the experience of being taken hostage and having their lives threatened? What have governments done to combat the terrorist threat? Is there a serious possibility that terrorist groups might acquire weapons of mass destruction?

The purpose of the remainder of this book is to provide answers to the questions just posed. The task is not an easy one. Despite an enormous volume of study and analysis of terrorism, there are still obvious gaps in our understanding of it as well as unresolved disputes among its observers over the meaning of what is known. Nevertheless, enough is known to make us feel optimistic about our ability to offer readers sensible answers.

Before assuming this responsibility, though, a final word is necessary. The succeeding chapters are concerned with what has been called terrorism from below, with private groups that have used terrorist violence to challenge or defend those in power. There will be commentary on the role of states in supporting terrorist groups, usually outside their own borders. But the role of states in waging open terrorist campaigns against their own populations will not be examined in any detail. The story of terrorism from above is sufficiently different as to require a separate volume in which to tell it. The job at hand is difficult enough.

KEY TERMS

guerrilla war	reactionary terrorism
insurgent terrorism	state terrorism
international terrorism	terrorism
nationalist-separatist terrorism	

NOTES

1 These descriptions of events were taken from Edward Mickolus, *Transnational Terrorism: A Chronology of Events 1968–1979* (Westport, Conn.: Greenwood Press, 1980), and National Foreign Assessment Center, *Patterns of International Terrorism: 1980*, PA81-10163U (June 1981); see also U.S. Department of State, *Patterns of International Terrorism: 1981* (July 1982), *Patterns of International Terrorism: 1982* (September 1983), *Patterns of Global Terrorism: 1983* (September 1984), *Patterns of Global Terrorism: 1985* (October 1986), *Patterns of Global Terrorism: 1986* (January 1988); *The Christian Science Monitor* (May 16, 1986), p. 11.

2 Alex Schmid, *Political Terrorism: A Research Guide to Concepts, Theories, Data Bases and Literature* (New Brunswick, N.J.: Transaction Books, 1983), pp. 119–152.

3 The remark is quoted by Kathleen O'Toole in her report of a symposium on terrorism held at Stanford University; see "Talking Terrorism," *Campus Report* (Feb. 10, 1988), p.11.

4 See, for example, Andre Maurois, *A History of France* (New York: Minerva Press, 1968), pp. 305–321.

5 Abraham Sofaer, "Terrorism and the Law," *Foreign Affairs* (Spring 1986), pp. 901–922.

6 Walter Laqueur, *Terrorism* (Boston: Little, Brown and Company, 1977), p. 5.

7 On the history of guerrilla warfare see Walter Laqueur, *Guerrilla: A Historical and Critical Study* (Boston: Little, Brown and Company, 1976).

8 Brian Crozier, *The Rebels* (Boston: Beacon Press, 1960) pp. 159–191; Thomas Thornton, "Terror as a Weapon of Political Agitation," in Harry Eckstein (ed.), *Internal War* (New York: The Free Press, 1964), pp. 92–95.

9 Schmid, op. cit., p. 101.

10 H. E. Vanden, "State Policy and the Cult of Terror in Central America," in Paul Wilkinson and Alisdair Stewart (eds.), *Contemporary Research on Terrorism* (Aberdeen: Aberdeen University Press, 1987), pp. 256–269.

11 Quoted in Ted Gurr, "The Role of the State in Political Violence" (a paper prepared for presentation at the World Congress of the International Political Science Association, Paris, July 1986).

12 On the purposes of terrorism see Schmid, op. cit., pp. 96–99; Thornton, op. cit., pp. 82–86; and Martha Crenshaw Hutchinson, *Revolutionary Terrorism* (Stanford, Ca.: Hoover Institution Press, 1978), pp. 18–39.

13 Brian Jenkins, *International Terrorism: The Other World War* (Santa Monica, Ca.: The Rand Corporation, 1985), p. 12.

14 Frederick Hacker, *Crusaders, Criminals, Crazies* (New York: W. W. Norton & Company, Inc., 1976), pp. 3–34.

15 For one example of this approach, see Paul Wilkinson, *Political Terrorism* (London: Macmillan & Co., Ltd., 1974), pp. 32–44.

CHAPTER 2

A SHORT HISTORY OF
POLITICAL TERRORISM

Murder carried out for political motives is hardly a new phenomenon in human history. The practice is almost as old as the historical record itself. It would be hard for someone growing up in the United States or any other Western nation for that matter to avoid hearing or reading about these events. The plays of Shakespeare (*Macbeth, Julius Caesar, Richard III*), the Old Testament, and the histories of Greece, Rome, and England abound with such tales.[1]

In general, these political murders have taken a very limited number of forms. The most obvious one is the slaying of a ruler; the assassinations of the Roman emperors Caesar and Caligula and the American President Lincoln come to mind. But there are also many cases in which the tables are turned and rulers have ordered the killing of some of their erstwhile advisers. For example, in 1170 A.D. Thomas à Becket, the Archbishop of Canterbury, was slain at the behest of Henry II ("What disloyal cowards do I have in my court, that not one will free me of this lowborn priest?") over a dispute involving the role of the church in his kingdom. There also have been many instances when conflicts over which individual or noble family should rule were resolved by a rival or group of rivals killing their opponents. The history of Italy during the Renaissance, Florence in particular, provides abundant illustrations.

But should these political murders also be considered as acts of terrorism? They certainly bear some resemblance. The motivation for the violence was political. The acts themselves were committed not on fields of battle, but in places—the Roman Forum, Canterbury Cathedral, Ford's Theater—where violence was not expected to occur and against individuals unprepared for its expression. Yet, those often legendary instances of political murder were not manifestations of terrorism. A crucial element was missing.

Terrorism, as we argued in the introduction, has an additional psychological component not present in these cases of political murder. There is the intent to use the violence to modify the behavior of some audience which is missing. The political murders we have mentioned were committed to achieve a direct political end, not, additionally, as a means to influence the outlook of relevant others. If political terrorism is identified with the latter, does it follow that its origins are quite recent, that to occur it requires the existence of modern means of mass communication by which the terrorists can make propaganda by deed?

The answer is no. Groups engaged in political terrorism were present long before the mass media transformed their sponsors and leaders into international celebrities. But, like much of the terrorism practiced in the Middle East during the 1980s, for example, the Party of God (Hizbollah) in Lebanon, the early outbreaks were inspired by a mix of religious and political motives. The audience with which these early terrorists sought to communicate included not only other individuals in their surroundings but also, and indispensably, God.

THE RELIGIOUS ORIGINS

The instances of this early form of political-sacred terrorism cited most frequently in the professional literature are drawn from Jewish and Muslim histories.[2] More specifically, the discussions focus on the roles of the Zealots in provoking the Jewish revolt against Rome (66–70 A.D.) and the Assassins, a sect from the Shiite tradition, which waged a campaign aimed at the purification of Islam for almost two centuries (1090–1275 A.D.). Although mentioned less often, the other major monotheistic religion, Christianity, also gave rise to extremist sects toward the end of the Middle Ages and, later, during the Reformation which pursued their goals by means of terrorism. Some commentary about these episodes may help us understand certain enduring features of terrorist logic.

The following quotation from the work of the Roman-Jewish historian Josephus captures some sense of the Zealots' modus operandi:

> The Sicarri committed murders in broad daylight in the heart of Jerusalem. The Holy days were their special seasons when they could mingle with the crowd carrying short daggers concealed under their clothing with which they stabbed their enemies. Thus, when they fell, the murderers joined in cries of indignation, and through this plausible behavior, were never discovered. The

first assassinated was Jonathan, the high-priest. After his death there were numerous daily murders. The panic created was more alarming than the calamity
itself; everyone, as on the battlefield, hourly expected death. Men kept watch
at a distance on their enemies and would not trust even their friends when they
approached.[3]

The message the Zealots (Sicarri was the name of their weapons)
wished to communicate to their fellow Jews was that all those moderates
who sought an accommodation with the Romans would meet the same
fate as befell those who had been killed. Not only were Jewish moderates
murdered, the Zealots also conducted provocative terrorist attacks
against Judea's Greek inhabitants and on the Roman rulers themselves.
The overall design was to eliminate dissent within the Jewish population
by terrorizing opponents into silence or acceptance and to provoke
Greeks and Romans into carrying out indiscriminate reprisals against
Jews, thus inflaming Jewish popular opinion and making war both justifiable and inevitable.

By using terrorist means the Zealots succeeded in provoking the conflict they had wanted, but the consequences of it, so far as the Jewish
population was concerned, proved disastrous. Thousands were killed;
Jerusalem was sacked and the Second Temple destroyed. A remnant of
Zealots fled and took refuge on top of Masada near the Dead Sea, where
they committed mass suicide in 73 A.D. rather than surrender to the Romans besieging them.[4] The memory of the Zealots' struggle and martyrdom lived on. Their exploits later served to stimulate additional rebel-
lions against Roman rule, ones whose outcomes proved even more
calamitous.

What led the Zealots to behave as they did? Did they believe Judea
could really defeat the forces of Rome? The answer has to do not with
the temporal balance of power but with the sacred audience to which
their terrorism was partially addressed. The Zealots lived during a period
in which there was widespread expectation, at least in Judea, that the arrival of a Messiah was imminent. They believed these turbulent last times
would be followed by the establishment of the Kingdom of God on earth.
The Messiah would arrive and deliverance would be forthcoming if they,
the Zealots, purified Judea and were themselves uncompromising in their
devotion to their goals. In short, members of this sect believed that their
terrorist activities would produce divine intervention and thereby lead to
Rome's defeat.

The Zealots were not the only religious sect to use terrorism in what
the historian Norman Cohn has referred to as the pursuit of the millennium. The Assassins (literally, from the Arabic derivation of the word,
hashish eaters), including the Fidayeen (rightly guided ones) of medieval
Islam, represent another such group.[5] Their origins are to be found in a

division among followers of the Shiite tradition and in particular with the formation of a sect known as the Ismalis. Followers of this group, centered in what is present-day Iran and Syria, believed in the need for a purification of the Muslim community in order to hasten the arrival of the Imam or Mahdi, "the heir of the Prophet, the Chosen of God, and the sole rightful leader of mankind," who would establish a new and just society.[6]

Outnumbered by the standing armies of Muslim rulers, the Ismalis' leaders sought to achieve their ends by unconventional means. Capturing strongholds in remote locales, they used these bases to stage protracted campaigns of terror against religious and political leaders of the dominant Sunni tradition. The latter had, in the Ismalis' judgment, usurped the leadership of Islam and then thoroughly corrupted its meaning and practice.

One example of the tactics used by the Assassins is contained in the following observation:

> A medieval Persian historian tells us the story of a certain theologian, one Fakhr al-Din, who used to write polemics attacking the Assassins. One evening he was sitting at his desk and writing. Suddenly from nowhere a man appeared before him and said, "My master has sent me to ask, Why do you attack us." The theologian said, "Of course, because you are in error." The man produced a knife, dug it into the desk, and said, "This could easily have been you." The theologian admitted this was so. Said the emissary of Assassin chief, "If you continue to write against us, the next time it *will* be you. However, if you change your views"—here he produced a bag of gold from under his cloak—"then this will be offered to you." At this point, says the chronicler, the theologian in question modified his views and began to write more favorably about the Assassins. When he was asked by a colleague why he had changed his attitude, he answered, "They have arguments that are both weighty and penetrating."[7]

Their tactics usually were much less amusing. Acting as instruments of God, the Assassins trained Fidayeen to seek the employ and confidence of their Sunni rivals. At unguarded moments the Assassin, using a short dagger, would then stab his enemy to death. Rather than flee, the Assassin would calmly await capture and execution. For his martyrdom, the Ismalis had promised the killer admission to paradise, a temporal replica of which was used as part of the Assassin's preparation.

Eventually the Ismalis strongholds were overrun by invading Arab and Turkish armies and the terrorist operations were brought to an end. Although the terrorism of the Zealots and the Assassins both were addressed to a sacred audience and required stealth in implementation, there were some differences. In the Zealot case, the terror was directed at both Jews and Gentiles, while for the Assassins it was restricted to other Muslims. Further, the Zealots sought to hide after their murders had been committed, while the Assassins did not and would have been considered themselves dishonored had they attempted to escape capture. Self-sacrifice was part of their ritual.

At least one of the circumstances surrounding sacred terrorism in the Christian tradition differed from its Jewish and Muslim variants. The sects involved made little effort to cloak themselves in secrecy, but carried out their operations in an open manner. Yet in many other aspects the similarities are impressive.

The first manifestations of terrorism intended to usher in the Christian millennium occurred on the European continent toward the end of the Middle Ages.[8] At the time of the Crusades, an era of periodic famines and epidemics, the belief, derived from the Book of Revelation, was widespread that Europeans were living through the last days. Before the advent of the millennium and the Second Coming of Christ, the world would have to be purged of its corruption and the ungodly punished for their sins.

In this context, from the end of the eleventh through the fourteenth century, there appeared in various parts of western and central Europe various "prophets." Claiming to be the reincarnations of long-dead kings or saints, the pseudo Baldwin or pseudo Frederick II, for example, these prophets announced that they had returned to purify Christendom. Often their messages were so persuasive that they were able to form itinerant bands of followers. The latter would move from community to community proclaiming the prophets' messages and, not uncommonly, also seek to carry them out. Accordingly, Jews, the most visible and close-at-hand symbols of ungodliness for these sects, were terrorized for the edification of the local town dwellers. Tortured, threatened, often given a choice of conversion or death, and sometimes massacred outright, the elimination of the Jews was defined as a precondition for the coming of Christ's reign on earth.

This sort of violence often was threatened and applied to other segments of the population as well. Bishops and other members of the church hierarchy became targets, as did the wealthy and high-born, all accused of avarice and other types of sinfulness.

The forces of change unleashed by the Reformation of the sixteenth century also provided the context in which some Protestant sects sought to fulfill their millennial yearnings by terrorist means.[9] The atmosphere was such that, later, groups such as the Fifth Monarchists in England came to believe that the execution of Charles I would be followed by the advent of King Jesus. It was in Germany and the Netherlands, however, that this sort of emotion produced terrorist violence. The targets were both Catholics and Lutherans. The Anabaptists, who were responsible for much of this violence, regarded themselves as the elect of God and defined Catholics and Lutherans as embodiments of the anti-Christ whose elimination was necessary before the millennium could begin. "Christ will give the sword and revenge to them, the Anabaptists, to punish all sins, stamp out all governments, communize all property and slay those who do not permit themselves to be rebaptized."[10] Accordingly, Anabaptist lay preachers and their followers proclaimed the city of Munster to be the new Jerusalem and waged a campaign of terror against its heretical inhabitants in order to establish God's kingdom before their efforts were repressed by the authorities.

Later, in the seventeenth century terrorism inspired by messianic visions spread to France. In Cévennes, Languedoc, and elsewhere, "prophets" from the Huguenot (Calvinist) community encouraged their followers in rebellion against the Catholic monarchy of Louis XIV. As part of this uprising, Catholics and those Protestants unwilling to participate in the violence became the targets of terrorist attacks. Women, children, entire families were murdered, and indeed whole villages were destroyed by those seeking to eliminate the ungodly, satanic forces that opposed them. The French military, using exceptionally brutal means, eventually put an end to the rebellion.[11]

So far in this commentary we have identified the earliest manifestations of terrorism with a particular type of extreme religious belief held, at different times, by dissident sects in Jewish, Muslim, and Christian traditions. Their terrorist activities, directed at both human and divine audiences, were intended to change and transcend history and make possible a perfect human condition of peace and harmony. But the purposes of these groups, though religiously inspired, were not exclusively religious in effect. Unlike the Thugs, a Hindu sect in India, that secretly murdered thousands of other Hindus as part of its ritual, the groups on which we have focused had to achieve political goals before their religious ones could be realized. In particular, secular rulers and "ungodly" segments of the population had to be terrorized into accepting the sect's viewpoint through the killing of selected members of the profane category. Furthermore, those under attack were not uncommonly dominant elites (religious, political, social) in their societies whose possession of wealth, power, and status were linked to the corruption of the temporal world. In short, we are dealing with attempts to modify the political order in the name of an ultimately religious purpose.

Another element in these groups' behavior which requires emphasis is the subjective outlook of their members. For not only did they often appear to see themselves as doing something for the world, they were also simultaneously doing something for themselves. By committing homicides for altruistic reasons, members of these sects also seem to have believed they were demonstrating their own proximity to God.[12]

TERRORISM FOR THE PEOPLE

It was as the result of the French Revolution that terrorism lost its sacred quality. As with so much about the modern world, the events following 1789 in France had profound consequences in the development of political terrorism as we have come to know it in our time.

As we observed in the introduction, the term "terror" was used originally to describe a violent episode, from the fall of 1793 to the summer of 1794, during this revolutionary upheaval.[13] Following the execution of Louis XVI, the Jacobins, led by Robespierre and the Committee of Public Safety, unleashed the process to which the term Reign of Terror has been applied. More than 12,000 French citizens lost their lives because they were suspected, however vaguely, of opposition to the new revolutionary regime in Paris. Before Robespierre was brought down, Jacobin agents all over France sought to protect the goals of the revolution by spreading panic through violence among segments of the population—would-be émigrés, nobles, clergy—suspected of plotting against these goals or merely harboring such sentiments in their minds.

We should bear in mind, however, that the French Reign of Terror was a policy carried out by a state, one authorized by the National Convention, not pursued by a sect or private group. Further, its objective was to protect a revolution already under way, not initiate one. For these reasons, the period during which terror reigned in France does not represent the first modern manifestation of the type of violence identified in the introduction as terrorism from below. Nonetheless, certain characteristics of the French revolutionary experience were to become exceedingly important in the development of this brand of terrorism.

First, much like the religiously motivated terrorism of earlier times, there is the vision of the world being made over. The violence would purge the corrupt and make possible the advent of a new age in which the hated old ways would have no place. Illustratively, the French revolutionaries even sought to establish a new way of telling the passage of time by creating a new calendar, one which ignored the earlier Christian-based one.

Second, if the revolution or the Reign of Terror were not made in the name of God, in whose name were they made? The answer, one with enduring effects, was the people. In the century following the events in France, revolution against the prevailing political order often was justified by its proponents in the name of the people, the masses, or the proletariat. Like God for the sacred terrorists, the people's will came to be viewed as transcendent, and one which would-be revolutionaries believed they were able to discern. Interestingly, the name of the first modern terrorist group was the People's Will (Narodnaya Volya in Russian).

This was true of many but not all nineteenth-century revolutionaries. The slogan of the French Revolution had been "Liberty, Equality, Fraternity." Each of these words formed the basis for separable types of revolutionary hopes during the nineteenth century.[14] Those revolutions attempted in the name of liberty were ones whose purpose was the establishment of republican government and representative institutions. Revolution in the name of fraternity reflected the desire for a national community, a people, to expel a foreign occupier and achieve national independence. Revolutions pursued on behalf of equality found their justification in opposition to major disparities in wealth and the private ownership of economic enterprises.

For revolutionaries who wished to make revolutions on the basis of equality (socialist, communist, anarchist) and fraternity (nationalist, anti-imperialist), the people, the masses, or the working class became a transcendent force, a substitute for God, in whose name everything became justifiable. Illustratively, James Billington quotes the Polish nationalist poet Adam Mickiewicz as referring to his homeland (in 1842) as the "Christ among nations.... He contended that a messianic mission had been imparted to three peoples: the ancient Israelites, the French and now the Slavs.... Mickiewicz regarded Poland's destruction twice in one life-time as a sacrificial offering for the sins of others, necessary to save the peoples of the world."[15]

And Raymond Aron has this to say about the idea of revolution in the name of equality:

> In Marxist eschaetology, the Proletariat is cast in the role of collective savior. The expressions used by the young Marx leave one in no doubt as to the Judeo-Christian origins of the myth of the class elected through suffering for the redemption of humanity. The mission of the proletariat, the end of prehistory thanks to the Revolution.... it is easy to recognize the source of these ideas: the Messiah, the break with the past, the Kingdom of God.[16]

Revolutionary sentiment stimulated by republican principles (liberty) was less likely to incorporate a view of the people as a quasi-sacred object; instead those holding the sentiment were more likely to see society as composed of individuals with individual rights to assert, or of regional or religious groups whose interests needed representation.

Another outgrowth of the French Revolution which needs mention is the array of secret revolutionary societies that emerged in Europe in its aftermath. After Napoleon was finally defeated in 1814 and the Congress of Vienna had restored the old royal houses he had toppled, a number of secret groups were formed (modeled initially after Babeuf's Conspiracy of Equals in France) whose members were committed to keeping alive the principles identified with the French Revolution. Societies such as the Carbonari and the League of the Just sprang up in various parts of Europe in order to provide a milieu in which the prospects for revolution could be discussed.

A final effect of the French Revolution on the development of modern terrorism was the model it provided for all those later nineteenth-century revolutionaries who hoped their societies could be transformed in analogous fashion. This model was based on a largely spontaneous mass uprising sparked by a crisis in the incumbent political regime. Before 1871 revolutionary groups throughout Europe continued to believe that revolutions would follow the French pattern: "A political crisis would inspire popular insurrection. Barricades would be thrown up in the capitals, and revolutionaries would seize public buildings and proclaim the Republic....little thought was given to organizing the masses ahead of time."[17]

It was out of disappointment with the failure of events to follow this model that modern terrorism, terrorism from below, emerged during the last third of the nineteenth century. There were several reasons for this disappointment. Despite popular uprisings in 1830 and 1848 in various countries, revolutionary changes were not forthcoming. Russia remained an autocracy under the czars; France became an empire under Napoleon III; monarchy prevailed in Germany; Italy was unified at least formally but under the leadership of the House of Savoy. After an abbreviated expression of fervor, the masses did not persist, as revolutionary intellectuals wanted and expected, in their enthusiasm for change. In spite of those who dreamed of a working-class–based revolution, the proletariat did not seem to share the dream. Even the popular rising of the Paris Commune in 1871, in the wake of the Franco-Prussian War, proved disheartening. The episode displayed how little poorly equipped urban masses could do in the face of a professionally trained army which employed modern weapons.

The frustrations attendant these failures to repeat the French Revolution as well as the mystifying reluctance of the people to be inflamed by revolutionary passion led to some rethinking. What should be done to ignite such passions and unleash social or national revolutions? Among European radicals of this era one such answer, but only one of several, was terrorism.[18] While some, like Marx, emphasized the need to wait until economic and social conditions became propitious, or emphasized the importance of careful planning and organization, those who became "alchemists of revolution" turned to the techniques of terrorism.

Czarist Russia offered the first manifestations. As early as 1869 Serge Nechayev, the author of the *Revolutionary Catechism* (an interesting title in light of previous discussion) and a follower of the anarchist Bakunin, sought to create a secret society among young Russian university students which would spark the revolution by assassinating leaders, supporters, and beneficiaries of the czarist regime.[19] These plans came to nothing, as did those of another ephemeral organization called "Hell" several years later.

Terrorism as practice as opposed to conception was performed in Russia first by the People's Will. The latter was a band of young Narodniviks, ex-students from middle-class backgrounds who had become disenchanted when their efforts to go to the people had been met with the indifference of the peasantry and police repression during the 1870s. It launched a terror campaign directed against czarist officials beginning in 1878, a campaign which culminated with the assassination of the reform-minded Alexander II in 1881. These activities did not evoke a popular uprising, with the Russian people rallying to the revolutionary cause, nor did they lead to the liberalization of the czarist regime. Instead, the result was a new and far harsher czar, the repression of People's Will, and the imposition of even more autocratic methods.[20]

This failure did not bring an end to Russian terrorism, however. There was another failed attempt, in 1887, to assassinate the czar, an initiative for which the brother of V. I. Lenin was executed. But terrorism on a larger scale was revived at the beginning of the twentieth century, this time not by a secret society but by a political party: the Socialist Revolutionaries. The latter was a non-Marxist socialist party whose revolutionary hopes were placed in Russia's urban working class. Between 1902 and 1908 the Combat Organization, the Socialist Revolutionaries' covert wing, assassinated a number of important czarist officials in the hope that these killings would paralyze the regime and inspire the proletariat.[21] The Russian workers were not so moved; their revolution would come later and under different auspices. For their part, the Socialist Revolutionaries' terrorist activities were curtailed after it was discovered that the head of its Combat Organization, Yevgeny Azef, had been a police spy who had collaborated with the authorities in tracking down his presumed colleagues.

In light of the frequency with which contemporary terrorist groups profess their fidelity to Marxism or Marxism-Leninism, it may come as a surprise to report that in the nineteenth century and early years of the twentieth, both the theory and practice of terrorism were developed not by Marx or Marxists but by anarchists whose views Marx and Lenin held in the utmost contempt.[22]

There is much to admire in nineteenth-century anarchist thought. It was a philosophy which emphasized the possibilities of human freedom and the ability or potential capacity of people to live in harmony with one another without the need for a formal government to coerce them into obedience. Furthermore, anarchists were internationalists in the sense they perceived nationalism or the allegiance of people to different national identities as unfortunate barriers to human brotherhood. But by far the worst of such barriers for the anarchists were private property, particularly to the extent it gave rise to greed, selfishness, and exploitation, and the institutions of governments with their inevitable commitments to oppress the weak, protect the wealthy, and stifle freedom. And it was these institutions which some anarchists set about to destroy by means of revolutionary violence.

Some anarchists who advocated or pursued the strategy of "propaganda by deed" believed they had devised a modern and scientific means for bringing on revolution. New weapons, dynamite in particular, would make it possible for revolutionaries to be selective in their choice of targets. While earlier revolutionaries had relied on mass bloodshed, the new ones would limit the carnage to those responsible for the oppression of the people. New means of mass communication could be used to spread the word of anarchist deeds to those expected to be inspired by them. This at least was the theory and justification. While others who wished to transform society on behalf of its exploited victims had sought in this era to form social democratic political parties to pursue this goal through democratic reform or, alternatively, had conceived a violent confrontation with capitalism to be the mechanical result of historical forces, the anarchists believed in the possibilities of direct action by individuals and small groups.

In practice, the period between 1880 and the outbreak of World War I saw a wave of terrorist activity carried out by anarchists.[23] The Italian king, the empress of Austria-Hungary, the presidents of France and the United States, and the prime minister of Spain, along with a long list of economic and social notables, were assassinated by anarchists. In other instances, the violence was less discriminate. Bombs were thrown into crowded cafés and theaters or exploded during public processions; other targets of anarchist bombs included the Chamber of Deputies in France and the Haymarket in the United States. In some countries, Italy, France, and Spain in particular, anarchism developed a popular following.

Revenge was a not uncommon motive for these acts of homicide. For example, the American anarchist Alexander Berkman tried to kill the steel tycoon Henry Clay Frick in 1892 because of the action his company had taken against striking workers in Homestead, Pennsylvania. But the underlying logic of anarchist terrorism was based not on retaliation against single cases of injustice and oppression, but on the broader ramifications the violence was expected to have; often these spectacular deeds were intended to inspire the masses, to show them in a way that pamphlets and street-corner assemblies could not, that those in power were vulnerable and that an end to capitalist exploitation was available. In short, these attacks could, by their propaganda effect, stimulate social revolution.

This did not happen; the anarchists failed. But anarchist terrorism during this era in Europe and America evoked strong responses from both the right and left. For those in power and their defenders in the press and elsewhere, the anarchists' actions were used to make propaganda of their own. Often, in Italy and the United States, for example, those in power used anarchist activity as an excuse to condemn all those organizations—political parties, trade unions, workers' circles—whose members were intent on modifying the existing economic and political order. Hair-raising stories were reported of secret societies and international conspiracies, vastly exaggerated accounts almost always, the purpose of which was to stimulate not social revolution but popular patriotic defenses of the status quo.

On the left, Marx and later Lenin and Trotsky viewed anarchist and social revolutionary terrorism as shortsighted and destructive of their own revolutionary objectives. Among other things, the communists argued that terrorism won popular sympathy for its victims. From their viewpoint, these acts invited repression from the authorities at a time before working-class organizations were strong enough to defend themselves. And worse yet, rather than mobilize the masses these adventures instead tended to increase their passivity, leaving them with the impression that this small-group violence *was* the revolution, not a supposed spark with which to ignite it. Terrorism inadvertently left the many with the impression that revolution could be accomplished through the efforts of the few.[24] Terror might make some sense only when the proletariat was already organized and self-conscious, when it followed rather than vainly sought to precipitate these developments.

So far we have discussed the use of terrorism in the modern world by small groups whose aims were the overthrow of the czarist autocracy in Russia and the destruction of the state and capitalism in Europe and America. But nationalism also became an important motive for the use of terrorist activity during the latter part of the nineteenth and beginning of the twentieth century. Terrorism's nationalist practitioners were influenced less by the abstract philosophical principles of the anarchists and others, but this did not make their deeds any less lethal.

The principal targets of the violence were the British, Austro-Hungarian, and Ottoman empires. The objective of those nationalist groups that pursued their goals through terrorism was the achievement of independent statehood for certain nations under imperial control. First to employ terrorism in the name of these nationalist causes were groups acting on behalf of Irish independence from Britain. A group known as the

Irish National Invincibles committed the Phoenix Park murders in Dublin in 1882. Apparently inspired by the assassination of the Russian czar, which occurred shortly before the event, the Invincibles murdered the British lord secretary and an associate while they were out for a stroll.[25] In the late 1800s another group of Irish nationalists, the Clan Na Gael, based in the United States, committed a series of dynamite bombings in England. Various public buildings, including Scotland Yard and London Bridge, were attacked in this fashion. Yet neither this dynamite campaign nor the Phoenix Park episode seems to have done much to advance the cause of Irish independence.

The failure though did not inhibit other nationalist groups from trying their luck. A small organization of Hindus, in pursuit of Indian independence from Britain, assassinated a British official in London in 1909. Armenian revolutionaries seeking freedom for their homeland from the Turks carried out attacks on Ottoman officials during the 1880s and 1890s. Likewise, a Macedonian organization, the IMRO (Macedonian Revolutionary Organization), sought to gain independence for its homeland from Ottoman rule by using analogous means, and with a similar lack of success. And finally, we should not forget that it was the member of a Bosnian nationalist group, Gavrilo Princip, who assassinated the Austro-Hungarian archduke at Sarajevo in July 1914. This event was one of a large number of terrorist attacks aimed at liberating southern Slavic nationalities from the Hapsburg Empire. But it was the one which served as the precipitating event of World War I.

The nearly two decades between the conclusion of the First World War and the outbreak of the Second World War were years during which a new motive emerged as a major cause of political terrorism, at least in Europe. Right-wing terrorism, or terrorist violence committed by groups seeking to preserve the status quo or restore previously existing circumstances, became a major actor in the drama. Some of this rightist terrorism had been prevalent elsewhere in earlier decades. In the United States, terrorist violence was employed by the Ku Klux Klan during the post-Civil War Reconstruction era as a means to prevent ex-slaves from exercising their constitutional rights of citizenship.[26] In czarist Russia a group known as the Black Hundreds, fearful of social change and the spread of revolutionary sentiment, directed attacks against Jews, liberals, socialists, and students at the beginning of the twentieth century, usually with the complicity of local authorities.[27]

In Europe two factors, hardly unrelated to one another, contributed to the outbreak of right-wing terrorism after World War I. First, the Russian Revolution of 1917 led elements within the socialist movements of many European countries to the conclusion that the Bolshevik triumph in the Soviet Union could be duplicated in their own nations. Indeed, it was widely believed that the Russian Revolution was simply the first explosion of worldwide communist insurrection. In fact, there were abortive attempts along these lines in Germany, Italy, Finland, and Hungary, all of which were violently repressed. Nonetheless, significant segments of the population in these countries as well as others where the perceived threat was less acute became fearful that red revolution posed a significant danger for their societies. The second ingredient in this brew was the rise of fascist movements, at first in Italy in 1919 and then in Germany, Austria, and other countries of Western and Eastern Europe. Despite some ostensibly radical and socialist components, fascist doctrine was ardently nationalist and violently anticommunist. Furthermore, adherents to fascist movements often stressed the values of direct action and violent combat for their own sake. Unlike earlier anarchist or even nationalist groups for whom violence was a means to an end, the fascist view was that it represented, like conventional warfare, an exhibition of virility and the spirit of adventure. Violence was good for the soul.

While a good deal of the violence practiced by fascist or protofascist organizations involved brawling and other forms of street-corner gang warfare directed against their leftist opponents, certainly some of it was terrorist in character. In the Po Valley of Italy, punitive expeditions carried out by Fascist squads during the 1920–1921 period were designed to intimidate an audience of radicalized farm laborers into quiescence.[28] In Germany, even before the rise of the Nazis, a number of Weimar politicians, including finance minister Matthias Erzberger and foreign minister Walter Rathenau, were assassinated by members of the right-wing Organization Consul. These were acts of vengeance intended to purge Germany of those "traitors" who had signed the Versailles Peace Treaty.[29]

At approximately the same time, Hungary was the site of a "white terror" campaign unleashed by rightist forces in reaction against the short-lived Hungarian Soviet Republic under Bela Kun. The purpose was to teach workers and peasants to "mind your own business and stop thinking of political rights and social revolution."[30] In Romania the Iron Guard or Legion of the Archangel Michael, a fascist formation, assassinated eleven political leaders and other notables between 1924 and 1937.

In general, then, the interwar period was one during which the strategy of terrorism came to be identified more with the behavior of rightist or fascist groups than leftist or anarchist ones.[31] The latter did not disappear entirely, however; anarchist opponents of Mussolini's dictatorship set off an occasional bomb in Italy and attempted to murder various diplomatic representatives of that country stationed in several European countries.

The left-to-right shift in the origins of much of the terrorist activity influenced the outlook of groups that used this form of violence to pursue nationalist objectives. Thus the Ustasha, the Croatian separatist organization responsible for the assassination of Yugoslav King Alexander and the French foreign minister during the former's visit to Marseilles in 1934, derived ideological inspiration as well as material support from the Italian Fascists.

The achievement of independence for Ireland after the Anglo-Irish War (1919–1921) did not bring an end to violence on that strife-torn island. As a price for its independence the Irish government agreed to a partition arrangement whereby Ulster, the Protestant-dominated northern region of the country, would continue under British rule. The Irish Republican Army (IRA) regarded this concession as a betrayal of its goal of a free and united Ireland. As a result the IRA launched a terrorist campaign against the new regime in Dublin. Terrorist attacks continued throughout the 1920s and 1930s despite the government's efforts to outlaw the organization and punish its adherents. The uncompromisingly anti-British IRA developed ties to the Nazi regime in Germany and in 1939–1940, just as World War II began, staged a series of bombings in Ulster and in England itself.[32]

The Middle East also was the site of nationalist terrorism during the 1930s. In Egypt the Muslim Brotherhood carried out a number of terrorist attacks against public officials it deemed too sympathetic to the British presence.[33] In the British mandate of Palestine, groups growing out of the revisionist Zionist movement, the Irgun and the Stern Gang, employed terrorism against the British after His Majesty's government had issued its exclusionary White Paper (a document which severely limited Jewish immigration) in 1939. The Irgun suspended these activities shortly after the outbreak of World War II, but the Stern Gang persisted in its use of violence.[34] The terrorism of the Jewish organization also had been stimulated by periodic terrorist attacks directed against the Yishuv (the Jewish settlement in Palestine) by Arab groups responsive to the anti-Semitic appeals of the Grand Mufti of Jerusalem.

World War II itself, although it brought indescribable horror to millions of noncombatants, did not involve much in the way of the small-group terrorism to which this study is devoted. Members of the Stern Gang assassinated Lord Moyne, the British Resident, in Cairo in 1944 and made an attempt on the life of Britain's high commissioner in Palestine. In those areas of Europe under German occupation, anti-Fascist and anti-Nazi resistance organizations occasionally carried out attacks against those they suspected of collaborating with the enemy. In Italy, for instance, the Resistance movement, basically a rural guerrilla endeavor, organized the Partisan Action Groups, which led attacks on officers of the German occupying force and Fascist remnants, including the murder of Fascist philosopher Giovanni Gentile, in the northern cities during the 1943–1945 period. In many cases the objective was to provoke the enemy into taking indiscriminate reprisals against the urban populations and thereby transform them into ardent and mobilized anti-Fascists. All too often the Nazi and Fascist forces obliged by committing horrifying atrocities against innocent bystanders.

The two decades following the conclusion of World War II in 1945 was a time of profound change. It was an era during which the vast transoceanic empires of the European powers—British, French, Dutch, Belgian—were replaced by a host of new independent nations in Africa, the Middle East, and Asia. Also, China, the world's most populous nation, was the site of a successful social revolution, as Mao and his Communist forces defeated the Nationalists in 1949.

In some places, for example, India, the process of decolonization was accomplished largely by peaceful means. In many instances, however, change involved violence. The Dutch were expelled from Indonesia as the result of a war waged against them by nationalist forces under Sukarno. The Viet Minh waged a guerrilla campaign aimed at eliminating the French presence in Indochina.

The dominant form of violence in the postwar period, aimed at either decolonization or social revolution, was rural-based guerrilla warfare. The major success stories were those of Mao Tse-tung in China, Ho Chi Minh in Vietnam, and Fidel Castro in Cuba. But there were also less publicized failures. Guerrilla insurgencies were defeated in Greece, Malaya, and the Philippines. In some of these instances, both the successful and unsuccessful, terrorism was used by those groups pursuing national liberation (Vietnam) or social revolution (Greece). But, nearly always, terror was an auxiliary means for these movements.

Terrorism as the principal or major weapon in the arsenal of national liberation and social revolutionary movements usually was confined to countries with highly urban populations. The Irgun under Menachem Begin staged its revolt against the continued British presence in Palestine.[35] In the mid- to late 1950s, the National Liberation Front carried out a number of indiscriminate attacks against the French population in Algeria for the purpose of achieving independence from France.[36] And toward the end of that struggle, elements in the French population reciprocated by indiscriminately murdering Algerian Arabs. Later these elements, committed to the preservation of a French Algeria, formed the Secret Army Organization, which, in turn, launched a terror campaign in metropolitan France, one which included several assassination attempts on President de Gaulle, who, they believed, had betrayed their cause by negotiating for Algerian independence.

During the 1950s the British were confronted by the Mau Mau rebellion in Kenya. In that country members of the Kikuyu tribe, reacting against the threat to their ancient customs (e.g., polygamy) posed by Christianity, European civilization, and the theft of their land, formed a violent cult committed to the expulsion of the British and the restoration of their traditional ways. Led for a time by Jomo Kenyatta, a British-educated anthropologist and later Kenya's first president, the Mau Mau waged a campaign of terror against white settlers, members of the Kikuyu tribe suspected of collaborating with them, and even ones who refused to go through the group's ritual oath-taking ceremony.[37]

The island of Cyprus in the eastern Mediterranean and the British protectorate of Aden, presently the People's Republic of South Yemen, also were places where terrorism played a significant role in nationalist conflicts. In the case of Cyprus, the right-wing Greek politician George Grivas organized the EOKA (Ethniki Organosis Kyprion Agoniston) in 1954 for two purposes: the expulsion of the British and the achievement of *enosis,* the union of the island with Greece. Some five years later, after more than 500 people had been killed by EOKA fighters, the British departed. But they left behind an independent country with the rights of its Turkish minority protected by law. Finally, the British evacuated Aden and its environs in 1964 after having been the target of terrorist attacks carried out by groups supplied by President Nasser of Egypt.[38]

Despite the dramatic changes of the postwar decades and the high volume of political violence that often accompanied them, terrorism, the above cases notwithstanding, was not a major factor in determining the outcome in most of these conflicts. In the context of guerrilla insurgencies, civil wars, and mass protests, terrorism played a role but a decidedly secondary one. From the late 1960s to the present time it would, as we shall see, assume a far more central place in the domestic politics of many nations and in the international arena as well.

THE LESSONS

What lessons may be learned about terrorism from this brief reading of the historical record? Because the various episodes of terrorist activity we have described occurred at so many different times and in so many different settings, the effort to generalize about them is difficult. Nevertheless, certain central themes seem to emerge. First, terrorism often has been depicted as a weapon of the weak. The various religious sects and political groups whose violent exploits we have mentioned certainly fit this characterization. Compared with those of their enemies—Rome, the British Empire, the Russian autocracy—their numbers and resources appear meager in the extreme. The reasoning employed in their use of terrorism against these powerful enemies often seems to have had a magical quality.[39] Their use of violence, in many cases, was not intended to defeat their opponents directly, but, instead, its purpose was to conjure up an all-powerful and all-good force—Jehovah, Allah, Christ, the People, the Masses, the Proletariat—whose intervention on the terrorists' side would, to put it mildly, change the balance of power. Even some of the right-wing groups whose terrorism was intended to prevent rather than accelerate change, for example, the Legion of the Archangel Michael, believed they were acting in the name of God or the Nation.

Second, the society to be created or restored through the application of terror, sacred or secular, was one which would be free of conflict and drained of corruption. This condition would be achieved because the sources of disharmony and imperfection—foreigners, the ungodly, the state, capitalism—would have been removed as a result of the terrorists' operations.

Finally, there is an element of frustration present in the behavior of many of the groups that turned to terrorism, a sense that their views, although obviously correct to their adherents, were not shared or appreciated sufficiently by others whose cause the group had sought to champion. This frustration with the indifference, moderation, or even opposition with which their views were met, not uncommonly, by those who theoretically should be sympathetic to them, coupled with the great power at the disposal of their enemies, frequently served to provoke terrorist responses. These generalizations may not apply to all the manifestations of terrorism we have discussed, but they at least seem to fit many of them.

KEY TERMS

anarchism	Reign of Terror
Assassins	right-wing terrorism
enosis	Viet Minh
left-wing terrorism	white terror
propaganda by deed	Zealots

NOTES

1 For a history, see Franklin Lord, *Political Murder* (Cambridge, Mass.: Harvard University Press, 1985).

2 David C. Rapoport, "Fear and Trembling: Terrorism in Three Religious Traditions," *The American Political Science Review,* 3:78 (1984), pp. 658–677.

3 Ibid., p. 670.

4 David C. Rapoport, "Terror and the Messiah: An Ancient Experience and Some Modern Parallels," in David Rapoport and Yonah Alexander (eds.), *The Morality of Terrorism* (New York: Pergamon Press, 1982), pp. 13–42; see also Yehoshafat Harkabi, *The Bar Kokhba Syndrome* (Chappaqua, N.Y.: Russel Books, 1983), pp. 3–23.

5 Bernard Lewis, *The Assassins: A Radical Sect in Islam* (New York: Oxford University Press, 1967).

6 Ibid., p. 27.

7 Bernard Lewis, "Islamic Terrorism," in Benjamin Netanyahu (ed.), *Terrorism: How the West Can Win* (New York: Farrar, Straus & Giroux, 1986), p. 69.

8 Norman Cohn, *The Pursuit of the Millennium* (New York: Oxford University Press, 1970), pp. 53–186.

9 For the context see Michael Walzer, *The Revolution of the Saints* (Cambridge, Mass.: Harvard University Press, 1965), and Christopher Hill, *The World Turned Upside Down* (New York: Viking Press, 1972).

10 Cohn, op. cit., p. 255.

11 Linda and Marsha Frey, "Terrorism in Early Modern Europe: The Camisard Revolt," in Paul Wilkinson and Alisdair Stewart (eds.), *Contemporary Research on Terrorism* (Aberdeen: Aberdeen University Press, 1987), pp. 107–120.

12 David Rapoport, "Why Does Religious Messianism Produce Terror?" in Wilkinson and Stewart (eds.), op. cit., pp. 72–88.

13 J. L. Talmon, *The Origins of Totalitarian Democracy* (New York: Frederick A. Praeger, 1960), pp. 122–148; Michael Phillip Carter, "The French Revolution; Jacobin Terror," in Rapoport and Alexander (eds.), op. cit., pp. 133–151; and Albert Parry, *Terrorism from Robespierre to Arafat* (New York: Vanguard Press, 1976), pp. 39–54.

14 For a commentary, see James H. Billington, *Fire in the Minds of Men* (New York: Basic Books, 1980), pp. 54–85.

15 Ibid., pp. 161–162.

16 Raymond Aron, *The Opium of the Intellectuals* (New York: W. W. Norton & Company, Inc., 1957), p. 66.

17 Martha Crenshaw, "The Strategic Development of Terrorism" (a paper presented at the 1985 Annual Meeting of the American Political Science Association, New Orleans, August 29–September 1, 1985), p. 9.

18 For some examples of this rethinking, see Walter Laqueur (ed.), *The Terrorism Reader* (New York: New American Library, 1978), pp. 53–108.

19 Lewis Feuer, *The Conflict of Generations* (New York: Basic Books, 1969), pp. 130–131; Walter Laqueur, *Terrorism* (Boston: Little, Brown and Company, 1977), pp. 30–31.

20 Sergei Pushkarev, *The Emergence of Modern Russia* (New York: Holt, Rinehart and Winston, 1963), pp. 184–186; Astrid von Borcke, "Violence and Terror in Russian Revolutionary Terrorism: The Narodnaya Volya, 1879–83," in Wolfgang Mommsen and Gerhard Hirschfeld (eds.), *Social Protest, Violence and Terror in Nineteenth and Twentieth Century Europe* (New York: St. Martin's Press, 1982), pp. 48–62.

21 Manfred Hildermeir, "The Terrorist Strategies of the Socialist Revolutionary Party in Russia, 1900–14," in Mommsen and Hirschfeld (eds.), op. cit., pp. 80–87.

22 On this theme, see Richard E. Rubenstein, *Alchemists of Revolution* (New York: Basic Books, 1987), pp. 141–157.

23 James Joll, *The Anarchists* (Cambridge, Mass.: Harvard University Press, 1980), pp. 99–129; and Marie Fleming, "Propaganda by the Deed: Terrorism

and Anarchist Theory in Late Nineteenth Century Europe," in Yonah Alexander and Kenneth A. Myers (eds.), *Terrorism in Europe* (London: Croom Helm, 1982), pp. 8–28.

24 Laqueur (ed.), *The Terrorism Reader,* op. cit., pp. 198–222.

25 Lord, op. cit., pp. 230–238; Peter Alter, "Traditions of Violence in the Irish National Movement," in Mommsen and Hirschfeld (eds.), op. cit., pp. 137–154.

26 David M. Chalmers, *Hooded Americanism* (Chicago: Quadrangle Books, 1965), pp. 8–21.

27 Hans Rogger, "Russia," in Hans Rogger and Eugene Weber (eds.), *The European Right* (Berkeley: University of California Press, 1966), pp. 483–488.

28 F. L. Carsten, *The Rise of Fascism* (Berkeley: University of California Press, 1969), pp. 55–57.

29 Lord, op. cit., pp. 261–263.

30 George Barnay, "The Dragon's Teeth: The Roots of Hungarian Fascism," in Peter Sugar (ed.), *Native Fascism in the Successor States, 1918–1945* (Santa Barbara, Ca.: ABC-Clio, 1971), p. 74.

31 Laqueur, *Terrorism,* op. cit., pp. 16–17.

32 Michael Laffan, "Violence and Terror in Twentieth Century Ireland," in Mommsen and Hirschfeld (eds.), op. cit., pp. 155–173.

33 George Lenczowski, *The Middle East in World Affairs,* 4th ed. (Ithaca, N.Y.: Cornell University Press, 1982), pp. 506–513.

34 J. Bowyer Bell, *Terror Out of Zion* (New York: Avon Books, 1977), pp. 77–125.

35 Ibid., pp. 129–315.

36 Martha Crenshaw Hutchinson, *Revolutionary Terrorism* (Stanford, Ca.: Hoover Institution, 1978).

37 Brian Crozier, *The Rebels* (Boston: Beacon Press, 1960), pp. 255–267.

38 Anthony Burton, *Urban Terrorism* (New York: Free Press, 1975), pp. 163–176.

39 Lawrence Freedman, "Terrorism: Problems of the Polistaraxic," in Lawrence Freedman and Yonah Alexander (eds.), *Perspective on Terrorism* (Wilmington, Del.: Scholarly Resources, 1983), p. 5.

CHAPTER 3

CONTEMPORARY TERRORISM

Conventional warfare between organized political entities has been a relatively continuous (if lamentable) factor in human history. The same cannot be said for outbreaks of political terrorism. Their occurrence has been far more episodic. Years, decades, or even centuries have elapsed without much evidence of terrorist activity. Then, in one country or another a wave of terrorism has struck, only to crest and subside shortly thereafter.

It is obvious that from the late 1960s to the present we have lived through what Walter Laqueur has titled an "age of terrorism." Is this age simply the latest and most flamboyant episode in the history of terrorism, one likely to subside in the not too distant future; or do contemporary terrorist operations reflect certain long-term changes in the structure of modern societies and in their relationships with one another for which the past offers no precedent? No clear-cut answer to this question is possible; however, there are a number of nations, Argentina and Turkey among others, which suffered severe terrorist episodes during the 1970s where the violence had subsided by the 1980s. Yet, on the other hand, nations and areas of the world largely free of terrorism in the last decade, South Asia for example, have become the sites of major terrorist activity in the present time.

A question we may ask with some confidence that a plausible answer will be forthcoming concerns the conditions existing in the world during the mid- to late 1960s from which the current era of political terrorism emerged. What combination of factors was at work in these years which transformed terrorism from a relatively minor annoyance into the global attention-getting phenomenon it is today?

The best way to organize a response to this question is by dividing it into two categories: preconditions and precipitants. The former refers to background conditions that set the stage for terrorism, while precipitants are specific events that precede and indeed stimulate the use of terrorism.[1]

PRECONDITIONS

If, as we have defined it, terrorism is a type of small-scale violence aimed at modifying the behavior of an audience, then the first factor to which attention should be paid is one that has to do with the ability to communicate. It was no accident that the Palestinian group Black September took Israeli athletes captive during the 1972 Olympic games in Munich. Nor was it random chance that led the Montoneros to stage an operation during the 1978 World Cup soccer tournament in Argentina.[2] In both cases the athletic events had television audiences estimated to number more than 800 million people. Thanks to technological developments in mass communications, i.e., satellite transmission of television pictures, the world has become a global village. News of events which in an earlier era would have taken years to make their way around the world can now reach millions instantaneously.

But developments in the technology of communication are one thing; access to the mass media is something else. Just as it was not chance that led Black September and the Montoneros to stage their attacks in ways designed to attract a worldwide audience, so too it is no accident that the Soviet Union and most of its Warsaw Pact allies have been largely immune to terrorist violence. In these nations access to the mass media is carefully controlled by those in power. Of course, it could be argued that access to the mass media in the industrial democracies is not totally free, especially for individuals or groups who wish to destroy these regimes, but there is really little comparison to societies where even the unauthorized use of photocopying machines is regarded as a crime against the state.[3]

In addition to changes in the technology of mass communication, there were material conditions in the 1960s that served to set the stage for the terrorist drama to follow. Changes were also at work in the technology of mass transportation, commercial aviation in particular. The widespread use of jet aircraft to carry large numbers of passengers from one congested airport to another at unprecedented speeds and according to predetermined schedules clearly had an effect. The planes and their passengers became vulnerable to skyjackers. The latter were also free to purchase tickets and travel rapidly from areas of the world which were the sites of their grievances, such as the Middle East, to other locations, such as Western Europe, where their attacks were not anticipated.

Commercial jet travel plus television would prove an especially combustible combination. In the United States, for example, an individual or small group would skyjack a plane bound for Miami and insist that it be diverted to Havana. Among the audience watching the event on television were other individuals and groups with their own grievances who would seek, a week or a month later, to duplicate the earlier achievement. And so on.

During the 1960s discussions about technological change in weapons often focused on the testing of hydrogen bombs and the means devised by the superpowers, ballistic missiles and nuclear-powered submarines, for their delivery to enemy targets. But these weapons of mass destruction were not the only implements of killing which were undergoing change. A whole range of weapons, from hand-held missile launchers to plastique explosives to teflon-coated armor-piercing bullets, were either developed or had their capacities improved over these years.[4] Such improvements—the miniaturization of previously existing weapons—made it easier for single individuals or small groups to conceal weapons until they were ready for use or to detonate explosives from a safe distance. In all, the effect was to make it possible for a small number of terrorists to kill large numbers of people in a way which facilitated the escape of the terrorists after the event and made it more difficult for the authorities to discern their intentions before the event.

Aside from these specific improvements in the techniques for communicating, traveling, and killing, we should not forget the extent to which modern industrial societies, by the 1960s, had become dependent upon a whole range of complicated and vulnerable technologies. Automobiles cannot run without gasoline, which must be produced from petroleum at refineries. City streets and homes cannot be lighted without electricity carried by power lines from generating plants. These circumstances, the givens of modern urban life, make it possible for a small group of terrorists to disrupt the lives of millions by setting off a modest explosion at a particularly vulnerable point in the system.[5] Furthermore, the threat proved to be more than merely potential. During the 1970s terrorist groups operating in Latin America and Western Europe staged attacks on refineries and electrical power grids in an effort to call attention to their various grievances.

Clearly, it took more than changes in the tools and implements of modern life to create the conditions necessary for the advent of contemporary terrorist activities. It was the human condition and the perception of it by those who later attempted to modify it by violence that promoted the age of terrorism.

The earth, of course, is a vale of tears, and the people who inhabit it have uncounted grievances against various aspects of their lives. But this is hardly a new development. In the nineteenth century terrorism was employed by groups seeking to end the poverty and exploitation of the masses and by others searching for the means to eliminate autocracy and political repression in Russia and elsewhere. If these were the preconditions for contemporary terrorism, we would expect such countries as Haiti and Bulgaria to have been swarming with terrorists by the end of the 1960s. But, of course, they were not.

In fact, some nations whose working classes were enjoying unprecedentedly high standards of living, West Germany and Japan, for example, were later struck by relatively serious bouts of revolutionary terrorism. Similarly, while some nations in Sub-Saharan Africa had governments that committed acts of torture and political repression which rivaled those of czarist Russia were largely immune to terrorism, some of the Western democracies were the targets of virulent terrorist campaigns whose perpetrators alleged they were fighting against the "fascist" essence of these constitutional regimes.

The fact that terrorism occurred in some nations where it should not have but did not occur in others where it should, at least in theory, has led a few observers to the conclusion that terrorism has no preconditions.[6] The search for broad social and political explanations is likely to prove fruitless because terrorism is an activity, unlike mass protests, guerrilla insurgencies, or civil wars, pursued by small groups whose members and milieu often seem idiosyncratic in the context of societies numbering in the millions.

Other observers, however, believe they have identified the exclusive precondition for contemporary terrorism. Its manifestations were the outgrowth of a single comprehensive conspiracy. Followers of this line of reasoning believe that the Soviet Union along with some of its Warsaw Pact allies, plus congenial movements and regimes elsewhere, embarked on a plan to use terrorism in order to destabilize the industrial democracies and pro-Western governments in the Third World.[7] Although opposed in Marxist-Leninist theory to terrorism, the Soviet practice was one of achieving its geopolitical goals by sponsoring small bands to take up arms against its enemies.

By now the evidence is persuasive that the Soviets did provide support on a selective basis to many terrorist groups.[8] But this analysis still falls short of a comprehensive explanation. Presumably the Soviets had as strong an incentive to destabilize Norway and Denmark as Italy and Turkey, all members of NATO. Yet the latter two countries had serious terrorist problems in the 1970s while the former remained unscathed. Evidently conditions existed in Italy and Turkey that promoted outbreaks of terrorism, while those conditions did not exist in Norway and Denmark, no matter how much the Soviets might have wished them into existence. Furthermore, the Soviets would seem to have little incentive to assist right-wing "death squads," neo-fascist groups, or certain separatist organizations whose terrorist activities were antithetical to Soviet interests or whose goals were ones to which the Russians were either indifferent or hostile. Consequently, the case for Soviet support of terrorism, on a selective basis, is convincing, but the assertion of a comprehensive conspiracy is not.

Despite obvious skepticism concerning the conspiratorial view, it seems clear that the international competition between the United States and the Soviet Union was an important precondition for contemporary terrorism. There are several ways in which the superpower conflict contributed to the outbreak. First, communist ideology and Soviet policy had long emphasized American imperialism as a principal cause of economic distress and political dependence in various nations, especially those located in the southern hemisphere. Many of the groups with which this chapter is concerned, including some active in the United States itself, derived their inspiration from the Soviet-originated view of America as the imperial power of the modern era. Tangible evidence to support this view could be found in the growing presence of American-owned multinational corporations whose business operations were spreading around the world during the 1960s.[9] Further evidence exists in the reality of American military bases, the stationing of American troops, and the training of local armed forces by American personnel in various nations. The buildup of the American military presence was, of course, an outgrowth of the antagonism between the two superpowers.

During the 1960s Soviet policies, along with those pursued by some communist parties in Western Europe and Latin America, also represented important preconditions for contemporary terrorism. Oddly, these policies had an unintentional rather than a deliberate effect. After the 1962 Cuban missile crisis both Soviet and American leaders saw the need to reach an accommodation which would place limits on their conflict in order to avoid nuclear catastrophe. By the late 1960s, the result was Soviet-American détente. Whatever its virtues or vices this policy left many radicals in Western Europe and Latin America with the impression that the Soviet Union was no longer a serious revolutionary force in the world. It had betrayed its historic mission and had become a protector of the status quo.

The same might be said, and indeed has been said, about the domestic roles of nonruling communist parties in such nations as Italy and France.

Instead of acting as revolutionary vanguards of the proletariat, these parties gave the impression that they, like the Soviet Union, were prepared to live with the existing economic and political order until such time as a peaceful transition to socialism would occur.[10]

For many young people radicalized by injustices in their own societies and the growing American role in Vietnam, these betrayals left them in search of revolutionary alternatives. Some young people found them in the apparently uncompromising examples of Mao in China and Castro in Cuba. The successful Chinese and Cuban revolutions, both based on rural guerrilla warfare, served as models to show that violence still could be used to dislodge domestic reaction and foreign imperialism. In short, by the late 1960s New Left political movements had emerged in many countries around the world, movements less interested in revolutionary rhetoric, Soviet or otherwise, than in direct action.

Certain aspects of American life during the sixties also provided preconditions for the coming terrorist age. The civil rights struggles in the south, the rioting by blacks in the northern cities, and the student-based protest against the Vietnam war were put on display via the mass media. Among other things, these occurrences showed audiences in different parts of the world that (1) the United States was vulnerable to turmoil and disorder, and (2) massive publicity could accrue to groups that used various forms of direct action to achieve their social and political objectives.

To this point the analysis has focused on developments in technology and on forces at work in the international environment. Now let us turn our attention to the domestic situations in areas of the world which would become, subsequently, the major locations for terrorist operations.

Here foremost consideration should be given to the existence of unresolved and widely felt grievances and discontents. The most serious cases were to be found in the Middle East and Latin America. In the Middle East, the Arab-Israeli conflict provided the background condition from which terrorism would emerge. There the inability of those Arab nations surrounding the Jewish state to relieve the plight of the Palestinians by defeating Israel was an obvious precondition for terrorist operations.[11] If Israel's legitimacy as a nation-state was denied by the nations surrounding it, legitimacy was also a significant factor in Latin American politics during this era. The issue was not, as in the Middle East, a challenge to the external legitimacy of a particular nation. Rather the question was the internal legitimacy of particular political regimes which sought to rule these nations. Vast differences in the distribution of wealth, power, and status among citizens within these countries, coupled with unpopular military governments in Argentina and Brazil or shaky democratic ones elsewhere, constituted the preconditions for insurgent violence in general and political terrorism in particular.[12]

In the countries of Western Europe and North America, two factors were at work. First was the existence of long-standing grievances concerning the status of various ethnic groups. In particular, the resentments found among the Basque population of northern Spain under the repressive Franco dictatorship comes to mind, a regime that denied Basques the most elementary rights of cultural expression.[13] But the democracies were not totally immune to these sorts of ethnic grievances either. The most notable example was that of Northern Ireland. As a result of the post-World War I territorial settlement, Britain retained sovereignty over Ulster, that part of Ireland with a loyalist Protestant majority and a significant Catholic minority. The latter was the habitual victim of various forms of discrimination, and elements within the Catholic community had never become reconciled to the area's membership in the United Kingdom. Their true allegiance was to Dublin and the Irish Republic to the south.[14]

Although the Basques in Spain and Catholics in Northern Ireland would prove to be the most serious cases, so far as terrorism is concerned, they hardly exhaust the list. The situations of French-speaking Quebecois in Canada, Puerto Ricans and blacks in the United States (among other groups), and Corsicans in France also require mention. There were also the émigré groups, members of ethnic groups who for economic or political reasons had left their homelands behind and settled in the democracies. Characteristically, the émigrés harbored resentments not against the nations to which they had fled but against the regimes that had compelled their flight. Living within the Western democracies were Croatians with grievances against Yugoslavia, South Moluccans hostile to Indonesia, Armenians with memories of persecutions suffered at the hands of the Turks, and, concentrated in the United States, anti-Castro Cubans—to mention the most obvious cases.

The second precondition for the development of contemporary terrorism in the democracies was based not on ethnicity but on ideology. Stemming from those forces at work in the international environment already observed, the Western democracies along with Japan were the countries within which New Left political movements evolved during the 1960s. These movements, in Italy and West Germany, for example, usually were rooted in the universities and composed of students, intellectuals, and others whose outlook on the world was to prove an important precondition for the formation of revolutionary terrorist groups.[15] In general, the movements were composed of people who believed that existing left-wing political parties provided inadequate channels for the expression of the emotions they were feeling. These emotions included hostility to the American involvement in Vietnam, sympathy for the plight of the poor in the Third World and in their own nations, and contempt for the consumer-centered societies in which they lived. In addition, these movements' followers developed a fascination with the tactics of direct action, not violence necessarily, but parades, public assemblies, and street-corner agitation (e.g., guerrilla theater). The Provos in the Netherlands with their playful send-ups of the Dutch establishment furnish an example.

In some of the democracies, Italy and West Germany among others, the rise to visibility and public performances of the New Left movements evoked a backlash on the part of right-wing political parties and other forces, such as the neo-Fascist Italian Social Movement and the Springer press in West Germany, which found the new style of politics fundamentally offensive to their sense of nationalism, morality, and public order. In the ensuing years these rightist elements would contribute to the growth of reactionary terrorism.

Finally, we should remember that those nations and regions of the world which were among the first to experience the contemporary episode of political terrorism had at least two things in common. First, they were areas with long histories of political violence, where there existed long-standing traditions of violent challenges to the prevailing political order. Indeed, a large repertoire of historical myths and symbols deriving from heroic armed conflicts in the past existed to provide guidance for those who turned to terrorism. The form the violence took may have been new, but political violence itself was hardly a new phenomenon in these areas.

Second, many of the countries which would become the sites of terrorism had recently experienced significant waves of urbanization. This was especially true for Latin American and Middle Eastern nations.[16] But even in Italy cities such as Rome, Turin, and Milan exhibited substantial population growth in the decade or two preceding the advent of the terrorist era. In a sense, urban terrorism represented a shift in both style and location, that is, to the major metropolitan areas, of conflicts which had been waged previously in rural environments.

PRECIPITANTS

With two exceptions the major events that had the greatest impact in precipitating the age of terrorism represented failures rather than successes from the point of view of those who had caused them to occur. But it was these frustrating defeats which served to inspire those who felt them most acutely to turn to terrorism. Also, in very specific instances clumsy acts of government repression, as in the quelling by the West German police of student protests against the state visit of the late Shah of Iran in 1967, led extremists to certain conclusions about the nature of political authority in their countries—conclusions that sparked terrorist operations.

So far as the situation in the Middle East is concerned, it was the outcome of the June 1967 Arab-Israeli war that is pivotal to understanding subsequent developments. For years various Palestinian fedayeen groups had done their utmost to provoke a war between Israel and its Arab neighbors. Yet when it finally came, the Six Day war resulted in a massive and humiliating defeat for the Arab cause.[17] Instead of wiping Israel off the map, the outcome was Israeli occupation of the Gaza Strip, the Sinai Desert, Jerusalem, the West Bank of the Jordan River, and Golan Heights. The magnitude of the Arab defeat led the Palestinian leadership to rethink its approach to the problem. The conclusion reached from this soul-searching was that conventional warfare by the Arab states would not produce the desired results, but the new Israeli occupation of so much territory with such sizable Arab populations provided the Palestinians with an opportunity. Instead of relying upon the Arab states to do their work for them the Palestinians would launch a "people's war" against the Israeli occupiers. Such a war would approximate the guerrilla insurgency being waged so successfully by the Viet Cong against American forces in Vietnam.

Accordingly, in the period between 1967 and 1969 efforts were made by guerrillas from fedayeen bases in Jordan to infiltrate the West Bank. A series of attacks were staged, some of which yielded modest successes which were then accorded enormous publicity in the Arab press—the Six Day war was being avenged. On balance, though, these operations were not successful. The terrain of the West Bank hardly approximated the jungles of Vietnam. It was hard for the guerrillas to find cover, especially since the local Arab population did not prove as sympathetic as expected. Further, the Israeli military was watchful and carried out retaliatory strikes against Palestinian bases in Jordan. Political leaders in Amman were not pleased by the development of semiautonomous Palestinian areas within their country either. For this reason Jordan proved to be less the safe haven for Palestinian fighters than North Vietnam was for the Viet Cong.[18]

Although political concerns in Latin America were vastly different from those prevailing in the Middle East, the events that precipitated terrorism in Latin America show some similarity with those in the Middle East. For many radical Latin Americans the great revolutionary achievement was that of Fidel Castro in Cuba. By the end of 1958 what had been a small band of guerrillas fighting in the Sierra Maestra mountains had managed to defeat the corrupt dictatorship of Fulgencio Batista and later to expel the Yankee imperialists in the bargain. Castro's success had widespread ramifications throughout the region. Between 1960 and 1967 over twenty rural guerrilla campaigns were launched in Latin America, including one in Bolivia led by Che Guevara, a hero of the Cuban revolution. The aims were similar: social revolution and the elimination of North American influence. And the results were similar as well: all the insurgencies were defeated, including Guevara's initiative.[19] Apparently other means would have to be found for the revolutionaries to achieve their objectives.

In the industrial democracies defeat took another form, one involving the decomposition of the broad New Left movements. For reasons we have discussed, the 1960s witnessed the formation of student-centered political movements. From the Zengakuren in Japan and the Students for a Democratic Society in the United States to *Potere Operaio* in Italy and similar groups in other Western European nations, movements had been organized to achieve through direct action objectives that conventional political parties, including communist ones, seemed unwilling to pursue.

By the end of the 1960s and the beginning of the 1970s these movements had begun to come apart. They were subject to internal factional disputes over tactics and ideology. In some cases their attempts to broaden their support among the masses were met with the scorn and derision of those whose cause they sought to lead. In Italy, for example, the unsuccessful effort by the millionaire publisher and New Left leader Giangiacomo Feltrinelli to enlist a band of Sardinian criminals in the revolutionary cause was treated as a comedy by the press.[20] In other instances attempts by the New Left to win power through the democratic electoral process provided a shock of recognition; when the ballots were counted little support was forthcoming. What could be done? For some groups within these movements the answer proved to be terrorism.

In the case of Northern Ireland, a Civil Rights Association had been organized by Catholics and some Protestants, not to achieve a union of Ulster with the Irish Republic but to end discrimination against the region's Catholic minority. Its efforts, which included peaceful civil rights marches and other nonviolent tactics borrowed from the civil rights movement in the United States, did not produce the desired reforms. What these manifestations did produce was a reawakening of ancient religious fears and hatreds.[21]

Aside from the Cuban revolution, the one major success that helped precipitate contemporary terrorism was the Vietnam war. Its occurrence made several enormous contributions. First, the Viet Cong showed the vulnerability of the American superpower to methods of unconventional warfare. Second, the fact that the Viet Cong had committed a wave of assassinations against local representatives of the Saigon regime in the villages of South Vietnam during the early phases of its operations led revolutionary observers elsewhere to believe that terrorism was a necessary first step in the escalation of a war of long duration against their nations' rulers. Popular support would follow rather than precede the terrorist phase of the struggle. Third, the mass media–transmitted accounts of atrocities committed by American forces and their South Vietnamese allies against the civilian population did little to endear the United States or its NATO allies to the anti-Vietnam opposition movements they confronted at home. The atrocities also seemed to show that repression would not work, that rather than weaken support for the Viet Cong they actually strengthened it.

Of course, the problem for those revolutionaries who sought to create a Cuba in the Mediterranean or 100 Vietnams elsewhere was that the conditions for the successful transplantation of these experiences often were not present elsewhere. But this was a lesson that would be learned only as the terrorist drama unfolded.

GOALS OF CONTEMPORARY TERRORISM

In reviewing terrorist activities over the last two decades we will use the ultimate objectives of terrorist groups mentioned in the introduction as the bases for our classification. As will be recalled, the goals or aims of terrorism were identified as nationalist-separatist, revolutionary, or reactionary in nature. Our accounts will reflect these distinctions.

Nationalist-Separatist Terrorism

By all odds the most widely publicized terrorist operations in the contemporary era have involved the Arab-Israeli conflict and the activities of the Palestine Liberation Organization (PLO). The reasons why this conflict has played a central role in international political life are not as obvious as they may seem at first glance. In the years after World War II millions of people were displaced as the result of newly defined borders and the creation or destruction of nation-states. Members of many ethnic groups found themselves living in less than ideal conditions as a consequence. Measured by the total number of people displaced as the result of Israeli independence in 1948, roughly half a million, and the size of the territory under dispute, tiny by global standards, the Palestinian question should not have received the attention it has been accorded.[22]

The difference between the scale of the dispute and the importance assigned to it is explicable for these reasons. First, the land in question contains sites considered holy by the world's major monotheistic religions. Second, the fate of the Jews, including its political and religious meaning, has been an important theme in European civilization for two millennia; its importance was reemphasized by the Holocaust. Third, unlike many other ethnic groups with outstanding territorial grievances, the Palestinians had powerful allies in the Arab world and beyond who came to see their interests, e.g., Pan-Arabism, as inextricably linked to those of the Palestinians. Finally, the use of terrorism, particularly operations carried out in Western Europe, helped transform an essentially regional issue into a global concern.

The defeat suffered by the Arabs in the 1967 war and the inability of the Palestinian fedayeen groups to mount an effective guerrilla campaign on the West Bank in its aftermath mark the context which may be used to understand subsequent developments. As an organization the PLO had existed since 1964, when it was created by Egyptian President Nasser, but it was only after 1967 that it assumed the role with which it is now widely identified. The PLO's position as the sponsor or perpetrator of terrorism derives from the fact that after the Six Day war it became an umbrella organization for a variety of the previously existing fedayeen groups, most of whom had their own Arab patrons.[23] The largest of such groups was the Palestine National Liberation Movement (Fatah) headed by Yasser Arafat and initially under Syrian sponsorship. It was Arafat who became the PLO's leader during this period.

Although it was by far the largest, Fatah was hardly the only fedayeen group to be found under the PLO umbrella. There were twelve such groups, the most important of which were the Popular Front for the Liberation of Palestine (PFLP) and its factional offspring, the Popular Democratic Front for the Liberation of Palestine (PDFLP) and the Popular Front for the Liberation of Palestine–General Command (PFLP-GC). By 1968 these and other groups had established bases within Palestinian refugee camps in Jordan.[24] With the failure of their guerrilla expeditions to the West Bank, these PLO groups began their terrorist activities. The most spectacular events involved the skyjacking of commercial airliners. The Jordanian government in Amman did not regard these exploits with indifference. King Hussein, the target of an assassination attempt, sought to impose limitations on the fedayeen. But his effort did not deter the PFLP, under the leadership of George Habash, from simultaneously skyjacking three airliners in 1970 and flying them to Dawson's Field in Jordan. The passengers were not harmed, but the planes were destroyed on the runway by the PFLP skyjackers. This was the last of a series of provocations the Jordanian government was willing to tolerate. The PLO had begun to act as a state within a state. King Hussein, with some reluctance, unleashed his army against the fedayeen.

The result was Black September. The Jordanian military destroyed the PLO bases, with many civilian casualties, and the organization was driven from the country. Syria almost went to war with Jordan in an effort to rectify the situation, but was deterred by threats of intervention from Israel and the United States. In turn, these developments had far-reaching consequences, the most important of which was the reconstitution of the PLO apparatus in Lebanon.

Given the ethnic and religious mix of its population and the weakness of its armed forces, Lebanon was a far more fragile entity than Jordan. Accordingly, the PLO groups were able to operate in it with a far greater degree of independence than they had enjoyed in their previous home. Bases were established in Palestinian refugee camps in and around Beirut as well as the other cities. A section of southern Lebanon came to be known as Fatahland in view of the extent of control that organization exercised over it.

For more than a decade the PLO was able to use Lebanon as a training center and staging area from which to launch terrorist attacks on several types of targets. First, there were cross-border assaults staged inside Israel in such northern communities as Ma'alot, Kiryat Shmona, and Naharia. These attacks were almost always fatal for their perpetrators and produced Israeli counterattacks on PLO centers in Lebanon. Second, PLO groups carried out terrorist operations against Israeli and Jewish targets in third countries. The killing of Israeli athletes at the 1972 Munich Olympic games may serve as a spectacular illustration, but the list is a long one, and as the 1976 Israeli rescue of kidnapped French airline passengers at Entebbe Airport in Uganda suggests, rarely cost-free to the PLO fighters themselves. There were also attacks in third countries, usually but not always European, against targets which were neither Jewish nor Israeli. Nations that had offended the PLO by virtue of their support for Israel or held PLO fighters in prison, for example, the United States and West Germany, found their own citizens the targets of attack.

In addition to this sort of event, a good deal of PLO and PLO-related terrorism has been intra-Arab in nature. Not only did the organization become embroiled in the Lebanese civil war from 1976 forward, but it also conducted terrorist activities against Arab regimes and leaders considered hostile to its concerns. For example, the Jordanian prime minister, Wasfi Al-Tal, was assassinated outside the Sheraton Hotel in Cairo because of his role in the destruction of the PLO organization in Jordan. And after the 1978 Camp David accord between Israel and Egypt, the latter's citizens became targets of PLO attacks because of their country's peace agreement with Israel.

Finally, the PLO has attacked itself on numerous occasions. Disagreements over aims and tactics, i.e., rejectionists versus moderates, coupled with the fact that the various groups for which it has provided an umbrella represent the interests of conflicting Arab nations, have led to terrorist violence committed by one faction against another. For example, the Fatah Revolutionary Council formed in 1973 by Sabri al-Banna, a.k.a. Abu Nidal, has carried out terrorist operations against various PLO spokespersons it regarded as too willing to compromise with the Israelis. Among Abu Nidal's victims have been PLO representatives in London, Paris, Brussels, and Kuwait.[25] In 1982 and in the aftermath of the PLO's defeat in Lebanon by the Israelis, another group of Fatah dissidents, backed by Syria, attacked PLO forces in the northern Lebanese city of Tripoli, thereby driving Arafat from his last base in the country.[26] Despite the infighting and its having been driven out of both Jordan and Lebanon, the PLO has some notable achievements to its credit. It has been recognized as the sole legitimate representative of the Palestinian people by Arab governments. Acting on its behalf, these same governments were able to have a United Nations General Assembly resolution passed that equated Zionism with racism. PLO missions and diplomatic representatives are to be found in many communist bloc and Third World nations. The PLO also enjoys "observer" status at the United Nations. Its activities have excited widespread admiration among many Arabs, including those resident on the West Bank. Arafat and other PLO figures have met many of the world's heads of state and religious leaders, including the Pope. From an organizational perspective, the PLO is both large and, thanks to contributions from oil-rich Arab nations and its own business dealings, wealthy as well.

What has not been achieved are any of the PLO's ultimate goals regarding either the Israeli-occupied West Bank or Israel itself. The future of the West Bank remains unclear, but its occupation by the Israelis appears unlikely to be brought to an end by further acts of PLO terrorism. And for an organization acting in the name of national independence, the fact that many of its operations have been sponsored and, in some cases, actually implemented by Arab nations is something to contemplate.

No other terrorist organization pursuing nationalist-separatist objectives has won the international acclaim received by the PLO. None of the others can count on the support of so many governments around the world. But at least in terms of publicity, the closest approximation to be found in Western Europe is the Provisional Irish Republican Army (PIRA). Over the years, it has received support from Libya and some of the Warsaw Pact nations. Also, assistance has been forthcoming from well-wishers in the United States, help furnished under the auspices of the Irish Northern Aid Committee (NORAID). Unlike the PLO groups, however, PIRA's various active service units have not engaged in the practice of skyjacking or carried out terrorist operations on a global basis. For the most part their activities have been confined to the Irish Republic, Northern Ireland proper, and other areas of the United Kingdom. The most spectacular, if not the most lethal, terrorist attacks growing out of Northern Ireland's "troubles" was the assassination of Lord Mountbatten, Queen Elizabeth's cousin, in 1979, and the unsuccessful attempt to kill British Prime Minister Thatcher at Brighton in 1984.

As we noted, the spark that ignited contemporary terrorism in Northern Ireland was the Catholic civil rights movement of the late 1960s and the hostile response to it by elements in the Protestant community, including the police. But the tinder for the fire was the profound alienation many Catholics felt about the conditions in which they lived.[27]

The onset of the troubles in 1969 and the inability of the existing Irish Republican Army to protect Catholic neighborhoods in Belfast and the other cities from Protestant mobs and the Protestant-dominated police (the so-called B specials) led to a division within the organization and the formation of PIRA. This development evidently was also encouraged by a few ministers in the Irish government in Dublin.[28]

On the other side of the Irish Sea, the British government viewed with alarm the surge of Protestant and Catholic protest. It reacted by urging Northern Ireland's provincial government at Stormont to undertake a series of reform measures intended to improve the status of Catholics. Also in 1969 British Prime Minister Wilson ordered troops sent to the area; their objective was to restore order by, among other things, protecting Catholic neighborhoods from Protestant assault. But the presence of British troops had an effect opposite to the one London had intended.

In patrolling Catholic areas and conducting house-to-house searches, the troops managed to antagonize those citizens it had been sent to protect. The PIRA portrayed the troops as an army of occupation which, in turn, symbolized continued British domination of Ireland, a circumstance it was committed to eliminating by violence. To this end, PIRA was successful in recruiting a large number of young men to its ranks from such Catholic working-class neighborhoods as Bogside in Derry.

Over the next several years PIRA carried out attacks on British troops and conducted a campaign of bombing public places where Protestants were likely to be found. Militant Protestant organizations reacted with their own wave of sectarian murders directed at Catholic targets.

Reactions to this escalating wave of terrorist violence included a policy of internment without trial which was begun by the provincial government in 1971 and was later adopted by London. This measure allowed the authorities to detain individuals suspected of terrorism without providing habeas corpus and other due-process protections.[29] Applied almost exclusively to PIRA suspects, the policy made matters worse by solidifying Catholic opinion against British injustice. There were more bombings in Belfast and still more troops were shot. The British government, now led by Conservative Prime Minister Edward Heath, responded by sending additional troops and by suspending the Stormont government. In March 1972 direct rule from London was imposed. This action was taken in the aftermath of Bloody Sunday, when British troops killed thirteen Catholic men in Derry.

The British then sought to recreate a new provincial government based on a Protestant-Catholic power-sharing arrangement. This effort failed because of Protestant hostility. In 1974 there was a general strike of Protestant workers organized to express their opposition to the proposal.

The same year also witnessed the formation of another terrorist group, the Irish Nationalist Liberation Army. Like PIRA it is committed to a united Ireland under the direction of a socialist regime. To further this end, it has committed such acts of terrorism as the assassination of the Conservative leader Airey Neave in 1979 and the bombing of Harrod's department store in 1983, both in London.

Despite a long list of other terrorist attacks, including some committed against British diplomats on the European continent, neither PIRA nor the Liberation Army has been successful in achieving their objectives. In 1985 the British and Irish governments reached an agreement that ended direct rule from London. The arrangement provided for a new provincial government, one organized with sectarian power sharing in mind. Most important, though, it established a consultative body which includes representatives from both Dublin and London to consider the province's long-term problems. It remains to be seen whether this initiative will succeed in bringing Northern Ireland's troubles to an end.

Terrorism in Northern Ireland was initiated by groups operating in a democratic context. Whatever the prejudices of the Protestant majority and the deficiencies of Stormont, the governments of Ireland and Great Britain are modern democracies. The same cannot be said about the situation in Spain at the time the first members of Euzkadi Ta Askatasuna (ETA) committed themselves to achieving independence for their Basque homeland (Euzkadi) from Spanish domination. Not only the Basque region but all of Spain was ruled by a right-wing dictatorship under General Francisco Franco.[30] The democratic regime in Madrid, which Franco defeated in a particularly destructive civil war (1936–1939) had extended regional autonomy to the Basques. From Franco's point of view, however, such a devolution of power represented an intolerable threat to Spanish unity. The victory of his forces in 1939 brought an end to Basque hopes for autonomy, much less independence.

The setting for Basque terrorism differed from the circumstances prevailing in Northern Ireland in several other ways. For one, the fact that Spain was a dictatorship whose leader had received support from Mussolini and Hitler ensured there would be a residue of sympathy for the Basque cause among Western Europeans, particularly among the French, that was not available to the PIRA. This fact inclined French governments to look the other way when ETA terrorists sought sanctuary among the Basque population of France, whose three southernmost departments are considered part of the Basque homeland. Second, while Belfast and the rest of Northern Ireland was and is an economically depressed region, the Basque provinces of Spain are more prosperous and industrialized than the rest of the country. Despite repeated claims by separatists to the effect that the Basque region is really an exploited colonial possession of Madrid, it is exceedingly odd for a colony to be more economically advanced than the imperial power that exploits it. Also, Northern Ireland's troubles are rooted in religious differences between Catholics and Protestants; in this case, however, both the Basque separatists and their opponents are Catholics.[31] Finally, ETA's origins are more like those of many revolutionary terrorist organizations than those of the PIRA.

ETA began as a study group of young university students in 1952; most of its founders were drawn from well-to-do families. Its early years were devoted to ideological struggles rather than violent confrontations with the Spanish authorities.[32] At assemblies and in pamphlets questions were debated concerning the extent of ETA's commitments to nationalism and socialism and the desirability of clandestine operations versus organizational efforts among Basque workers. In the mid-1960s ETA became committed to a policy of armed struggle, and an Activist Branch was formed whose purpose was the acquisition of sufficient money with which to launch such a campaign. Accordingly, from 1965 forward ETA commandos staged a series of bank robberies and other holdups.

By the late 1960s, and despite a succession of factional divisions, ETA was clearly in business. Inspired in part by the revolutionary theories of Che Guevara and the successes of the Viet Cong, the organization began its armed struggle against the Franco regime.

Fundamentally this struggle consisted of two sorts of terrorist operations. First, members of the Guardia Civil, Franco's paramilitary police force, were assassinated in the Basque region and other parts of Spain along with other police and military officers. Second, Basque industrialists and other business executives were kidnapped and held for ransom. ETA terrorism was rarely of the indiscriminate variety.[33]

Targets were selected with these purposes in mind: inviting repression from Madrid as a means of building popular support among the Basques and convincing Basque workers of ETA's commitment to their social class. The payment of ransom by the industrialists' families, of course, had a more than symbolic aim.

The most spectacular achievement during the Franco era occurred in 1973. Admiral Carrero Blanco, the Spanish prime minister and Franco's likely successor, was assassinated in Madrid. As may be imagined, this act, as well as less dramatic terrorist exploits, led to a large number of arrests. The trials of ETA terrorists, particularly those which ended in death sentences, became opportunities for making propaganda based on the self-sacrifices of ETA's cadres. Yet, when Franco died in 1975, the Basque region seemed no closer to winning autonomy than it had before the violent campaign began.

Cultural freedom and the establishment of a regional government for the Basques were achievements of Spanish democracy. After Franco's death Spain underwent an unexpectedly smooth transition to democracy. Political parties were organized, elections were held, and a new constitution was drafted. A Basque Nationalist party participated in all these developments. Further, in 1979 Basque voters approved a statute which provided a framework for the formation of an elective regional government. The following year another election was held in the Basque region, which, for the first time in the area's history, produced a popularly selected assembly to direct the region's public business.

Yet, despite the advent of Spanish democracy and the achievement under its auspices of Basque autonomy, ETA-based terrorism did not come to an end. In fact, during these transitional years, the level of terrorist attacks actually increased in comparison to what it had been under the Franco dictatorship.[34] ETA, by now split into three separate entities, persisted in its violence largely because of its dissatisfaction over the fact that complete national independence had not been won. But these terrorist operations, carried t in the new democratic context, apparently had the effect of the organization losing rather than gaining popular support in the region.

In recent years the number of terrorist attacks has declined somewhat. But, as in Northern Ireland, it is unlikely that the attempt at compromise will lead to the disappearance of terrorism from the Spanish landscape.

More optimistic conclusions can be reached with respect to terrorism perpetrated by other nationalist-separatist groups in the Western world. In Canada, the Front for the Liberation of Quebec (FLQ), a group seeking independence for that province from the Canadian federation, carried out a few highly publicized terrorist operations during the early 1970s. These activities included the kidnapping of James Cross, the British trade commissioner, and the murder of Pierre La Porte, Quebec's transport minister. But a combination of political reform, popular revulsion, and state repression led to the FLQ's demise.[35] The United States was not immune to nationalist-separatist terrorism either. During the 1970s, the Armed Forces for the Liberation of Puerto Rico, and elements within the American Indian Movement and the Black Panther party, among others, staged terrorist attacks in order to advance their own separatist goals. But as with their Canadian counterparts, these activities had largely disappeared by the 1980s.[36]

In France groups seeking independence for Corsica and Brittany began to launch violent attacks, largely bombings, during the 1970s; these activities have persisted through the present decade. For the most part the targets have been symbolic ones, such as public monuments and government offices, and their impact has been distinctly limited.[37]

The stories of émigré groups in pursuit of nationalist-separatist objectives are much the same. Despite the widely publicized exploits—which include bombings, acts of air piracy, kidnappings, and assassinations—of groups seeking freedom for Croatia, Armenia, and South Molucca (from Indonesia) during the 1970s, their terrorist activities have declined in recent years. While their violence managed to call attention to what were previously regarded as obscure causes, this consciousness raising has not led to any tangible accomplishments.[38]

These remarks should not lead the reader to conclude that nationalist-separatist terrorism has disappeared. It has not. Instead, it has undergone a change of venue from Europe to South Asia.

The assassination of Indian Prime Minister Indira Gandhi in 1984 and the destruction of an Air India 747 jet over the Atlantic the following year (which killed 329 people) were the principal events that focused worldwide attention on the problems of India's Sikh minority. Members of the Sikh religion represent about 2 percent of the country's population and are geographically concentrated in the Punjab.[39] In economic terms the Sikhs do not constitute an impoverished minority. Instead they are overrepresented at the upper end of Indian society; Sikhs are to be found disproportionately among India's professional military establishment. Nor, prior to the outbreak of terrorism, did the Sikhs lack a political organization to give voice to their concerns. In fact, the Akali Dal, the Sikh political party, had begun to demand an autonomous state (to be called Khalistan) in the early 1970s.

The current terrorist episode grew out of a conflict between Hindus and Sikhs. Expressions of sectarian antagonism involving the reciprocal desecration of various religious symbols led to the formation of an armed Sikh resistance movement. Some members of this youth organization, the dal Khalosa, were arrested after having committed acts of violence; others stationed themselves within the Golden Temple in the holy city of Amristrar. In 1984 Indira Gandhi ordered Indian Army units to invade the temple. Many Sikhs were killed in the defense of their shrine. This event ignited a series of terrorist attacks by Sikhs against Hindus. Later, Hindu mobs took vengeance against Sikhs for the violence done their brethren.

Terrorism in Sri Lanka bears some resemblance to the situation in India. Once again it is a geographically concentrated religious minority, the Tamils, that is at the center of the conflict. But unlike the Sikhs, the Hindu Tamils have been the object of long-term and governmentally sanctioned discrimination practiced by the country's Buddhist Sinhalese majority. In response to anti-Tamil riots in 1977, several Tamil separatist groups were formed, the most prominent of which was the Liberation Tigers. The first major attack launched by the Tigers, who hoped to achieve an independent state of Eelam, occurred in 1983 and involved the assassination of thirteen Sri Lankan soldiers. Since that year the violence has escalated with the separatist groups carrying out indiscriminate slaughters of Sinhalese women and children in the country's major cities.[40]

By 1987 the conflict had reached the point of civil war, with the Tamil groups able to exercise de facto control over large sections of their home region. The Indian government (its interest stems from the fact southern India has a large Tamil community) has sought to bring about a compromise settlement. The Indians have sent their own troops to Sri Lanka in order to enforce the agreement and disarm the Tamil organizations. The outcome of this situation, however, is far from clear.

Contemporary nationalist-separatist terrorism has been prevalent in the Middle East, in the Western democracies, and most recently in South Asia. Conspicuously missing from the list is Sub-Saharan Africa, an area of the world whose population is divided into thousands of separate tribal units and one whose postcolonial history has not been noted for its political stability. In short, the ingredients for this type of terrorism appear to exist, but in practice there has been little of it.[41] Tribal and religious communities have pursued their goals through mass protests and guerrilla warfare campaigns rather than terrorism. The notable exception concerns events presently unfolding in South Africa.

Organized terrorist operations in that country are carried out by the Spear of the Nation, the military branch of the African National Congress (ANC).[42] Most of its activities have been centered in the Johannesburg and Durban metropolitan areas, where car bomb explosions, rocket attacks, and shootings have been directed against industrial facilities, police and military installations, shopping malls, and white residential neighborhoods. The frequency of these terrorist attacks has increased substantially in recent years, and barring an end to South Africa's system of white supremacy, seem likely to continue into the foreseeable future. Attempts by the South African government to eliminate the terrorism by, among other things, assassinating various ANC representatives in other countries have not proved successful.

Revolutionary Terrorism

Terrorist campaigns intended to bring about a fundamental change in the distribution of wealth, power, and status in society have been prevalent in Latin America, where they have posed serious challenges to several incumbent regimes, and in the industrial democracies, where, with two exceptions, they have not. While terrorist groups pursuing nationalist-separatist objectives commonly assert their commitments to socialism and opposition to capitalism, it is sometimes forgotten that there are distinct traces of nationalism in the views of groups which employ terrorism for social revolutionary purposes. Capitalist forms of economic enterprise are commonly associated with the presence of foreigners, foreign-owned multinational corporations, and foreign military presence. Accordingly, for revolutionary terrorists there is often an identification between capitalism and an American presence, with an end to the former requiring the expulsion of the latter. Among other things, the affinity of nationalist-separatist groups for socialism and the affinity of revolutionary organizations for anti-American nationalism have facilitated a degree of cooperation between the two types of groups, for example, Palestinian nationalists with West German revolutionaries, in committing acts of international terrorism that probably would not have been possible without their mutual hostility to the forces of American imperialism.

The link between anti-American nationalism and social revolution has been particularly strong in Latin America, where opposition to Yankee imperialism has been a central theme in the doctrines of left-wing political movements for a very long time. Aside from a brief wave of terrorism in Venezuela initiated by the activist wing of the Communist party in the 1962–1963 period, the three Latin American nations to be the principal sites of urban terrorism in the late 1960s and 1970s were Uruguay, Brazil, and Argentina.[43] At the time their terrorist experiences began, Uruguay had a democratic government, whereas Argentina and Brazil were ruled by the military. What these nations had in common were highly urbanized populations and social structures that exhibited vast disparities in wealth.

The National Liberation Movement (the Tupamaros) of Uruguay was in several ways prototypical of revolutionary terrorist groups in Latin America and elsewhere. Formed in 1962 in Montevideo as a small circle of revolutionary intellectuals headed by Raul Sendic, a labor union organizer, the Tupamaros spent the first years of their existence refining their ideological perspective and developing an organizational apparatus.[44] In regard to the former, the Tupamaros absorbed many of the ideas of a refugee Spanish anarchist, Abraham Guillen. Since more than half the Uruguayan population lived in and around Montevideo, Guillen believed: "Today the epicenter of the revolutionary war must be in the great urban zones, where heavy artillery is not as efficient as in the countryside for annihilating guerrillas tied to the land."[45] The city had other advantages as well; it was the center of the mass media and government, and there were potentially hundreds of thousands of sympathizers to be found among the urban masses.

Guillen's views, as well as those to be found in early commentaries of the Tupamaros, also emphasized the importance of organizational links to these urban masses, the need to avoid unprovoked cold-blooded killings and large-scale "Homeric" battles with government forces, at least in the early stages of armed struggle. Unprovoked killings would lead to popular revulsion and alienate the masses the Tupamaros hoped to win over. Homeric battles were ones which the urban guerrillas would lose.

The Tupamaros managed to violate all three admonitions in the course of their revolutionary campaign. Things went smoothly enough during the early "Robin Hood" phase of their operations when the emphasis was more on publicity than on confrontation with the authorities. For example, in February 1969 a unit of the Tupamaros robbed a gambling casino and distributed the proceeds to the poor.[46] Also, pamphlets were distributed exposing the corruption of various Uruguayan officials. But by the end of 1969 the organization sought to commemorate the second anniversary of Che Guevara's death by seizing the town of Pando. This Homeric undertaking produced the inevitable defeat.

A wave of violence followed this defeat, with Tupamaro assassinations of prominent police and military officers from 1970 onward. Included in this terrorist campaign were the abductions of several foreign officials, notably the American police adviser Dan Mitrione, later killed, and the British ambassador, Sir Geoffrey Jackson. The more serious the challenge the Tupamaros posed to the government, the worse things became for them. The police offered bribes to informers and employed torture to extract the information they required. The government also encouraged the formation of right-wing death squads to carry out extralegal killings of Tupamaros and their collaborators.

In the end the Tupamaros helped to bring about the collapse of Uruguay's democratic regime. But its replacement was not the one on which they had planned. In 1973 the military seized power and proceeded to liquidate what remained of the Tupamaro organization.

The military was already in control of Brazil when that nation's terrorist experience began. The generals had staged a coup against the populist President Joa Goulart in 1964.[47] At first, opposition to military rule came from the old civilian political elite, the Catholic Church, and the official Communist party. But their peaceful protests and other initiatives amounted to very little. As it turned out, armed opposition from revolutionary terrorist bands did not count for all that much either, but their operations were at least more spectacular.

If Guillen had been the Tupamaros' revolutionary theoretician, the equivalent role in Brazil was played by Carlos Marighella. A long-time member of the Communist party and author of the famous *Minimanual of the Urban Guerrilla* (1969), Marighella proposed a three-stage approach to revolutionary warfare. The first and preparatory phase was urban terrorism; this would be followed by guerrilla activity in the countryside. When the insurgency reached a sufficiently high level of intensity, a people's army would be formed that would then confront directly the government's forces. Terrorism, in other words, would play only a complementary not a central role in these proceedings.

Unlike Guillen, Marighella chose to put his theory into practice. In 1968 he left the Communist party to found and then lead National Liberation Action (ALN), one of several urban guerrilla groups to pursue an armed struggle against the Brazilian military government.[48]

The ALN, along with the Popular Revolutionary Vanguard (VPR), an organization headed by Carlos Lamarca, an ex-army officer, and the Movement of October 8 (MR-8), began terrorist operations in São Paolo, Rio de Janeiro, and a few smaller cities. In the 1969–1971 period kidnappings and assassinations of foreigners and the bombing of foreign-owned business enterprises became the principal means by which the terrorists sought to win the support of Brazil's urban masses. American, Japanese, West German, and Swiss diplomats were taken hostage or shot at. In some cases the freedom of foreign diplomats was exchanged for the release of imprisoned terrorists. Banks, both domestic and foreign-owned, were bombed and robbed, with the proceeds, in some instances, distributed to slum dwellers.

As in Uruguay, the authorities applied torture to extract information from terrorists they had taken prisoner. Some died rather than reveal their secrets, but many others were willing to disclose the whereabouts of their colleagues. Massive roundups followed these disclosures. Marighella and Lamarca were shot to death by the police after their hiding places were revealed to the police by prisoners under torture. Efforts to apply Marighella's theory outlived its author, but not for long. By 1974 the regime had managed to dismantle the major terrorist organizations, and the violence subsided.

In Argentina the use of torture by the authorities was far more pervasive than in Brazil. Thousands were killed.[49] But the magnitude of terrorist violence in Argentina also was far higher.

At the time Argentine terrorism began, the nation was ruled by a military regime that had deposed the widely popular though quasi-fascist President Juan Perón in 1955. Perón, who in his youth had been an admirer of Mussolini, had gone into exile in Franco's Spain. Much of the violence committed by the country's terrorist organizations in the late 1960s and early 1970s was aimed at restoring Perón to power. The expectations were that Perón would take Argentina in a nationalist (anti-American) and socialist direction.[50] The major terrorist group that sought Perón's return was the Montoneros. Formed in the years from 1968 to 1970, its origins were not rooted in Marxism. The Montoneros' organizers drew both doctrine and recruits from Catholic and Argentine fascist sources. The fascist contribution was provided by the Tacuara, an anti-Semitic youth organization that stressed the values of courage, sacrifice, and struggle.[51] As far as the Catholic component is concerned, the Montoneros derived inspiration from Pope Paul VI's *Populorum Progressio,* a statement which attacked such sins as the profit motive and economic inequality. Translated by liberation theologians into a justification for social revolution, these views attracted many idealistic Catholic youth to the Montoneros' cause.

The other organization that came to play a central role in Argentine terrorism was the People's Revolutionary Army (ERP). In contrast to the Montoneros, the ERP represented the armed wing of the Worker's Revolutionary party. Instead of *Populorum Progressio* and idealistic Catholic opposition to pervasive injustice, ERP members found their inspiration in the works of Leon Trotsky. Che Guevara was their martyred hero.[52] Furthermore, unlike the Montoneros and several smaller groups, the ERP did not regard Perón's resumption of power as a panacea which would solve Argentina's manifold economic problems.

Between the beginning of 1969 and the spring of 1973, when the Perónist Hector Campora was inaugurated as president of Argentina, the Montoneros, the ERP, and smaller groups committed a great number of terrorist attacks. One compilation of these activities goes on for more than twenty pages.[53] Along with less dramatic events, it includes the kidnapping and subsequent assassination of Pedro Aramburu, the country's ex-president. Another source reports that in 1973 alone, there were 178 kidnappings of foreign and Argentine businesspeople; included in this number were executives of Kodak, Exxon, Coca-Cola, Firestone, Swissair, and Peugot.[54] Millions were paid in ransom to secure the release of these individuals.

The volume of terrorist violence subsided during 1973 to 1974. Campora's election was followed by the much-awaited return of Perón. New elections followed his return; Perón and his second wife, Isabel, were elected president and vice president, respectively, of Argentina after Campora stepped aside. In exile Perón had appeared, if not all things to all people, relatively close to it. After his return and resumption of the presidency, the situation became clearer. Perón was not interested in the sort of radical economic changes his leftist admirers thought would be forthcoming. In addition, his attitude toward the Montoneros' "Perónist" violence was one of hostility. For a group that had heralded Perón's election by proclaiming "Today, Perón is Argentina; he is Fatherland," the letdown was considerable.[55]

A man of 77, Perón died in 1974. His vice president and widow, Isabel, succeeded to the presidency. A former professional go-go dancer, Isabel

Perón was hardly equipped to direct the affairs of a modern state, much less one as troubled as Argentina. During her period of leadership terrorist violence reached and then exceeded pre-1973 levels. High-ranking police and military officers were among the principal targets. In 1976, the military removed Isabel Perón and then proceeded to wage its brutal "dirty war" against the terrorist organizations and those suspected of sympathizing with them.

The defeat of guerrilla groups in Argentina, Brazil, and Uruguay has not brought an end to revolutionary terrorism in Latin America. The most recent manifestations suggest that the newer groups have learned something from the failures of the earlier ones. In Peru and Colombia especially, violent revolutionary organizations have tended to combine acts of urban terrorism with rural guerrilla warfare techniques in their efforts to displace incumbent political regimes. It may be the case also that the terrain in these countries is more favorable for such combined operations than in Argentina, Brazil, and Uruguay.

The rise of the Shining Path (Sendero Luminoso) movement in Peru coincided with the return of democratic rule to that country in 1980. The decision to create the Shining Path was made by a dissident communist (Maoist) philosophy professor, Abimael Guzman, along with some of his colleagues and students at the University of Huamanga.[56] The socially isolated and economically impoverished province in which the university is located was conceived as ideal for guerrilla operations. Indeed Shining Path's revolutionary program represents a restatement of the classic principles associated with this strategy. Initially, however, most of the movement's violence was of the terrorist variety. In 1980 and 1981 the Shining Path announced its presence by bombing public buildings and, incredible as it may seem, hanging dogs from lampposts (symbolic of its attitude toward those in power) in Lima and smaller Peruvian cities. Since that time it has carried out other terrorist attacks: one to coincide with a visit of the Pope to Peru, one in which sections of Lima were blacked out when power lines were destroyed, and one during an international conference of democratic socialists. The police have reacted to these occurrences with brutality; their response has included the mass execution of Shining Path prisoners during an attempted jailbreak.

But unlike the revolutionary groups in Argentina, Brazil, and Uruguay, the Shining Path has been able to sustain a guerrilla campaign along with its terrorist operations. Government military outposts in the Andes have been attacked with some frequency and, at times, villages have been seized and their Indian inhabitants subjected to political reeducation techniques.[57]

In Colombia not only have revolutionary groups sought to strike a balance between guerrilla warfare and urban terrorism, they have also be-

come involved with that country's wealthy narcotics dealers.[58] Among
the nine revolutionary organizations active recently in Colombia three
have attracted substantial international attention: the April 19 Movement
(M19), the Armed Revolutionary Forces of Colombia (FARC), and the
National Liberation Army (ELN).[59] Like the Shining Path, their operations have been directed at overthrowing not a military dictatorship but a
popularly elected democratic government. All three organizations have
combined efforts to establish liberated zones in the countryside with terrorist activities in Bogotá and other cities.

Terrorist attacks have included the kidnapping of foreign business executives and diplomats and the assassination of public officials; these
killings often have been done at the behest of the cocaine barons. In
1985, Colombia's ex-President Bentancur was able to persuade the legis-
lature to enact a liberal amnesty law for revolutionaries willing to abandon violence. The results have been mixed. FARC, an outgrowth of the
country's Communist party, accepted the offer tentatively, but M19 and
the others did not. In November 1985 the M19 expressed its feelings
about this attempt at national reconciliation by having fifty of its followers seize the palace of justice in Bogotá. In the ensuing violence, M19
killed the head of Colombia's supreme court along with eleven other senior judges. The police, acting on instructions from the president, attacked the building and killed all the revolutionaries who had barricaded
themselves inside it.[60]

Revolutionary terrorism, as a supplement to guerrilla insurgencies,
has become of some significance in Central America. In El Salvador, for
example, groups seeking to topple the democratic regime of President
Napoleon Duarte have staged a large number of terrorist attacks in San
Salvador, including the kidnapping of Duarte's daughter.

In Chile the Communist Patriotic Front has killed several officials of
that country's military dictatorship. In 1986 General Pinochet was himself the target of an unsuccessful assassination attempt. These episodes
were then used by the general as an excuse to delay the restoration of
democratic rule in his country.

So many of the world's industrial democracies have experienced revolutionary terrorism in recent years that it seems useful to introduce a
distinction before proceeding to the analysis of these developments. It is
true that Great Britain has had its Angry Brigade and that the United
States witnessed operations carried out by the Weather Underground
and Symbionese Liberation Army, but these organizations counted for
very little despite the publicity they received. On the other hand, there
are two nations, Turkey and Italy, where revolutionary terrorism has
posed serious threats to the prevailing political order. Standing some-
where between these two poles are such democracies as West Germany

and Japan, where revolutionary terrorists have had some impact, though not on the order of their Turkish and Italian counterparts.

Related to these differences in scale is the nature of the revolution the terrorist groups have sought to achieve. In general, though there are some exceptions, the weaker the group the more grandiose its plans. Members of such organizations as the United Red Army had little hope that their minuscule band could topple the Japanese government or bring about the collapse of capitalism in their country. Accordingly, their actions were directed less at winning the support of the indifferent Japanese working class and more on freeing the entire world from imperialism and the capitalist yoke. Their frame of reference was not Japan but the oppressed masses of the Third World.[61] On the other hand, revolutionary terrorist groups active in Turkey and Italy were able to attract thousands of recruits and had sizable constituencies of sympathizers and well-wishers in their countries. In these circumstances, the terrorists' objectives were more narrowly focused on achieving revolution in one country. Revolutionary groups composed of a small number of adherents need broader causes or movements whose situations of deprivation or oppression become justifications for terrorism. Where such causes and movements are missing at home, they are usually found abroad.

Terrorism in Turkey has exhibited nearly the full range of possibilities. Social revolutionary organizations committed to Marxist-Leninist objectives did not have a monopoly on the violence. There were, in addition, several right-wing groups, most prominent of which was the Grey Wolves, dedicated to the elimination of Marxism from Turkish life, as well as Kurdish and Armenian groups, which have used terror in order to advance their separatist objectives.

The first generation of revolutionary terrorists emerged from a pool of radical Turkish university students in 1970. Left-wing student politics itself had been stimulated by the student protest movements in Western Europe and by events in the Middle East during the late 1960s. The first and most important groups to appear were the Turkish People's Liberation Army (TPLA) and the Turkish People's Liberation Front (TPLF).[62] These organizations sought to liberate Turkey from its democratic government and its membership in NATO.

The several hundred members of TPLA and TPLF were helped in their pursuit of these goals by Palestinian groups and the Soviets, both of whom had an interest in changing Turkey's role in international politics. The revolutionaries received training in the PLO camps and weapons from the Russians.[63]

The level of terrorist violence perpetrated by TPLA and TPLF was sufficiently high to cause the military to declare martial law in 1971. The army then proceeded to decimate both revolutionary organizations by arresting or killing their militants, including their most visible leaders. Persuaded that it had brought an end to the violence, the military ended martial law in 1973. New elections brought a center-left government to power under Bulen Ecevit. Working under the same assumption as the military, the Ecevit government extended amnesty to those revolutionaries it held in prison.

This decision proved premature, to say the least. Many of the freed revolutionaries resumed their violent careers. This time they were joined by thousands of new recruits. A new generation of terrorist groups, including Revolutionary Road (Dev Yol) and Revolutionary Left (Dev Sol), carried out operations in Istanbul, Ankara, and other cities. During the late 1970s more than 4500 people were killed as a result of the ensuing anarchy, with the revolutionaries engaged in daily battles with the right-wing groups and various sectors of Turkish society.

By 1980 Turkey's major cities were on the verge of what one analyst has referred to as "Beirutization."[64] In a context in which political killings were occurring at a pace of more than one per hour, the military seized power. Civil liberties were suspended, and over the next several months thousands of revolutionaries were rounded up by special antiterrorism units. As in Uruguay and Argentina, terrorism in Turkey was defeated through the intervention of the military. But the price these countries had to pay for the repression was a high one—the end of democratic politics.[65]

Fortunately, Italians have not had to bear this same cost. Their democratic regime, despite all its well-known flaws, has been able to withstand the pressures created by the bout of terrorism Italy has suffered for more than a decade and a half. During this period revolutionary terrorist groups committed thousands of acts of violence, one of which, the kidnapping and assassination of Christian Democratic leader Aldo Moro in 1978, disrupted delicate interparty negotiations and shook the ruling coalition government to its foundations.[66]

As in Turkey, far-left terrorism in Italy is best understood in generational terms. That is, a first generation of terrorist groups emerged in the early 1970s. These included the Partisan Action Group (GAP) of Feltrinelli, an organization active in some of the northern cities, and the Nuclei of Armed Proletarians (NAP), whose operations were largely confined to Naples and Rome. The third formation to appear in these years was the Red Brigades (BR), an organization that has displayed far greater endurance than the others and one whose operations have been staged all over the country.[67]

To the extent that Italy had a serious terrorist problem in the first half of the 1970s, it came not from the left but from the right. Neo-Fascist groups such as the New Order (ON), National Vanguard (AN), and National Front (FN), mobilized in opposition to the mass protests of the New Left, carried out a number of anonymous bombings in public places in the hope they would be able to bring about the collapse of Italian democracy by means of a coup d'état. The neo-Fascists had well-wishers within the police and military establishments who were willing to help achieve this goal.

In contrast, the leftist groups carried out a series of "exemplary actions" involving the abduction of business executives, actions intended to convince Italian workers of their revolutionary potential. There were a handful of bank robberies and other events, but nothing on the scale of neo-Fascist violence. Furthermore, the authorities displayed much greater skill in dealing with leftist terrorism than with its neo-Fascist counterpart.

By 1976 it appeared to many as if revolutionary terrorism had been played out. The GAP and NAP had been destroyed, a result in part of their own ineptitude, and the BR's founders, members of its "historic nucleus," had been captured and put on trial in Milan.

The BR, along with a list of new second-generation groups, was able to recruit a large number of new adherents, many of whom came from such New Left movements as Worker Power (POTOP) and Continuous Struggle (LC). The optimism of these movements about the prospects for revolution through mass mobilization and political struggle had been dampened by a series of defeats.

In this period the BR's National Direction decided to strike at the "heart of the state" by directing the organization's attacks against Christian Democratic leaders, public officials, judges, journalists, and all those believed responsible for the maintenance of Italian capitalism. The BR was joined in this endeavor by Front Line (PL), another clandestine group, which waged "campaigns" of violence with the same purpose in mind. In addition, the authorities had to confront the practice of "diffuse" terrorism. Unlike the BR and PL, groups whose militants were full-time terrorists living lives of perpetual clandestinity, revolutionaries belonging to the Workers' Collective Autonomy (AO) began to commit acts of violence while trying to lead normal lives.

In the late 1970s the level of killings, "kneecappings," and bombings escalated. Not only Aldo Moro, but many prominent and some not so prominent Italians fell victim to the revolutionary terrorist campaigns. Nonetheless, the authorities were able to turn the tide. They did so not by the imposition of martial law and the suspension of civil liberties but through the application of new antiterrorist legislation. A new law provided reduced sentences for terrorists who were willing to repent and disclose the whereabouts of their comrades. By the early 1980s and particularly after the liberation of American General James Dozier from his BR kidnappers in 1982, enough revolutionaries had repented to permit the authorities to break the back of the terrorist groups.

Mass trials of the revolutionary terrorists were held in Italy's major cities in 1983 to 1984. Yet, some terrorists unwilling to abandon the struggle were able to avoid arrest and flee abroad; Paris was their favored destination. Others remained in Italy, where they have continued to recruit new members for the revolutionary cause and to commit additional acts of violence. In short, revolutionary terrorism in Italy has subsided but not disappeared.

Revolutionary terrorism in the Federal Republic of Germany has neither disappeared nor subsided, at least not by much. The Bonn government recorded 331 terrorist attacks carried out by leftist revolutionary groups in 1985, more than twice the number for any one year during the 1970s.[68] Compared with their counterparts in Turkey and Italy, however, the West German groups have been less successful or more selective in inflicting casualties on their fellow citizens. While Turkish revolutionaries killed thousands and the Italians hundreds, the West German terrorists were responsible for a total of twenty-five deaths between 1969 and 1979.[69] The vast difference between the severity of the violence and the amount of publicity it has attracted is likely the result of two factors. First, during the 1970s West German terrorists staged a number of spectacular operations in conjunction with the Palestinians: the kidnapping of OPEC oil ministers in Vienna, for example. These actions were sufficiently dramatic to capture the headlines all over the world. Second, given the contours of twentieth-century German history, there exist broad concerns, both in the Federal Republic and in the West in general, with events that seem to weaken the country's democratic institutions and international reputation.

Revolutionary terrorism in West Germany was hardly the outgrowth of economic distress and broad working-class discontent. Its origins are to be found, as in the other industrial democracies, in the rise of student protest and the formation of a youth-centered counterculture during the late 1960s. A distinctively generational element should be added to these ingredients. There was a sense that the older generation dominant in West German society when the terrorism began bore responsibility for the Nazi dictatorship. Despite abundant evidence to the contrary, many young leftists came to believe that not all that much had changed. Both the Hitler regime and the bourgeois democracy that replaced it were thought to be inherently fascist in character.[70]

The first German organization to launch attacks in the name of revolution was the Red Army Faction (RAF) or Baader-Meinhof Gang, a name based on the group's founders Ulrike Meinhof and Andreas Baader.[71] The RAF was later joined in its revolutionary activities by two

other groups which also attracted considerable attention: the Revolutionary Cells (RZ) and the Second of June Movement. While the RAF was
and continues to be a clandestine organization whose full-time terrorists
operate in an atmosphere of secrecy, the Revolutionary Cells, like the
Workers Collective Autonomy in Italy, has become adroit at the practice
of diffuse terrorism. It is a collection of groups whose members lead normal lives while committing acts of violence after hours on a part-time basis. From a theoretical point of view the two organizations are not identical. RAF has emphasized students as the social base of the revolution,
while RZ publications assign a comparable role to the working masses.
The Second of June group, which shared the same general orientation as
the RAF, abandoned the armed struggle in 1980, and most of its followers
joined the latter organization.[72]

Aside from a perception of West Germany as an intrinsically fascist
regime, the two organizations have been bound together by a rejection of
consumer society with its emphasis on mindless acquisitiveness. In this
regard, the RAF's first armed terrorist attack was not directed at the
heart of the state but involved the bombing of a department store. Further, as in Japan, the West German groups had no domestic constituency
to speak of. Consequently, they defined themselves as waging an armed
struggle on behalf of Third World liberation movements at war with the
forces of imperialism.[73] Israel and Zionism came to be identified with the
latter, so that ironically the revolutionaries, at war with the ghost of
Hitler, wound up collaborating with those who wish to destroy the
Jewish state.

Thus during the 1970s RAF members received training at Palestinian
camps in Lebanon and South Yemen. They carried out joint operations
with PLO commandos. These actions included the skyjacking of French
and German aircraft in 1976 and 1977. These events ended in disasters for
their perpetrators when Israeli and West German antiterrorist units liberated the passengers and killed most of those responsible (at Entebbe
and Mogadisho). The second defeat was particularly costly for the terrorists because it led directly to the suicides of RAF leaders being held in
West German prisons.

On the domestic scene, the revolutionaries focused their attention on
leaders of German business and government. Those they killed included
Gunter Von Drenkman, president of the West Berlin high court, and the
business leader Hans Martin Schleier.

Despite the arrest of many of their leaders and other mishaps the West
German groups have displayed a considerable capacity to endure. The
number of terrorist attacks for which they were responsible actually increased during the first half of the 1980s.[74] In this decade though they
have undergone some notable changes. First, in order to exploit the large

West German peace movement, attacks have been directed at NATO targets, including American military personnel and installations located in both the Federal Republic and Belgium.

Second, the 1980s also have witnessed some shift in alliance partners. While the Palestinians have not been abandoned, the West German groups have forged ties to new Western European organizations: Direct Action in France, the Communist Combatant Cells in Belgium, and the Fighting Popular Forces in Portugal. These groups, now active in countries largely free of domestic revolutionary terrorism during the seventies, share with their West German counterparts a desire to eliminate the American military and economic presence from the continent.

Just as nationalist-separatist terrorism has spread to South Asia and South Africa in recent years, so too revolutionary terrorism has undergone some migration. Despite serving as the location of much terrorist violence committed by groups from the Middle East and elsewhere, France was largely immune from terrorist violence of home-grown revolutionary groups during the 1970s. The situation has changed in the present decade. Direct Action (AD), a collection of semiautonomous bands, has carried out a long list of attacks in recent years, most of them in the Paris area. Not only does AD share RAF's hostility to the American presence in Europe and Israeli behavior in the Middle East, but its publications condemn French "neocolonialism" in Africa, which, in turn, is tied to the exploitive needs of the country's capitalist economy. Accordingly, AD pursues a global revolutionary strategy on behalf of the international proletariat.[75]

The presence of NATO and the European Economic Community headquarters on Belgian soil had provided the Communist Combatant Cells (CCC) with both rhetorical and physical targets. The CCC's emergence in the cause of Euro-terrorism owes little to the student protest movement, which in Belgium has been rooted in ethnic conflict, but instead was the outgrowth of contacts between AD and RAF leaders and local Marxist-Leninists. The latter have been sufficiently inspired by their French and German counterparts to carry out bombing attacks against NATO installations and the offices of multinational corporations in and around Brussels.[76]

Reactionary Terrorism

Popular political debate over the meaning and consequences of contemporary terrorism has tended to leave the impression that it is an almost exclusively leftist phenomenon. Since the most publicized nationalist-separatist and revolutionary groups usually have professed commitments to one or another version of Marxism-Leninism, the impression is perfectly natural. But the reality is something else. Organizations seeking not to change the social or political status quo but to preserve it, or, in some important cases, to recreate a world long past, have made substantial contributions to the volume of terrorist violence.

It seems reasonable to identify these terrorist organizations by the nature of the conditions their activities are intended to preserve or recreate. These circumstances are three in number: (1) ethnic and/or racial dominance, (2) a society free of communist influence, and (3) a society dominated by religious values.

The changing status and rising visibility of racial and ethnic minorities in Western Europe and the United States have evoked a terrorist backlash by groups attempting to champion the cause of the majority population. In Western Europe the presence of millions of "guest workers" from North Africa and the Middle East has stimulated a violent reaction in several countries.[77] While these guest workers usually occupy positions at the bottom of the occupational ladder and are often newcomers to the countries to which they have been invited, violence has also been directed at European Jewish communities whose members, for the most part, are of higher economic status and are long-time citizens of their countries of residence.

In West Germany such organizations as the Military Sports Group Hoffman, Action Front of National Socialists, Viking Youth, and other neo-Nazi formations emerged as the country's right-wing National Democratic party (NPD) was in the process of decline during the 1970s.[78] Animated by such slogans as "German jobs for German workers" and "foreigners out," these groups were bound together by their endorsement of Holocaust revisionism, a view that the Holocaust never occurred or has been vastly exaggerated by Jews for anti-German propaganda purposes. Though characteristically less articulate than the revolutionary terrorists, the neo-Nazis, nonetheless, were responsible for over 150 acts of violence in 1983 to 1984.[79] Desecrations of Jewish community institutions and assaults on Turkish workers are among the activities of choice, although in 1980 two Southeast Asian refugees were burned to death and a bomb was detonated at the Munich *Oktoberfest* that killed a dozen passersby.

The development of neo-Nazi violence in France has followed a somewhat different path. Compared with the West German experience, racist vandalism and terrorist operations preceded the rise rather than followed the decline of a mass right-wing political party. The National Front party of Jean Marie Le Pen is currently a significant force on the French political scene, but its ascendance came after a wave of violence perpetrated by small neo-Nazi organizations. In 1978, for example, a group identifying itself as the Charles Martell Club attacked a camp of guest workers in

Nice. This assault was followed by its bombing of the African-Muslim Student Association headquarters and the Algerian consulate near Paris. After another group, the French National Liberation Front, claimed responsibility for bombing the Paris office of a travel agency, it professed to be liberating the country from African, Arab, and Jewish influence.

The "Marxist" Popular Front for the Liberation of Palestine, operating under the PLO umbrella and in search of marriages of convenience, apparently furnished assistance to the French neo-Nazis as long as they were willing to attack Jewish targets.[80] Accordingly, in 1979 and 1980 such groups as the Fighters against Jewish Occupation, Odessa, and the European National Fascists (FNE) carried out a number of terrorist attacks, including the spraying of machine-gun fire at five Jewish institutions in Paris. The FNE also claimed responsibility for detonating a bomb in front of a Parisian synagogue in 1980. The explosion killed four people. In recent years these neo-Nazi bands, like their counterparts on the left, have included NATO and American targets on their hit lists.

In the United States contemporary reactionary terrorism, based on racist principles, has been stimulated by the Identity religious movement. Adherents to this theology believe that the Anglo-Saxon race is the one chosen by God to inhabit the North American continent. Other races have no right to live in the United States, a nation now overrun by "dusky hordes." Further, in opposition to divine intent, Jews have come to dominate American life to such an extent that there now exists a Zionist Occupation Government (ZOG) which must be brought down if the country is to be restored to its rightful owners.

Inspired by this religious doctrine, a group known as the Aryan Brotherhood carried out a series of terrorist attacks, bank robberies, and murders in the western part of the United States during the mid-1980s.[81] Now subdued by the FBI, the Brotherhood is not the only group of its kind: others include Aryan Nations, the Posse Comitatus, the Covenant, the Sword and the Arm of the Lord, and the Christian Patriots' Defense League. In addition to their adherence to Identity theology and their not uncommon veneration of Adolf Hitler, these organizations have created paramilitary training camps at various rural sites in preparation for the struggles to come.

A second type of reactionary terrorism is structured around political ideology rather than racism. The particular ideology linking various terrorist organizations in Europe and Latin America is anticommunism. It is true that such groups as the Grey Wolves in Turkey; the New Order, the National Vanguard, the Third Position, and the Nuclei of Armed Revolutionaries in Italy; and the Apostolic Anti-Communist Alliance in Spain have articulated views which emphasize the virtues of tradition in culture, hierarchy in society, and authoritarian leadership in government, but their resort to terrorism has been a reaction against left-wing groups and political parties that threaten, however remotely, to bring Marxist-Leninist regimes to power.

In view of its Fascist heritage, Italy has been the one European nation most susceptible to right-wing terrorism. Despite the fact that the revolutionary groups have received far greater publicity, the neo-Fascist ones have been responsible for a higher number of casualties.[82] Further, the modus operandi of left- and right-wing terrorists has differed. While the revolutionaries have tended to select specific individuals as their targets, the neo-Fascist groups have specialized in detonating bombs in public places. One such place was the waiting room of the Bologna railway station, where in August 1980 neo-Fascists exploded a bomb that killed eighty-five people, in the hope of randomly murdering as many as possible.

It is clearly no accident that the wave of neo-Fascist violence Italy has experienced in recent years coincided with the rise of New Left movements and the formation of revolutionary terrorist groups and with the electoral successes achieved by the Italian Communist party. The neo-Fascist organizations were intent on preventing red domination of the country's political system, much in the manner of Mussolini and his cohorts in 1922.

If anything, terrorism carried out in the name of anticommunism has been more virulent in certain Latin American countries than in Italy. Generically called death squads, groups have been formed in nations where violent leftist insurgencies have been mounted, ones either of the terrorist or rural guerrilla variety. In Argentina, for example, the Triple A (Argentina Anticommunist Alliance) emerged in 1974 and proceeded to publish a death list of journalists, priests, students, lawyers, and others its leadership suspected of sympathizing with the revolutionary groups. Those on the list were warned to either leave the country or face the consequences.[83] A series of Triple A executions followed. Likewise, during the late 1960s Brazilian leftists had to confront the Communist Hunting Command (CCC). And a Tupamaro Hunting Command was formed in Uruguay to help repress revolutionary activity in that country. In Colombia more than 450 members of the Patriotic Union, a leftist political party, have been killed by death squads since 1986.[84] The Secret Anticommunist Army, Purple Rose, and White Hand organizations in Guatemala have executed thousands of people suspected of leftist sympathies. Other Central American nations have had their own right-wing groups. Church and human rights organizations have been particularly hard-hit.[85]

These anticommunist vigilante groups differ from other terrorist organizations in two ways. First, they have commonly received financial and technical assistance from elements within the governments of the countries in which they operate. This has been true not only in Latin America but also in Italy, where a number of high-ranking military and civilian intelligence officers were arrested eventually for having participated in various neo-Fascist schemes. Second, the attitudes these rightist organizations have adopted concerning the publicity value of their operations have usually been more ambiguous than that of insurgent terrorist groups. In many cases the preference has been to avoid attracting the mass media's attention out of fear that reporters will then investigate their ties to figures in positions of authority. The audience with which these right-wing bands wish to communicate by their killings often can be reached by word-of-mouth rumors. In other instances, however, especially when they seek to create a general atmosphere of turmoil, these groups have acted like their revolutionary or nationalist-separatist counterparts and have sought widespread publicity.

The nation of Mozambique, a former Portuguese colony in southern Africa, has been ruled by a nominally Marxist regime since it won independence during the 1970s. It is presently confronted by an armed opposition movement, the Mozambique National Resistance, which has carried out a large number of terrorist attacks against helpless civilians. Casualties have been extraordinarily high. There is evidence that the government of South Africa has furnished assistance to this movement in the hope that its operations will inhibit Mozambique from providing sanctuary to its antiapartheid opponents.[86]

In Western Europe reactionary terrorism conducted for an essentially religious purpose can be found in Northern Ireland. There the violent campaign conducted by the Ulster Defense Association (UDA) and other Protestant bands has been anti-Catholic in character. Not only do its practitioners abhor Catholicism as a religion, they also oppose measures intended to improve the status of Catholics in the region. And, of course, the possibility that Ulster might some day be ruled by "papists" in Dublin fills them with horror.

In recent years a good deal of terrorism emanating from the Middle East has not been directly related to the Arab-Israeli conflict. Attaching a label with which to identify such terrorism is not easy. Yet if we ask ourselves what its ultimate goals are, the answer is that they are religious. Groups drawn from both the Sunni and Shiite traditions of Islam have used terrorism as a means to attack secular trends in Muslim societies and to preserve or revive the role of religion in daily life. Not only has this sort of terrorism been directed against Americans and Europeans, it also has been employed in efforts to dislodge regimes, even politically radical ones, regarded as insufficiently committed to Islamic principles. It is possible, therefore, to call this religiously motivated terrorism revolutionary. But, if we do so, we should bear in mind that the social and political order its practitioners wish to bring about is one out of the middle ages, not the twentieth century.

Those responsible for the assassination of Egyptian President Sadat in 1981 and the killing of 241 American Marines in 1983 belonged to groups inspired by the Iranian revolution. Yet they were offshoots of Islamic fundamentalist organizations that existed before the Ayatollah Khomeini came to power in Tehran. In at least one case, that of the Muslim Brotherhood in Egypt, its clandestine operations date from the 1930s. In most cases, there is a desire to repay the West and those perceived as advancing Western interests in the Middle East for humiliations suffered in the past.

In Middle Eastern nations where the Sunni tradition predominates, religiously motivated terrorist attacks have been carried out against the governments of Tunisia, Egypt, and Syria. In Tunisia, the most secular and Europeanized nation in the Arab world, the Islamic Tendency Movement (MII) has employed a combination of mass protests and acts of terrorism in an attempt to topple the existing regime. Among other things, Islamic Tendency followers have been offended by the improved legal status women have acquired during the leadership of ex-President Habib Bourguiba; as they see it, the new status of women represents a violation of important Islamic teachings.[87]

Islamic Liberation, a splinter group of Egypt's Muslim Brotherhood, attacked a military academy on the outskirts of Cairo in 1974 and killed eleven people. Its objective was to overthrow the Sadat government and replace it with an Islamic republic. In 1977 another fundamentalist group kidnapped a former cabinet minister and demanded that a message be broadcast that Egypt would then be governed in accordance with Islamic principles. When the demand was turned down the captive was murdered. Over 400 Egyptians were arrested in connection with this operation. Then in 1981 another Muslim Brotherhood splinter group, the Holy War Organization, assassinated President Sadat while he was reviewing a military parade in Cairo. The killing was intended not merely as an act of revenge for Sadat's treatment of other fundamentalists and his peace agreement with the Israelis, but also as part of a plan to spark a general insurrection against the overly secular Egyptian state.[88]

The fact that Syria has a radical regime hostile to Israel with close ties to the Soviet Union and amicable relations with revolutionary Iran has not immunized that country against religiously motivated terrorism. It is the secular nature of this Baath socialist government, symbolized by its 1977 constitution, and a political leadership dominated by the small Alawite minority, that has evoked terrorist violence. Followers of the Muslim Brotherhood opposed to atheism and in support of an Islamic state began to wage an assassination campaign against Syrian officials in

1977, two years before the fundamentalists came to power in Iran. In 1979 members of the Muslim Brotherhood killed thirty-two military cadets at a school in Aleppo. And in 1982 the Sunni fundamentalists briefly seized control of the city of Hamma, where they executed 250 supporters of Syrian President Asad. Consistent with this high level of violence and in keeping with the radical character of the regime, acts of government repression have been far more brutal than in either Tunisia or Egypt.[89]

Terrorists deriving their inspiration from the Shiite tradition have been active in Iraq and, most of all, in Lebanon. Like Syria, Iraq has a secular socialist regime, one with close links to the Soviet Union. It is also the only Arab country with a Shiite majority. Prior to the outbreak of the Iran-Iraq war in 1980, leaders of the Al Dawa (the Call) movement denounced the non-Islamic character of Iraqi President Saddam Hussein's regime and expressed the intent to establish a political order in alignment with the Iranian fundamentalists. Along with a series of mass demonstrations, followers of Al Dawa carried out a number of terrorist attacks, including an attempted assassination of the only Christian member of Iraq's political leadership. President Hussein believed, with some reason, that these activities had been stimulated by Tehran. In turn, this belief contributed to his decision to launch an invasion of Iran. Since the gulf war began, followers of Al Dawa, now operating from exile in Iran, have staged terrorist operations against Iraqi targets located in various Middle Eastern and Western European nations.[90]

The principal reason Shiite terrorism has attracted so much attention in the Western media, however, is because of events in Lebanon. The recent kidnappings of American and other Western journalists, teachers, and business executives, and the devastating bombings of American and French embassies and military posts along with the skyjacking of TWA flight 847 to Beirut in 1985, were all the work of Shiite organizations whose bases are located in that strife-ridden country.

Most of the groups responsible for these terrorist acts have been identified as components of Islamic Jihad, or Holy War.[91] The latter name has been applied to at least three separate organizations; Islamic Amal, Islamic Al Dawa, and the Hizbollah (Party of God) are the most important. Hizbollah was formed in southern Beirut by the religious leader Sheikh Fadallah. The other organizations began as dissident factions within the broad Shiite Amal movement, headed recently by Nabih Berri, a Western-educated lawyer. Dissatisfied by Berri's moderation, these groups broke away from Amal in order to pursue their Islamic objectives through violence. With bases of operation in southern Lebanon, Beirut, and the Bekáa Valley, they have carried out their attacks in conjunction with a detachment of revolutionary guards and other agents sent from Tehran.

STATE SPONSORSHIP

At the beginning of this chapter we sought to describe the preconditions and precipitating events in the absence of which the age of terrorism would not have occurred. In other words, an effort was made to identify those factors that *initiated* terrorist activity. But any understanding of contemporary terrorism would be incomplete if it did not examine other developments that have served to *sustain* and amplify the violence.

Clearly, a variety of factors has been at work, but chief among them has been state sponsorship. While no single state, i.e., the Soviet Union, has masterminded terrorist operations around the world, the evidence is compelling that several states, including the Soviet Union, have sponsored many of the terrorist organizations discussed in this chapter. Along with the U.S.S.R. and its various Communist bloc allies, the major sponsors include Iran, Syria, Libya, and South Yemen.[92]

Why have these and other regimes undertaken the sponsorship of terrorist groups? The most practical answer is that it is relatively cheap. In exchange for a handful of weapons and a few airline tickets, the sponsor is able to inflict damage, at low cost, on countries regarded as its enemies. Second, by directly committing acts of violence against a state, a sponsor runs the risk of a direct military confrontation. Systematically murdering another state's officials or sabotaging its economic enterprises are acts of war. Provoking a war against any country, particularly if it is one as powerful as the United States, is a risky undertaking. If, on the other hand, there exist terrorist groups willing to undertake such activities on a sponsor's behalf, the cost and risk are reduced. The sponsor will deny its involvement and will achieve the same effect without incurring the danger.[93] Thus, Syria and Iran can sponsor the murder of hundreds of Americans in Lebanon without much fear the United States will wage war against them. And if this is true of a superpower, what of weaker states like Saudi Arabia and Kuwait?

State sponsorship of terrorism takes a number of forms.[94] First, there is material and financial support. Illustratively, the various PLO factions have received enormous quantities of weapons from the Soviet Union and massive cash contributions from the oil-rich Arab states. Second, there is operational support. Sponsoring states provide facilities for the training of terrorists on their territories. They offer intelligence concerning the vulnerability of the terrorist group's targets. And they also provide assistance in the form of documents, e.g., passports and visas, which permit terrorists entry to and exit from countries in which their operations are staged. Sponsoring states also not uncommonly offer terrorists access to their legally protected diplomatic pouches; the latter may then contain weapons the terrorists would otherwise find difficult to smuggle into countries where their actions are planned to occur.

In addition, sponsors reduce the risks of terrorist operations by providing sanctuaries for their perpetrators. After retiring from a life of violence, Carlos, the Venezuelan-born international terrorist, took up residence at a seaside villa in Libya. Abu Nidal's organization had an office in Baghdad for a time during the early 1980s. Later its base of operations was moved to Syria and Libya. Apparently Abu Abbas, the man who planned the *Achille Lauro* operation, has found a safe haven in the People's Republic of Yemen. Demands for extradition and international arrest warrants are of little relevance to sponsoring states which commonly deny that these individuals are present within their borders. In some cases sponsors are able to provide political and ideological support for terrorism through their endorsement of such broad concepts as national liberation and anti-imperialism in such international forums as the United Nations General Assembly. These concepts, the equivalents of motherhood and apple pie for much of the Third World, are then used to justify any and all acts committed in their name by the terrorist groups.

Finally, in thinking about the role of state sponsorship we have assumed that the groups receiving help are in some sense autonomous actors, with goals and interests to pursue which coincide with but are not identical to those of their sponsors. In recent years, evidence has accumulated that certain states have, in effect, cut out these go-betweens. They have begun to practice low-intensity warfare without the use of surrogates. North Korea, Libya, Syria, and Iran have all used their own agents to carry out terrorist attacks on foreign soil. Sometimes these operations have been committed against their own nationals, prominent individuals who have gone into exile because of their opposition to conditions prevailing in their nations of origin. Thus, exiled Iranian and Libyan dissidents have been the targets of assassination attempts carried out by agents from Tehran and Tripoli. But it has also been true that such states as Syria, Libya, and Iran have used their own personnel to conduct assassination and sabotage campaigns against the citizens and property of other nations. This type of warfare by terrorism would seem to be a higher-risk undertaking because of the absence of surrogate terrrorist organizations to absorb the blame. When the possibility of denying responsibility is reduced, the likelihood of a state victimized by the violence actually retaliating against its source is increased, especially if the attacks persist.

A SUMMARY OBSERVATION

Some observers have likened contemporary terrorism to an epidemic disease to which different countries and regions of the world have become susceptible. If the comparison between terrorism and disease, including infection and contagion, makes any sense, then this chapter has largely been concerned with the etiology and presenting symptoms of the disease. It has discussed those conditions existing around the world over the last decades which served, first, to promote and then to sustain political terrorism. In addition, many of the major experiences of nationalist-separatist, revolutionary, and reactionary terrorism were scrutinized. On the other hand, there has been little discussion of the impact the terrorist disease has had on its bearers and victims as well as the various remedies those seeking its eradication have prescribed. These important subjects will be considered in the next chapters.

KEY TERMS

Beirutization
conventional warfare
death squads

kneecapping
reactionary terrorism

NOTES

1 Martha Crenshaw, "The Causes of Terrorism," *Comparative Politics*, 13:4 (1981), pp. 379–397.
2 Richard Gillespie, *Soldiers of Perón* (Oxford: Clarendon Press, 1982), pp. 257–258.
3 Alex Schmid and Janny de Graaf, *Violence as Communication* (Beverly Hills, Ca.: Sage Publications, 1982), pp. 5–57.
4 Christine Ketcham and Harvey McGeorge II, "Terrorist Violence: Its Mechanics and Countermeasures," in Neil Livingstone and Terrell Arnold (eds.), *Fighting Back: Winning the War against Terrorism* (Lexington, Mass.: Lexington Books, 1986), pp. 25–33.
5 See, for example, Maynard M. Stephens, "The Oil and Natural Gas Industries a Potential Target of Terrorists," in Robert Kupperman and Darrell Trent (eds.), *Terrorism: Threat, Reality, Response* (Stanford, Ca.: Hoover Institution Press, 1979), pp. 200–223.
6 Walter Laqueur, *The Age of Terrorism*, rev. ed. (Boston: Little, Brown and Company, 1987), pp. 142–173.
7 See, for example, Claire Sterling, *The Terror Network* (New York: Holt, Rinehart and Winston, 1981); Claire Sterling, *The Time of the Assassins* (New York: Holt, Rinehart and Winston, 1983); Ray Cline and Yonah Alexander, *Terrorism: The Soviet Connection* (New York: Crane, Russak, 1984); and Roberta Goren, *The Soviet Union and Terrorism* (London: George Allen & Unwin, 1984).
8 See, for example, David Shipler, *Arab and Jew: Wounded Spirits in a Promised Land* (New York: Penguin Books, 1986), pp. 108–110.
9 Richard Barnet and Ronald Muller, *Global Reach: The Power of the Multinational Corporations* (New York: Simon and Schuster, 1974).

10 See Donald Blackmer and Sidney Tarrow (eds.), *Communism in Italy and France* (Princeton: Princeton University Press, 1975).

11 For the background, see John Norton Moore (ed.), *The Arab-Israeli Conflict* (Princeton, N.J.: Princeton University Press, 1977).

12 Andrew Hoehn and Juan Carlos Weiss, "Overview of Latin American Insurgencies," in Georges Fauriol (ed.), *Latin American Insurgencies* (Washington, D.C.: NDU Press, 1985), pp. 9–40.

13 Robert P. Clark, *The Basques: The Franco Years and Beyond* (Reno, Nev.: University Press, 1979).

14 For an account, see Paul Arthur, *Government and Politics in Northern Ireland,* 2d ed. (Essex: Longman Group, 1984), pp. 1–15.

15 See, for example, Seymour Lipset and Philip Altbach (eds.), *Students in Revolt* (Boston: Beacon Press, 1969).

16 See, for example, Carl Brown, "The Middle East: Patterns of Change," *The Middle East Journal,* 41:1 (1987), pp. 26–39.

17 For an account, see Nadav Safran, *Israel: The Embattled Ally* (Cambridge, Mass.: Harvard University Press, 1978), pp. 240–256.

18 Jillian Becker, *The PLO* (New York: St. Martin's Press, 1984), pp. 59–67.

19 Hoehn and Weiss, op. cit., pp. 15–16.

20 Stefan Possony, "Giangiacomo Feltrinelli: The Millionaire Dinamitero," *Terrorism,* 2:3 (1979), pp. 213–230.

21 Alfred McClung Lee, *Terrorism in Northern Ireland* (New York: General Hall, 1983), pp. 77–97.

22 Laqueur, op. cit., pp. 215–223.

23 For these developments see William Quandt et al., *The Politics of Palestinian Nationalism* (Berkeley: University of California Press, 1973), pp. 52–78.

24 Arthur Day, *East Bank/West Bank* (New York: Council on Foreign Relations, 1986), pp. 31–33.

25 Christopher Dobson and Ronald Payne, *The Never Ending War* (New York: Facts on File, 1987), pp. 229–232.

26 Becker, op. cit., pp. 226–227.

27 Adrian Guelke, "Loyalist and Republican Perceptions of the Northern Ireland Conflict," in Peter Merkl (ed.), *Political Violence and Terror* (Berkeley: University of California Press, 1986), pp. 91–122; and Edward Moxon-Browne, "Alienation: The Case of the Catholics in Northern Ireland," in Martin Slann and Bernard Schechterman (eds.), *Multidimensional Terrorism* (Boulder, Col.: Lynne Rienner, 1987), pp. 95–109.

28 J. Bowyer Bell, *A Time of Terror* (New York: Basic Books, 1978), pp. 215–217.

29 Edward Moxon-Browne, "Terrorism in Northern Ireland: The Case of the Provisional IRA," in Juliet Lodge (ed.), *Terrorism: A Challenge to the State* (New York: St. Martin's Press, 1981), p. 150.

30 For an account, see Max Gallo, *Spain under Franco* (New York: E. P. Dutton & Co., Inc., 1974).

31 Laqueur, op. cit., p. 223.

32 Robert Clark, *The Basque Insurgents* (Madison: University of Wisconsin Press, 1984), pp. 28–56.

33 On this theme see Robert Clark, "Patterns of ETA Violence: 1968–1980," in Merkl (ed.), op. cit., pp. 123–142.

34 Clark, *The Basque Insurgents*, op. cit., pp. 103–116.

35 Jeffrey Ian Ross and Ted Gurr, "Why Terrorism Subsides: A Comparative Study of Trends in Terrorism in Canada and the United States" (a paper presented at the annual meeting of the American Political Science Association, Chicago, September 1987).

36 Ibid.; see also Frederic Homer, "Terrorism in the United States," in Michael Stohl (ed.), *The Politics of Terrorism* (New York: Marcel Dekker, 1983), pp. 145–177.

37 Philip Cerny, "France: Non-Terrorism and the Politics of Repressive Tolerance," in Lodge (ed.), op. cit., pp. 107–109.

38 See, for example, Valentine Herman and Rob Van der Laan Bouma, "Nationalists without a Nation: South Moluccan Terrorism in the Netherlands," in Lodge (ed.), op. cit., pp. 119–145.

39 John Thackrah, *Encyclopedia of Terrorism and Political Violence* (New York: Routledge and Kegan Paul, 1987), pp. 224–225.

40 Dobson and Payne, op. cit., pp. 257–262; see also *The Economist* (Oct. 10, 1987), pp. 35–36.

41 Robert Denemark and Mary Welfing, "Terrorism in Sub-Saharan Africa," in Stohl (ed.), op. cit., pp. 327–376.

42 Fredrick Clifford-Vaughn, "Terrorism and Insurgency in South Africa," in Paul Wilkinson and Alisdair Stewart (eds.), *Contemporary Research on Terrorism* (Aberdeen: Aberdeen University Press, 1987), pp. 270–289.

43 Ernest Halperin, *Terrrorism in Latin America* (Beverly Hills, Ca.: Sage Publications, 1976), pp. 7–21.

44 Arturo Porzecanski, *Uruguay Tupamaros* (New York: Praeger Publishers, 1973), pp. 52–53.

45 Quoted in Halperin, op. cit., p. 10.

46 James Kohl and John Litt, *Urban Guerrilla Warfare in Latin America* (Cambridge, Mass.: MIT Press, 1974), p. 202.

47 Ibid., pp. 38–41.

48 John Sloan, "Political Terrorism in Latin America," in Stohl (ed.), op. cit., pp. 381–382.

49 See, for example, Amnesty International, *Torture in the Eighties* (London: Amnesty International Publications, 1984), pp. 143–145.

50 Kohl and Litt, op. cit., pp. 311–312.

51 Gillespie, op. cit., pp. 48–49.

52 Peter Waldmann, "Guerrilla Movements in Argentina, Guatemala, Nicaragua and Uruguay," in Merkl (ed.), op. cit., pp. 261–263.

53 Kohl and Litt, op. cit., pp. 342–364.

54 Halperin, op. cit., p. 17.

55 Gillespie, op. cit., p. 144.

56 Raymond Bonner, "Peru's War," *The New Yorker* (Jan. 4, 1988), pp. 31–58.

57 David Palmer, "The Sendero Luminoso Rebellion in Rural Peru," in Fauriol (ed.), op. cit., pp. 67–96.

58 James Adams, *The Financing of Terror* (New York: Simon and Schuster, 1986), pp. 215–234.

59 Gary Hoskin, "Colombia's Political Crisis," *Current History* (January 1988), pp. 9–12, 38–39.
60 Peter Janke with Richard Sim, *Guerrilla and Terrorist Organizations: A World Directory and Bibliography* (New York: The Macmillan Company, 1983), pp. 449–459.
61 Christopher Dobson and Ronald Payne, *The Terrorists,* rev. ed. (New York: Facts on File, 1982), pp. 54–56.
62 Sabri Sayari, *Generational Changes in Terrorist Movements: The Turkish Case* (Santa Monica, Ca.: The Rand Corporation, 1985), pp. 2–3.
63 Goren, op. cit., pp. 180–181.
64 Sayari, op. cit., p. 1.
65 Dankwart Rustow, *Turkey: America's Forgotten Ally* (New York: Council on Foreign Relations, 1987), pp. 57–83.
66 Robin Erica Wagner-Pacifici, *The Moro Morality Play* (Chicago: University of Chicago Press, 1986).
67 Leonard Weinberg and William Eubank, *The Rise and Fall of Italian Terrorism* (Boulder, Col.: Westview Press, 1987); see also Leonard Weinberg, "The Violent Life: An Analysis of Left and Right-Wing Terrorism in Italy," in Merkl (ed.), op. cit., pp. 145–167.
68 Eva Kovinsky, "Terrorism in West Germany," in Juliet Lodge (ed.), *The Threat of Terrorism* (Boulder, Col.: Westview Press, 1988), p. 61.
69 Klaus Wasmund, "The Political Socialization of West German Terrorists," in Merkl (ed.), op. cit., p. 92.
70 Schura Cook, "Germany: From Protest to Terrorism," in Yonah Alexander and Kenneth Myers (ed.), *Terrorism in Europe* (London: Croom Helm, 1982), pp. 164–167.
71 For the origins of the RAF, see Jillian Becker, *Hitler's Children* (Philadelphia: J. B. Lippincott Company, 1977).
72 Hans Horchem, "Terrorism in Germany," in Wilkinson and Stewart (eds.), op. cit., pp. 141–163.
73 Geoffrey Pridham, "Terrorism and the State in West Germany during the 1970s," in Lodge (ed.), op. cit., pp. 23–24.
74 Bonnie Cordes et al., *Trends in International Terrorism* (Santa Monica, Ca.: The Rand Corporation, 1984), pp. 36–40.
75 Edward Moxon-Browne, "Terrorism in France" in Lodge (ed.), *The Threat of Terrorism,* op. cit., pp. 213–228.
76 Bruce Hoffman, *Right-Wing Terrorism in Europe* (Santa Monica, Ca.: The Rand Corporation, 1982), pp. 6–11; David Lauferr, "The Evolution of Belgian Terrorism," in ibid., pp. 179–211.
77 Peter Merkl, "Rollerball or Neo-Nazi Violence?" in Merkl (ed.), op. cit., pp. 229–255.
78 Ekkart Zimmermann, "Terrorist Violence in West Germany: Some Reflections on the Recent Literature" (a paper presented at the World Congress of the International Political Science Association, Paris, July 1985), p. 4.
79 Martin Lee and Kevin Coogan, "Killers on the Right," *Mother Jones,* 13:4

(1987), pp. 45–54; see also Gill Seidel, *The Holocaust Denial* (Leeds: Beyond the Pale Collective, 1986), pp. 43–50.

80 Stephen Singular, *Talked to Death* (New York: Simon and Schuster, 1987).

81 Leonard Weinberg and William Eubank, "Neo-Fascist and Far Left Terrorists in Italy," *The British Journal of Political Science* (April 1988); see also Thomas Sheehan, "Italy: Terror on the Right," *The New York Review of Books,* 27:21 (1981), pp. 23–26.

82 Gillespie, op. cit., pp. 153–156.

83 Hoskin, op. cit., p. 11.

84 John Sloan, "State Repression and Enforcement Terrorism in Latin America," in Michael Stohl and George Lopez (eds.), *The State as Terrorist* (Westport, Conn.: Greenwood Press, 1984), pp. 83–98.

85 Gerald Butt, *The Arab World* (Chicago: Dorsey Press, 1987), pp. 136–137. For a general discussion of the subject, see Robin Wright, *Sacred Rage* (New York: Simon and Schuster, 1986).

86 Steven Metz, "The Ideology of Terrorist Foreign Policies in Libya and South Africa," *Conflict,* 7:4 (1987), pp. 379–402.

87 Adeed Dawisha, *The Arab Radicals* (New York: Council on Foreign Relations, 1986), pp. 115–119.

88 Ibid., pp. 117–119.

89 Ibid., pp. 120–122.

90 Dobson and Payne, *The Never Ending War*, op. cit., p. 29.

91 Ibid., pp. 3–26.

92 Robert Oakley, "International Terrorism," *Foreign Affairs,* 65:3 (1987), pp. 611–629; see also Rushworth Kidder, "State-Sponsored Terrorism," *Christian Science Monitor* (May 14, 1986), pp. 17–19.

93 Neil Livingstone and Terrell Arnold, "The Rise of State Sponsored Terrorism," in Livingstone and Arnold (eds.), op. cit., pp. 11–24.

94 M. Asa, "Forms of State Support to Terrorism and the Possibility of Combating Terrorism by Retaliating against Supporting States," in Ariel Merari (ed.), *On Terrorism and Combating Terrorism* (Frederick, Md.: University Publications of America, 1985), pp. 119–133.

CHAPTER 4

THE TERRORISTS AND THEIR ORGANIZATIONS

The purpose of this chapter is to answer a number of questions fundamental to understanding contemporary terrorism. Specifically, we would like to know: Who are the terrorists? Where do they come from? What sorts of people join organizations that commit acts of terrorist violence? We also need to know something about their motivations. Why do people become terrorists? Should we take at face value their often professed commitments to whatever cause on behalf of which their violence is committed, or are there other motives at work? Related to the question of motivation is one concerning recruitment: How do people become terrorists? Is the process like that of joining a religious cult, a criminal gang, or a political party?

In addition to knowing something about the terrorists as individuals, we need to understand something about the nature of the organizations which they join. After all, most contemporary terrorism is not the work of isolated individuals, of demented gunslingers whose violence is the product of personal fantasy. Instead it is the outgrowth of groups of people acting together whose behavior is coordinated in some manner. What are these terrorist groups like? To what extent, for example, do they conform to popular stereotypes of small, clandestine bands of desperate individuals constantly on the run from the authorities?

The public record concerning terrorists and their organizations and the professional literature that attempts to analyze it present a mixed picture. Unlike many other political organizations, terrorist groups normally are unwilling to provide observers with much information concerning their members' backgrounds, internal structures, decision-making methods, and the like. Given this reticence, the evidence available to outsiders is limited. Some of it comes from terrorists who have been arrested by the authorities and who later have become willing to supply facts about their lives as well as about the organizations of which they were a part. But even if they are not arrested but simply achieve a certain degree of public notoriety, it has been possible for the authorities, journalists, and scholars to acquire substantial information about the biographical characteristics of certain terrorists even though they are still at large.

In the absence of data or in the presence of only fragmentary information about terrorists and their organizations, social scientists have been inclined to apply understandings derived from individuals and groups they believe bear some resemblance to them. A good deal of knowledge has been accumulated, for example, about the pressures toward conformity and consensus that exist among members of small groups who see each other on a daily basis over long periods of time. Some analysts have applied these understandings to the logic of decision making within terrorist bands by reasoning that there is a common set of rules that fit all such groups irrespective of their purposes.[1] In short, the present level of understanding about terrorists and terrorist organizations is based on a combination of fact and armchair theory. But enough of the facts are known and enough of the armchair theories have been tested by subsequent discoveries to make it possible to offer the reader some coherent answers to the questions with which this chapter began.

WHO ARE THE TERRORISTS?

Terrorist celebrities, individuals whose exploits have caught the attention of the general public, have been the subjects of a great deal of biographical writing. Sometimes published accounts of their lives have been reported in approximately the same way as biographies of important politicians, star athletes, theatrical performers, and other glamorous figures. Here are some examples:

Ilich Ramirez Sanchez, a.k.a. "Carlos the Jackal," is the son of a wealthy left-wing Venezuelan lawyer. As a youth Carlos lived the life of a playboy both in his native country and then in London where his parents sent him to be educated. Flabby, overweight, and less successful with women than he had hoped, he nonetheless attended cocktail parties and diplomatic receptions in that city before deciding to enroll at Patrice Lumumba Friendship University in Moscow. After some disruption there he was expelled (some accounts say that he was recruited by the KGB), after which he went to the Middle East, where he joined the Popular Front for the Liberation of Palestine (PFLP). Later still, Carlos led a number of terrorist attacks in Western Europe on behalf of that organization. He is now retired and reportedly lives in Libya, where he enjoys Colonel Ghaddafi's hospitality.[2]

Renato Curcio, a founder of the Italian Red Brigades, was born near Rome in 1941. His father, the brother of a well-known film director, fought on the Russian front during World War II. Raised as a Catholic (he was later married in church) by his mother and an uncle, who was killed while fighting in the anti-Fascist resistance, Curcio became a sociology student at the University of Trento, where he got caught up in the student protest movement of the late 1960s. In 1970 he moved to Milan, where he obtained a job with a publishing firm and helped organize a small leftist group that published revolutionary polemics and interviews with Tupamaro and Palestinian spokesmen. Shortly thereafter, Curcio, his wife, Mara Cagol, and others formed the Red Brigades in the hope of liberating Italian workers from capitalist exploitation.[3]

Sabri al-Banna, a.k.a. Abu Nidal, is the son of a wealthy Palestinian Arab merchant who grew up in Jaffa. His family also had homes in Turkey, France, and Egypt. When Israel was created in 1948, he and his family moved to the West Bank, which was then under Jordanian control. Sabri al-Banna studied engineering in Cairo and later took a job with an oil company in Saudi Arabia. While in that country, he began to discuss politics with other Palestinian exiles. These conversations led him to join Fatah. In 1969 he was appointed as that organization's representative in Baghdad. After the 1973 Arab-Israeli war, he concluded that Yasser Arafat was too willing to compromise with the Israeli enemy. He left Fatah in order to create his own organization.[4]

Ulrike Meinhof, the late founder of the West German Red Army Faction, was the daughter of an art historian. After the death of her parents, she was raised by a foster mother, a Christian pacifist. While a student at Marburg University in the 1950s, Meinhof became active in the cause of nuclear disarmament. She was animated by her strong religious convictions. In 1961 she married the publisher of a fashionable left-wing magazine and began to write articles for it. She also became the mother of twin girls. As a journalist she not only wrote but also produced films whose point of view was the plight of the underdog in German society. By the mid-1960s Meinhof became something of a radical chic celebrity as the result of her appearances on television talk shows. After she and her husband were divorced, Meinhof became a resident of a New Left commune in West Berlin. There she made the acquaintance of people with whom she would later follow the terrorists' path.[5]

Mehmet Ali Agca, the man who attempted to assassinate Pope John Paul II, was born in 1958 on the outskirts of a provincial Turkish city. He came from a very poor Sunni Muslim family, one in which his father drank and his mother suffered. His elementary school teacher reported that he was a quiet but bright student who believed he would be famous some day. A student of geography at Ankara and Istanbul universities during the turbulent 1970s, Ali Agca also spent some time at a Palestinian camp in Syria. In 1979 he killed a prominent Turkish journalist, allegedly on behalf of the right-wing Grey Wolves organization. Arrested for this murder, he later escaped from prison and fled to Bulgaria. Later still he traveled through various European nations until his fateful encounter with the pope in front of St. Peter's.[6]

Robert Jay Mathews was a native of Marfa, Texas, who joined a tax protest group, the Sons of Liberty, in 1974 while he was in his early twenties. Feeling hounded by the Internal Revenue Service, he and his family moved to a small town near the Idaho-Washington border. There he found a job as a worker in a cement factory. At night he took to reading. Spengler's *Decline of the West* left a strong impression on him. Mathews was particularly taken with a novel, *The Turner Diaries,* written by William Pierce, an American neo-Nazi activist. This book describes the efforts of a small band of patriots to overthrow the Jewish-controlled federal government and rescue the United States from racial contamination. In addition to his readings, Mathews also became a follower of the Christian Identity movement, the Idaho-based Church of Jesus Christ Christian in particular. The political outlook of this church approximated the one found in *The Turner Diaries.* At the end of 1983 Mathews, along with several other church members and ex-Ku Klux Klansmen, formed a terrorist group, the Order, whose goals were identical to those portrayed in *The Turner Diaries.* After a spree of bank robberies and synagogue bombings and the murder of Alan Berg, a talk radio personality in Denver, most members of the band were arrested. Mathews died in a shootout with the FBI in 1984.[7]

These faces in the crowd provide us with glimpses into the lives of individuals whose terrorist exploits have caught the attention of the mass media. For journalists these stories are intrinsically interesting because of the nature of the acts, murders, massacres, holdups, and so on, perpetrated by the subjects of their reportage. But as analysts of contemporary terrorism it is important for us to know how representative these individuals are of terrorists in general. Over the last two decades thousands of people have participated in terrorist operations in different parts of the world; generalizing about their backgrounds from a handful of prominent personalities may not take us very far in understanding who the thousands are and how they came to behave as they did. These days few reporters would attempt to generalize about the voting preferences of the American electorate by interviewing several passersby on a crowded street or a handful of shoppers at a supermarket. The number of cases is simply too small and unrepresentative for the reporter to arrive at any general conclusions. The same applies to terrorists.

It is worth beginning our investigation of what sorts of people become terrorists by pointing out a disagreement between two leading analysts of the subject. Richard Rubenstein and Walter Laqueur come away from their review of the same body of evidence with very different conclusions. For Rubenstein, most modern terrorists are isolated and alienated middle-class intellectuals who have become frustrated by their inability to develop organic ties to the oppressed and discontented masses. His interpretation, of course, is consistent with the earlier conclusions of Marx, Lenin, and Trotsky.[8] While Rubenstein is precise in locating the social backgrounds of contemporary terrorists, Laqueur's understanding emphasizes their diversity. For him, terrorists have emerged from all types of backgrounds. Their only common denominator has been their age. Most terrorists are young people.[9]

The wide difference of opinion between these two analysts over such a basic matter as who the subjects of their inquiries are, what types of people they are dealing with, will not leave the reader feeling very optimistic that plausible generalizations will be forthcoming. At this point, there is a need for some rethinking.

First, consider the observation that terrorists, their youthfulness aside, have come from so many different social circumstances that generalizations about them are virtually impossible. Basically the problem with this view is that it clusters people together on the basis of their participation in a particular form of group activity, terrorism, without considering the causes on whose behalf the violence is planned or committed. If we were to apply the same logic to members not of terrorist organizations but of political parties the same results would be forthcoming. That is, if we combined people who belonged to the Conservative, Labour, and Liberal parties in Great Britain, for example, we would discover a substantial diversity in their social backgrounds and conclude, therefore, that political party activists came from working, middle, and upper classes. However, if we took into consideration which particular political party they adhered to, some meaningful differences would emerge. Conservatives would have somewhat higher incomes and would have completed more years of schooling than the Labourites, for example. Likewise, since terrorist groups are political organizations after all, ones with different goals in mind, it seems reasonable to suspect that their social composition would somehow reflect these political differences.

Terrorist groups are not only political organizations, they are also extremist in their outlook and resort to direct action to achieve their ends. Some things are known about the social composition of extremist political parties and protest movements, even nonviolent ones, that operate in democratic contexts. There is some evidence that their support comes disproportionately from young males.[10] Impatience and freedom from family and job responsibilities are often linked to this phenomenon. From these observations we would expect terrorist groups to reflect some variation in their membership based on their political objectives, but, notwithstanding these variations, they would be composed not exclusively but disproportionately of young men.

Rubenstein's observation that modern terrorists are isolated and alienated middle-class intellectuals also needs to be placed in a more general context. In this case, the context is provided by the fact that such middle- or even upper-class figures characteristically form the initial leadership group of many violent political movements, not just terrorist ones. The major revolutionary movements of the twentieth century—ones that later succeeded in winning the support of millions of workers and peasants—were created not by people from these segments of the population, on whose behalf the revolution was to occur, but by the educated, whose social backgrounds were far removed from the masses they eventually came to lead. It should not be forgotten that Lenin's father was a school administrator and a member of the Russian nobility. Ch'en Tu-Hsiu, the founder of the Chinese Communist party, came from a wealthy mandarin family. Fidel Castro's father was a rich Cuban plantation owner. Che Guevara was a physician and the son of an architect. And, of course, Karl Marx himself was hardly of working-class background. "Nor are these isolated examples. The higher leadership cadres of most revolutionary movements on the left collectively share the same characteristics describing the very top leaders themselves."[11]

Despite the fact that the objectives of the Italian Fascist and German Nazi movements were not those of the Russian, Chinese, and Cuban revolutionaries, their founders' social roots were not all that different. While the Fascists and Nazis appealed for support not on the basis of social class—workers and peasants—but on the basis of nationalism and racial supremacy, their founding elites were drawn from roughly the same social backgrounds as the Communist ones. For example, among those who attended the organizational meeting of the National Fascist Movement at Milan in 1919 were nine lawyers, five professors, five physicians, five army or navy officers, three accountants, and a like number of parliamentary deputies.[12] A snapshot of the Nazi movement in Munich at the same early stage of its development also discloses its largely middle-class composition.[13]

The bearing these observations have on the social composition of terrorist groups has to do with the time at which they are made. In general, we would expect that the closer in time to the point of its formation, the more likely a terrorist group would be composed of middle-class intellectual elements. On the other hand, if a terrorist group is able to sustain itself over a long period of time, the more likely it is to be able to recruit members from whatever segments in the population its operations are intended to advance. If a terrorist group is quickly repressed by the authorities at an initial stage of its development, the more likely the social profile of its members will be skewed toward the middle class because we would expect the founders to be drawn from this background. Since most terrorist groups do not endure for very long, overall we would expect their memberships to exhibit this social bias. In sum, we would expect the social backgrounds of terrorist groups that do last for some time to be a combination of middle-class intellectuals or professionals plus others, with the identity of the "others" dependent upon the group's political objectives.

The reader also should be aware of the political implications involved in describing the memberships of terrorist groups, particularly revolutionary ones, as middle class. Sometimes this is done to achieve a polemical effect rather than an analytical purpose. That is, the middle-class backgrounds of many terrorists have been used to challenge the authenticity of their revolutionary credentials by suggesting, among other things, that they are really dilettantes playing at revolution without strong ties to the masses. Of course, in some cases this is true, but in others it is not. With these ideas in mind let us consider the social profiles of contemporary terrorists.

An early effort to paint such a portrait was made by Charles Russell and Bowman Miller.[14] Their work was based on a sample of over 350 individuals who were active in terrorist groups from 1966 through 1976. The time span involved is restricted to the first decade of the contemporary terrorist era. The groups whose members they included were the major revolutionary and nationalist-separatist organizations discussed in Chapter 3. Thus members of terrorist groups committed to such reactionary goals as racial and ethnic dominance or anticommunism were not subjects of investigation, and the groups whose members were considered, revolutionary and nationalist-separatist ones, were treated as if their distinctive political objectives would make no difference in their social makeups.

The profile of modern terrorists that is revealed in the Russell and Miller study is one that confirms our expectations about the dominance of young males. Most terrorists were between twenty and thirty years of age, although the leaders of these groups tended to be substantially older. Women constituted less than 20 percent of the sample and, despite some well-publicized exceptions, were likely to have confined their activities to logistical and support roles. Ironically, the female terrorists tended to play the same sorts of subordinate roles vis-à-vis males that women in general have performed in the wider society. Further, given the sorts of lives they lead, most terrorists, males and females, were unmarried.

So far as their origins were concerned, the roots of most terrorists were found to be in large cities. For the most part these urban guerrillas had either been born in or were long-time residents of the metropolitan areas in which their violent acts were committed. In general, their socio-economic backgrounds conform to our earlier expectations. The terrorists tended to have come from middle- or even upper-class family backgrounds and to have displayed a high level of educational attainments. Some had become terrorists while attending colleges and universities, others after they had received their degrees.

More than a decade has elapsed since Miller and Russell completed their work. Does subsequent work offer any modifications in their findings? If we introduce distinctions among terrorist groups based on their political objectives and the length of time a particular terrorist episode has lasted, the answer is positive and dramatically so.

In some cases where evidence is available differences in the terrorist groups' goals are reflected in the backgrounds of their memberships. Such conventional differences as left versus right, or revolutionary versus reactionary, serve to distinguish among the terrorists.

In the industrial democracies, terrorist groups committed to the preservation of racial or ethnic dominance have tended to draw their adherents from the lower strata of these societies. In the United States, most members of the Order or the Aryan Brotherhood were not college-educated nor were they the sons and daughters of the establishment. For the most part they had held blue-collar jobs before drifting into terrorist violence.[15] Similar conclusions have been reached concerning the backgrounds of right-wing terrorist groups in France and West Germany. Illustratively, the information reported in Table 4-1 shows the relatively limited educational performances and low occupational status of convicted right-wing terrorists in West Germany.

As one observer put it: "The terrorist right in Germany and France is drawn almost exclusively from the lower classes. Its members are mostly young, uneducated common laborers who lack the skills necessary for employment in their countries' highly technical industries.... The youth-

TABLE 4-1
EDUCATIONAL LEVEL AND OCCUPATIONAL BACKGROUND
OF RIGHT-WING TERRORISTS IN WEST GERMANY IN 1980

	Right-wing terrorists, %
Education:	
Volksschule (elementary)	49
Technical	22
Grammar (high school)	17
University	10
Other	2
	100%
Occupation:	
Self-employed	8
White collar	9
Skilled worker or artisan	41
Unskilled worker	34
Other (unemployed)	8
	100%

Source: Eva Kolinsky, "Terrorism in West Germany," in Juliet Lodge (ed.),
The Threat of Terrorism (Boulder, Col.: Westview Press, 1988), pp. 75–76.

ful converts to neo-Fascism have been described by a Paris police inspector as 'political punk rockers,' searching for comrades, simplistic answers to their dilemma, scapegoats, and a good fight."[16] The reasons for the susceptibility of some working-class youth to the appeals of racist violence are not all that hard to come by. Any number of public opinion studies have disclosed the vulnerability of the poorer and less-educated strata to ethnic and racial prejudice, at least in multiracial and multiethnic societies.[17]

There are few studies available devoted to the social backgrounds of the members of terrorist groups committed to the use of violence for the preservation of religious values in the Middle East or anticommunist defense of the death squad variety in Latin America. In regard to the former, however, we should note that although the Islamic fundamentalist groups in Lebanon were organized by religiously educated clerics, they have apparently been most successful in recruiting their followers among the slum dwellers of south Beirut.[18]

We would expect terrorist groups committed to the eradication of communist influence in society would draw their followers disproportionately from sectors of society most likely to be threatened by the consequences of red revolution. And while the composition of the Latin American "death squads" remains obscure, the impression exists that many members are off-duty police and military officers. There is at least one study which reports the occupational backgrounds of neo-Fascist terrorists active in Italy between 1970 and 1984. The data recorded in Table 4-2 are consistent with this interpretation. Although students are well-represented among members of the violently anticommunist neo-Fascist groups, they are outnumbered (taken together) by individuals from the Italian business community, the free professions, and the country's police and military corps. In other words, individuals who had the most to fear from the Red Brigades' violence or the electoral successes of Italy's Communist party are strongly represented in the neo-Fascists' ranks.

The difference between left and right produces a meaningful distinction in the gender of terrorist organizations. There is evidence that racist and anticommunist groups are almost exclusively male aggregations.[19] Aryan Brothers in the United States, New Order militants in Italy, and neo-Nazi bands in West Germany seem to have had few women adherents. But, notwithstanding Russell's and Miller's findings, revolutionary groups active in the same countries have exhibited substantial female representation. By contrast to their rightist counterparts, the Symbionese Liberation Army and Weather Underground in the United States, the Red Brigades and Front Line in Italy, and the Red Army Faction in West Germany have had many women members, including ones playing active leadership roles.[20] The same observation applies to some of the major revolutionary groups active in Latin America during the 1970s.

This differential representation of women is largely explicable in political or ideological terms. Reactionary groups commonly emphasize military values and the traditional role of women in society; both notions are incom-

TABLE 4-2
OCCUPATIONAL BACKGROUND OF ITALIAN NEO-FASCIST TERRORISTS, 1970–1984

Occupation	Number	Percent
Criminal, subproletarian	5	2
Student	50	21
Manual worker	20	8
Police, military worker	37	16
Shopkeeper, small businessperson, sales clerk, artisan	29	12
White-collar clerk	20	8
Teacher	14	6
Free professional (physician, lawyer, architect)	35	15
Industrialist, business manager, aristocrat	<u>27</u>	<u>11</u>
	237	99%*

*Percentages add to 99 because of cumulative effect of rounding.
Source: Leonard Weinberg and William Eubank, "Italian Neo-Fascist Terrorists: An Effort to Distinguish Left from Right in the Study of Violent Group Members," *British Journal of Political Science* (October 1988).

patible with an acceptance of females as equal participants in the "manly" art of political violence. Revolutionary bands, on the other hand, often stress economic and social equality as goals, and consequently are most likely to be accepting of women as equals in their struggles.

Some information is also available concerning the occupational characteristics of revolutionary terrorists in different countries. Table 4-3 provides information about this factor for the Tupamaros in Uruguay and members of the major left-wing terrorist groups active in Italy. In both cases the strong representation of students and middle-class professionals is indisputable: it is what we have been led to expect. But a fact that leaps to our attention is the presence of large numbers of manual workers and others at the bottom of the occupational scale. In Italy and Uruguay the revolutionary groups were able to recruit roughly one-third of their members from precisely that segment of the population on whose behalf they sought to make a revolution. This figure is particularly impressive in light of the intensive campaign waged by the authorities, especially in

TABLE 4-3
OCCUPATIONAL BACKGROUNDS OF REVOLUTIONARY TERRORISTS IN URUGUAY AND ITALY

Occupation	Number	Percent
Captured Tupamaros, 1966–1972		
Student	99	29.5
Professional, technical	109	32.4
Worker	109	32.4
Other (includes unemployed)	19	5.7
	336	100 %
Terrorists* identified or arrested in Italy, 1970–1984		
Criminal, subproletarian	58	5.2
Worker	335	29.8
Student	301	26.7
Military, police officer	14	1.2
White-collar clerk	198	17.6
Shopkeeper, small businessperson, sales clerk	29	2.6
Teacher	110	9.8
Free professional	61	5.4
Industrialist, business manager, aristocrat	8	0.7
Housewife	11	1.0
	1125	100 %

*Members of the Red Brigades, Front Line, and other revolutionary groups.
Source: Arturo Porzecanski, *Uruguay's Tupamaros* (New York: Praeger Publishers, 1973), p. 29; Leonard Weinberg and William Eubank, *The Rise and Fall of Italian Terrorism* (Boulder, Col.: Westview Press, 1987), p. 86.

Uruguay, to repress the terrorist organizations before they could pose truly serious threats to the existing political order. Working-class representation is somewhat higher in Italy than in Uruguay, but the former country is one in which the terrorist groups were able to operate over a longer period of time than the Tupamaros in Uruguay. It should be remembered, however, that in these two instances we are not dealing with trade union organizations or other above-ground workers' groups that may take decades to develop a strong working-class clientele.

We should also bear in mind the "provincialism" of the Italian and Uruguayan terrorists. Their leaders sought to achieve revolutions in their own countries. Unlike their counterparts in West Germany and Japan, active during the same time, they were not seeking to facilitate the liberation of the exploited in the Third World.[21] Rubenstein's judgment and Russell's and Miller's findings about the highly educated and middle-class character of revolutionary terrorists seem more appropriate for the German and Japanese settings, conditions in which the local working classes were largely indifferent to revolutionary appeals.

The two major cases of nationalist-separatist terrorism in the Western world we discussed in Chapter 3 were those of Northern Ireland and the Basque region of Spain. Fortunately some information is available concerning the backgrounds of both Provisional IRA and ETA terrorists. Insofar as the latter are concerned, it will be recalled that the ETA was organized by a small group of young Basque students in the early 1950s whose families were of middle- or upper-class backgrounds. But by 1970 the picture had changed substantially. According to a study reported by Robert Clark, the class composition of a sample of ETA members in that year shows a dramatic increase in the representation of people at the lower end of the scale. As shown in Table 4-4, well over one-third of the sample was comprised of people who either were unemployed or came from working-class backgrounds. In addition to its commitment to the goal of Basque separatism, the fact that the ETA also became an organization with an affinity for Marxism and an additional commitment to socialism may be related to its ability to recruit adherents among working-class Basques.

In Northern Ireland the discriminatory policies pursued by the Protestant-dominated provincial government were felt most acutely by members of that region's Catholic working class, especially those living in Belfast and Derry. This pattern is reflected in the composition of the Provisional IRA (PIRA). Most of its cadres and leaders have not been drawn from Northern Ireland's small Catholic middle class, but from the far larger pool of unemployed and working-class Catholics living marginal lives in the cities.[22] And, as with the ETA, we cannot help but notice that PIRA is also an organization that stresses the goal of socialism

TABLE 4-4
SOCIAL CLASS OR OCCUPATIONAL IDENTITY OF ETA
MEMBERS

Social class, occupation	Percent*
Working class	30.9
Lower middle class	12.3
Middle class	29.6
Upper class	2.5
Student or priest	18.5
Unemployed	6.2
	100 %

*N = 81.
Source: Robert Clark, "Patterns in the Lives of ETA Members," in Peter
Merkl (ed.), *Political Violence and Terror* (Berkeley: University of California
Press, 1986), p. 288.

in conjunction with its hope for a united Ireland. It wants a socialist republic for the whole island.

The social composition of terrorist groups may be affected not only by
the political objectives of the groups but also by their duration. Like
other revolutionary bands those in Turkey initially drew their members
from university student populations and other radicalized intellectuals.
This was true in the early 1970s for the first generation of terrorists. But
the thousands of young people who were caught up in the violence at the
end of that decade present a far different social profile. Many were illit-
erates who had recently arrived in the big cities from rural areas where
they had been the offspring of poor peasant families.[23] A similar pattern
was at work in Italy. There members of the Red Brigades, Front Line,
and other revolutionary groups who were arrested or identified by the authorities in 1977 and later tended to have been younger and were more
likely to have come from working-class backgrounds than their predeces-
sors who were involved in the violence during the early 1970s.[24]

In seeking to answer the question of who the terrorists are, we are limited by the incomplete nature of the biographical evidence available to
us. Nonetheless, certain central themes are apparent. First, it is true that
the terrorists have been drawn from a wide variety of backgrounds. But
this does not mean that participation in terrorist groups is based on random chance and that no generalizations are possible. Instead, our observations about the social composition of such groups are that it bears a
meaningful relationship to the political objectives of the group in approximately the same way that the memberships of other political organizations, such as political parties, do to theirs. Second, it is true that terrorist groups are often initiated and led by alienated middle-class

intellectuals. But this is also true of most extremist groups that pursue their goals by violent means. Yet, if terrorist groups are able to last over any appreciable length of time, chances are their memberships will expand to include followers from segments of society on whose behalf the groups claim to be acting. These relationships are far from perfect, but they do represent central tendencies.

WHY DO PEOPLE BECOME TERRORISTS?

Terrorists, as well as their various defenders, offer explanations for their motivations that differ radically from those of their opponents. Stefano delle Chiaie, the leader of an Italian neo-Fascist band, once referred to the members of his National Vanguard organization as an "elite of heroes."[25] His observation was made before he and several other "heroes" had attempted to detonate a bomb in front of an elementary school. The terrorists and their defenders, in other words, commonly describe their motives in laudatory terms. The practitioners of terror are described as selfless champions of whatever cause their violent deeds are intended to advance. The violence, it is claimed, has been forced upon them as a result of intolerable and long-suffered conditions. We are dealing then with modern-day knights of the round table.

Not surprisingly, the terrorists' opponents hold rather different views on the subject. "Animals," "wild beasts," and "lunatics" are terms they frequently attach to the terrorists. For example, any number of his opponents have diagnosed the president of Libya as suffering from mental illness as the result of his support for various terrorist enterprises. What should we make of these competing interpretations of motive? Are the terrorists altruistically inspired heroes or deranged killers of the innocent?

First, compared with lone assassins, serial killers, and mass murderers, contemporary terrorists rarely act alone. They are members of organizations, sometimes exceedingly complex ones. Truly demented individuals would have a difficult time maintaining the sorts of human interactions necessary to belong to organized groups. Furthermore, the members of terrorist organizations whose lives often are precarious enough as it is would be reluctant to admit to their ranks individuals whose behavior is so unpredictable and appears to be so crazy that it would endanger the groups' persistence as an organized entity. For these and other reasons most psychologically informed observers have concluded that, in general, contemporary terrorists are not mad people.[26] To say this is not to deny, however, that from time to time profoundly disturbed individuals will appear in terrorist groups. Kozo Okamoto, one of the members of the Japanese United Red Army who machine-gunned two dozen Puerto Rican pilgrims at the Tel Aviv airport in 1972, believed his victims would be reincarnated as stars in the firmament.[27] A few other captured terrorists have impressed their interrogators by their fanciful views of reality. Yet a Belfast psychiatrist who conducted a long series of interviews with convicted murderers found a dramatically higher incidence of mental disturbance among those who had killed out of purely private motives than that among those who had belonged to and acted in the name of Northern Ireland's various terrorist organizations.[28]

The allegation that terrorists are mentally ill also carries with it a certain political meaning. If they are simply crazy people living out their private delusions in the political arena, there is no need to take their political concerns seriously. Thus one effect of applying the label "mentally ill" to terrorists is to discredit whatever cause their actions are designed to promote.

It does not follow, however, that we should dismiss all psychologically grounded explanations of terrorist motivation or that we must accept the self-serving descriptions of the terrorists themselves in answering the why question. Even if we were to accept the premise that people are drawn to terrorism because of oppressive conditions, most people living under or witnessing such conditions do not resort to terrorist practices as a means of rectifying them. Many suffer in silence, others turn to various forms of political action, but only a few become members of groups that randomly kill passersby at an airport. What drives the few?

Approaches to the study of terrorist motivation may be divided into those that emphasize the push provided by internal psychological attributes and those that emphasize the pull offered by the organizations to which these individuals become attached. In both cases, however, the evidence to support the interpretation rests on a relative handful of interviews with imprisoned terrorists who have been willing to talk to psychologists while in confinement in West Germany, Italy, Israel, and the United States, and on a reading of the same public record available to the rest of us by observers trained in psychology and psychiatry. First, let us consider the matter of push.

It has been argued that persons predisposed to recruitment by modern terrorist organizations have learned to see the world in very simple terms. For many of them things are either white or black, all good or all bad. They are also collectors of injustice, people extremely sensitive to slights and humiliations inflicted on themselves or on members of social groups to which they belong or with which they identify themselves.[29] As one observer remarks: "The terrorist seems to be hypersensitive to the sufferings and injustices of the world at large, but totally insensitive to immediate, palpable suffering directly around him, especially if he has produced it himself."[30] This paradox of being sensitive to the suffering of some while simultaneously being indifferent to the injuries inflicted on their victims may be the product of the terrorists' propensity to dehumanize the latter by regarding them as objects or impersonal concepts.[31]

In addition to these characteristics, some observers have speculated that many terrorists are stress seekers, individuals with a need to interrupt the monotony of their daily lives by the pursuit of adventure and excitement. A need to feel a sense of omnipotence, of being powerful and in control of the situation, has also been mentioned as a quality in the minds of some terrorists. This feeling may be achieved when the individual is able to instill fear in others. Rather surprisingly, given the nature of their activities, the evidence is mixed concerning the outlook of terrorists toward violence. In some cases analysts have detected underlying feelings of aggression and hostility in a few imprisoned terrorists, while others have pointed to a pattern of ambivalence over the use of violence after having interviewed different individuals in similar settings.[32]

If these are the symptoms that present themselves, what are their causes? Or, put another way, are there certain types of people likely to display the psychological traits just mentioned? The literature here directs our attention to childhood experiences and personality development.

One such account links the narcissistic personality with a propensity for terrorism.[33] For reasons having to do with their relationships to their parents, certain children experience great difficulty in forming close personal bonds with other people. They also sustain a grandiose sense of the self, a sense of their own perfection, beyond the point where such an outlook is considered normal, while seeing people around them as deficient and flawed. When such individuals experience defeat and humiliation in adulthood, they may react by expressing feelings of "narcissistic rage" and manifest this anger by displaying some of the traits we have mentioned. For example, "the self renounces any suggestion of inherent limitations and attributes all failures and weaknesses to others. The Ayatollah Khomeini's pronouncement 'Carter is the Devil' illustrates the form that this...can take."[34]

The fact that many terrorists are young people in their early twenties has not gone unnoticed by psychologically informed observers. The human development theories of Erik Erikson have affected these observers' views of what influences some young adults to become terrorists.[35] According to this understanding, late adolescents commonly confront the crisis or problem of establishing a stable individual identity for themselves. This identity, an answer to the question of "Who am I?" requires the development of a sense of the self as a whole, complete human being whose life has some meaning. Further, the formation of an adult identity requires some young people to establish a faith in someone or something outside themselves and then to be trustworthy in its service.

This concept is what Erikson refers to as "fidelity." When individuals experience great difficulty in establishing personal identities or in overcoming what he calls an identity crisis, for reasons relating to childhood problems, they become vulnerable to "totalism." The latter is an inclination to resolve their identity problems by submerging themselves completely in some collectivity or group that will provide an identity for them. A weak or poorly developed sense of the self often leads young adults to make total commitments to various groups and ideologies. In some cases this may mean affiliation with exotic religious cults, but in other instances it may mean absorption into a terrorist group. As Crenshaw writes in connection with the lives of West German terrorists:

> The group became the family that had never provided the warmth, protection, security and support the individual had needed. The opportunity to join a terrorist organization allowed the individual to submerge himself in a collective identity and thus to lay down the burden of personal responsibility. The group met a need to idealize authority figures, to express aggressive tendencies, to feel omnipotent, and to belong. Its ideology of violent resistance to the state and to imperial domination allowed collective identification simultaneously with the victims of oppression and the aggressive authority figure, while neutralizing guilt through intellectual and emotional justifications. The group provided the structure and integration lacked by the isolated individual.[36]

In view of the highly abstract character of these assertions and the theories on which they are based, it is necessary to reemphasize what is being claimed for them. It is not contended that these personality problems or sets of psychological traits determine the decision of an individual to become a terrorist, only that they influence it. And further, the influence or predisposition applies to some terrorists active recently in the democracies, but not others.

In rethinking the problem of terrorist motivation it will be helpful to introduce three distinctions. First, in some nations and social milieu, West Germany and Japan, for example, terrorist organizations are small, deviant groups whose members must make radical breaks with the surrounding society in order to join or form them. In other situations, however, the terrorist organization is more a part of its surroundings; rather than representing social or political deviance the organization is considered a relatively normal expression given these surroundings. For example, joining the Provisional IRA for a Catholic youth in Belfast or becoming a member of a PLO group for a young Palestinian growing up in a Beirut refugee camp involves a different type of decision than becoming the member of the Red Army Faction in Germany or the United Red Army in Japan. The kinds of choices associated with joining the PIRA or PLO seem more normal in the context of the existing social environment of these organizations than the choices involving those organizations named in Germany or Japan. In Northern Ireland, interviews with members of both the PIRA and the Protestant Ulster Volunteer Force suggest these terrorists lead normal family lives, usually are able to hold regular jobs over long periods of time, and are less prone to alcohol abuse than the general population.[37] It follows from these observations that the individual psychological peculiarities suggested in the literature may be more influential in pushing people into the more deviant terrorist organizations than in cases where the organizations represent broader social forces at work in the society.

A second distinction relevant to the psychological disposition toward terrorism is linked to the goals of terrorist groups. There is at least fragmentary evidence, based on the Italian and West German experiences, that neo-Fascist and neo-Nazi groups are more likely to attract truly disturbed individuals than their left-wing revolutionary counterparts. To the extent this is true, the difference may be related to the fact the rightist organizations articulate ideologies that glorify violence for its own sake as an inherently manly activity. They are, therefore, likely to attract followers with deep-seated feelings of hostility. In contrast, the ideologies of the revolutionary groups typically emphasize violence not as an end in itself but as an instrument necessary to foment major social change.[38]

Third, it is important to remember that individuals vary in the intensity of their commitments to and in the roles they play within terrorist organizations. Some become deeply involved while others remain on the fringes. Some members become leaders while others remain followers. It seems likely that these differences would be related to the individual psychologies of terrorists. For example, interviews with some imprisoned West German terrorists indicate that followers were motivated primarily by the desire to join a group per se. Leaders, on the other hand, often displayed characteristics associated with narcissistic personality types. They were uninhibited, inconsiderate, self-absorbed, and unemotional, with deeply rooted feelings of hostility.[39]

In the above account we have mentioned some of the factors that may be at work in making certain people susceptible to recruitment by terrorist groups. In addition to these intrapersonal factors that push people toward terrorism, we should also consider the possibility that there are things about terrorist organizations that pull people into them.

The writing on this subject begins from the premise that terrorist groups are voluntary political organizations which must offer people incentives to join them and then contribute effort toward maintenance of those incentives.[40] The most obvious of such incentives is the achievement of whatever purpose stimulated the formation of the group in the first place. And no doubt this is sufficient reward to cause some deeply committed individuals to become members. But the reality may be some-

what more complicated. For instance, Charles Glass, the American journalist who was kidnapped by a Shiite group in Beirut, reported overhear-
ing a conversation among his youthful abductors. Their talk focused not
on the virtues of the Ayatollah Khomeini or the sufferings of the Shiite
community in Lebanon, but on the small amount of money they were being paid in compensation for the hazardous duties they were
performing.[41] This story suggests that even in terrorist organizations re-
putedly composed of fanatical believers there are other incentives at
work.

Among the incentives terrorist organizations have to offer potential recruits are (1) the opportunity for action, (2) the fulfillment of a need to
belong, (3) the promise of social status, (4) the acquisition of material reward, and (5) the occasion for vengeance.[42] It is important to remember
that these incentives need not be totally independent of one another. An
individual may be pulled into a terrorist organization because it provides
two or more of these incentives. Further, and consistent with this view,
people may be simultaneously attracted by the group's political goals and
any combination of the above-mentioned incentives.

Whether or not such expectations are met once recruits become members, terrorist groups seem to offer opportunities to translate words into
action. One of the ways that terrorists differ from other radicals is that
they often have grown tired of political rhetoric. After endless arguments
over ideology and countless denunciations of their opponents in cafés,
coffeehouses, schools, and student centers, terrorist groups give potential recruits the impression they may actually do something about the
problems which have stimulated so many words. Indeed, terrorists often
exhibit contempt for the empty pronouncements of those who support
the cause but are unwilling to put themselves at personal risk in its behalf. For many young people, even those without strong political commitments, the allure of instant action may be very strong; in fact, it may
be so strong that the acquisition of a detailed understanding of the terrorist group's goals sometimes may follow rather than precede their
membership in it. The incentive of direct action also may help explain
why terrorist groups find it hard to be cautious in situations where it
would pay them to be. Risks may have to be taken in order to retain the
involvement of those members for whom the opportunity for action was
the primary incentive for their affiliation.

Group membership itself may provide another basis for joining a terrorist group. We have already mentioned this motive in connection with
the push toward terrorism stimulated by internal psychological traits.
Here it should be sufficient to point out that terrorist groups offer opportunities for participation in a total community and a sense of complete
immersion that more impersonal political organizations do not.

Ordinarily we would not think that membership in a terrorist group would do much to enhance a person's social status. These aggregations are not the equivalent of exclusive social clubs or elite university societies. Yet, in some cases it is clear that belonging to a terrorist group does improve an individual's reputation in his or her community. This is what Connor Cruise O'Brien writes on the subject:

> As a young man in a Catholic slum of Belfast or Derry, you are nobody unless you are in the IRA. In a Palestinian slum "camp" in Lebanon, you are nobody unless you are in the PLO. Nor is the ambition purely personal. You are also winning enhanced status for your family, and if you are killed in action, your family's status will be still further enhanced. Furthermore, a rise of personal and familial status is not in any way dependent on the organization's attaining its political objectives. Indeed such success might well cause your status to collapse.[43]

For some young men the opportunity to carry a gun and appear dangerous to others is a strong incentive for membership. If we add to this the reputation afforded individuals fighting on behalf of a popular cause, the attraction becomes stronger still. Even further, there may be the opportunity to achieve a kind of immortality. In Ireland songs and stories have been composed in honor of IRA gunmen who have died for the cause. In Latin America and Western Europe new terrorist units often take their names from deceased members of old ones. And in the Middle East the expectation of immortality may be quite literal. According to the Ayatollah Taleghani, "When martyrs undergo an inner transformation and perceive the truth, when they are killed, God, having given a pledge, insures and preserves their existence."[44] For people who believe in the Islamic principles of Jihad and martyrdom, the role of being a terrorist in the name of God can carry with it an exceedingly high status.

Like improved social status, material reward is not an incentive we commonly associate with membership in a terrorist group. But as the conversation Charles Glass overheard in Beirut suggests, it is often a relevant consideration. Some terrorist groups are very wealthy, particularly those in the Middle East, which receive financial support from oil-rich nations. Their leaders often enjoy standards of living, such as seaside vacations at Mediterranean resorts, comparable to those of business executives or celebrities from the entertainment world. But even groups without state backing are able to acquire large sums from ransoms paid for their kidnap victims, bank robberies, and related criminal undertakings. And, as was the case with Feltrinelli in Italy, they may be the objects of large cash donations from philanthropically minded sympathizers. All this permits terrorist organizations, at least ones that last over any length of time, to pay their members monthly stipends with occasional bonuses for particularly harrowing adventures. Presently, PIRA regulars are paid $36 a week if they are single, more if they are married. For young adults living in areas of high unemployment like Belfast, even the prospect of a relatively small income in exchange for little work is a meaningful incentive. Not too long ago members of a youth gang from the South Side of Chicago offered their services to Colonel Ghaddafi with the clear understanding they would perform acts of terrorism against American targets if he would compensate them adequately for their work.

Finally, we should consider the possibility that an opportunity for vengeance is an inducement for many individuals to become terrorists. For example, the first manifestations of terrorism carried out by the Tamil Tigers in Sri Lanka followed a massacre in which members of their ethnic community were the victims. An opportunity to avenge the victims of massacres also would appear to be an important incentive at work for terrorist groups active in Lebanon, the slaughter of Palestinians at the Sabra and Shatilla camps in particular. And in the United States the violence directed at police officers by members of the Black Panthers and Black Liberation Army during the early 1970s seems to have attracted new members to the ranks because of their previous run-ins with law enforcement officers.

In reviewing the reasons why people become terrorists, both the psychological traits that may provide a push and the organizational incentives that offer a pull, we should avoid the pitfall of overdetermining or overexplaining these reasons. Just as the victims of terrorist violence sometimes happen to be in the wrong place at the wrong time when the bomb goes off, so too there is an element of happenstance in the process by which some people become members of terrorist groups. The same set of psychological traits mentioned in connection with terrorism will predispose some people just as easily to become followers of a religious cult or a criminal gang, or to perform some private act of violence. On the other hand, some individuals join terrorist groups without a clear understanding of what it is they are getting themselves into. On occasion, all that is required is knowing someone else such as a friend, relative, husband, wife, or lover who has become a terrorist for the particular individual to develop the affiliation himself or herself.

HOW PEOPLE BECOME TERRORISTS

Becoming a terrorist requires not only motive but opportunity as well. Many people can have the appropriate motives and be responsive to the relevant incentives and still not become the members of terrorist organizations—if, for example, such organizations do not exist in their countries or if they are somehow outside their field of vision, that is, if potential members remain unaware of the existence of such organizations. Thus, we need to know something about the process. How do people become terrorists?

One possibility is by public appeal. Claire Sterling reports that the following advertisement appeared in the October 23, 1970, issue of a right-wing Munich newspaper:

> Wanted! Courageous comrades to join us, a group of politically committed friends, for a tour of several months in the Middle East as war correspondents to study the war of liberation of the Palestinian refugees to reconquer their homeland. If you have tank experience apply at once. Money is no obstacle. What matters is a comradely spirit and personal courage. Information on the Palestine Liberation Organization free on request.[45]

Likewise, Walter Laqueur has pointed out that Colonel Ghaddafi has placed similar announcements in newspapers all over the Muslim world from time to time.[46] Sometimes the publicity is free. Italian lawyers defending the members of the Red Brigades (Brigate Rosse, or BR) at their trials recall receiving telephone calls from young people who wanted to know where they should go to sign up. These people had been excited by pictures they had seen of the BR's exploits on television. So to respond to the question of how people become terrorists by saying they have answered "want ads" in the papers is not a totally facetious reaction. Here, as elsewhere, the mass media play a role. However, in terms of the overall pattern of recruitment this type of public appeal has had a limited impact.

Most of the literature on the subject emphasizes that recruitment is based on personal contacts among people who already know each other. There are certain places where potential terrorists are likely to be found and where they are likely to interact with individuals who are terrorists or who know terrorists. University campuses and other locations where students congregate are often appropriate places.[47] In some countries prisons have been the sites for the recruitment of terrorists. Convicted terrorists have used their confinement as an opportunity to politicize other inmates. Palestinian refugee camps in the Middle East provide obvious locations for recruitment to the PLO. Sometimes it is the workplace. The Red Brigades were able to attract members who were employed at a Fiat automobile factory in Turin. In other instances recruitment may be based on the place of residence. There are certain neighborhoods in Belfast, West Berlin, and Rome where a particular climate of political opinion existed that facilitated the recruitment process. The important factor in all these places of recruitment is an opportunity for personal interaction.

The process by which people become terrorists usually is not one that involves a sudden conversion. Typically it is not a matter of a revelation, a complete break with the past; instead becoming a terrorist commonly involves a series of steps which gradually removes people from their old lives and leads them into new ones. Furthermore, there are really two separable situations to consider: (1) the choice made by members of a previously existing group to practice terrorism, and (2) decisions made by people to affiliate with a terrorist organization after it is already a going concern.

At least for individuals who take the path of clandestinity by joining an existing terrorist group, there seems to be an initial phase that one observer has labeled "disassociation."[48] As the name suggests, this step involves a loosening of or distancing from previous social and emotional ties. A move away from home, a broken marriage, a departure from school, a growing dissatisfaction with a job are factors that set some people adrift in search of new meanings and personal associations.[49] The next step for potential terrorists is reached when they come into contact with other individuals whose ideas and ways of living they find attractive or similar to their own. In short, they find a group of other people with whom they feel comfortable, where there is some sense of shared values, including political ones. The more absorbed individuals become in their new setting, the more likely they are to be resocialized or repoliticized by the standards prevailing in the group. If the group is on the fringes or contains individuals sympathetic to the terrorist cause, the involved oftentimes will participate in political activities, usually ones of an open, above-ground but semilegal character. A turning point is reached when the individuals come to the attention of the terrorist group. Some members will then evaluate their backgrounds to make sure they are "clean," i.e., are not likely to be government informers, and to determine if these persons are able or willing to go underground. On occasion the recruits will follow friends or relatives who have taken the same path earlier. Oftentimes new recruits will be asked to commit an act of violence as a means of testing their commitment and, also, of binding them to the group.

The second pattern involves the decision of an already existing group or a faction of it to become a clandestine terrorist band.[50] The choice here is not that of an individual but of a whole group. Some event or series of experiences may lead the members of this body to engage in a debate over the desirability of pursuing their aims through terrorism. As we have seen in the cases of the Tupamaros and the ETA these discussions may be protracted ones. There is some evidence drawn from the literature on Groupthink (the idea that the way members of a group interact with one another in itself shapes the outcome of its deliberations) which suggests that such units are likely to make far riskier decisions than each member of it would as separate individuals.[51] In any case, if members have become dependent on the group, they are likely to be drawn into terrorism as the result of peer pressure toward conformity.

The two patterns discussed above apply to cases of clandestine terrorist groups, ones that require their members to establish new identities and live subterranean lives. The Red Brigades and the Red Army Faction have operated in this fashion. But not all terrorist groups are like this. Some groups, such as the German Revolutionary Cells and Worker Collective Autonomy in Italy, are composed of "after-hours" terrorists who commit occasional acts of violence while leading normal lives most of the time. In situations, as in the Middle East, where terrorist groups enjoy safe havens in sympathetic countries, most members will also lead perfectly normal lives most of the time. In these cases, where there is no need to establish whole new identities, it does not seem likely that the two patterns we have discussed fit the recruitment process. Joining such groups is more like joining a conventional military force or a political party.

TERRORIST ORGANIZATIONS

Terrorist organizations have been classified in a number of ways. One effort focuses on their targets and bases of operations. The Israeli analyst Ariel Merari distinguishes between *xenofighters,* groups whose violence is directed at foreign targets, and *homofighters,* ones whose enemies are their own compatriots. He further divides them into those which operate from foreign bases and those which function inside the countries that are the objects of their attention.[52] Researchers at the Rand Corporation have devised a conceptual scheme for classifying terrorist groups based on a list of ten attributes which are more focused on their internal characteristics.[53] These frameworks are helpful because they call attention to an important point: they emphasize the fact that terrorist organizations are not all alike. If we are willing to consider as terrorist all nonstate organizations that engage in this type of violence, then we are struck by the variety of forms these groups display. Some of the major sources of variation are discussed below.

Origins

Some groups are formed out of circles of like-minded individuals explicitly for the purpose of committing acts of terrorism. They represent new aggregations which after a period of preparation or incubation begin their violent campaigns. The Italian Red Brigades, German Red Army Faction, and French Direct Action furnish examples. The origins of other terrorist groups are to be found in decisions taken by previously existing groups, usually political movements and political parties, to change their

methods of operation. The PLO existed for some years before its leadership became committed to terrorism.[54] In other cases, it is not an entire
political organization that is transformed into a terrorist group but only
part of it. In these situations a militant faction or, commonly, the youth
wing of the original organization will separate itself from the main group
for the pursuit of terrorist purposes. The neo-Fascist Nuclei of Armed
Revolutionaries in Italy was composed of disaffected members of the
Rome branch of the Italian Social Movement's youth organization.

Size

Since terrorism involves small-group violence, it is easy to believe that
the total membership of any given terrorist group is also quite small. This
is only true, however, for the units that actually carry out terrorist attacks. Seizing a hostage or skyjacking an airliner is obviously the work of
a handful of individuals. But this is not to say that the whole terrorist
organization of which these units are a part is itself small. In reality,
there is considerable variation. To be sure the Symbionese Liberation
Army and the Order or the Aryan Brotherhood in the United States did
not consist of many more than a few dozen members at the height of their
operations. But some terrorist groups have thousands of members at any
one time. One estimate made in the early 1970s put the number of PLO
armed fighters at close to 15,000.[55] In Argentina, the Montoneros were
able to mobilize more than 1500 members to carry out a single campaign
in 1974. Terrorist organizations with over 1000 members are more the exception than the rule, however. The majority have less than fifty members at any one time.[56]

There is evidence that the size of a group influences the type of operations it is able to conduct. Large groups are more likely than small ones to
carry out such difficult tasks as kidnapping, hostage taking, and the occupation of buildings. Smaller groups, with fewer resources, are more likely
to confine themselves to setting off bombs and shooting at targets.[57]

Complexity

Related to variations in their size, terrorist groups also differ from one
another in terms of the complexity of their organizational structures. The
stereotype we have of a terrorist group is that of a small band of desperate people living clandestine lives and under the direction, perhaps, of a
few charismatic leaders. This picture conforms to what one observer has
referred to as terrorist groups with centrifugal infrastructures. He writes:
"This centrifugal infrastructure resembles that of a solar system: the
leader is the sun, and the members are surrounding planets, usually

within the range of his direct impact.''[58] No doubt many small terrorist bands look like this, but what of those with memberships in the thousands? The evidence is that often despite themselves (they wish to retain flexibility) large terrorist groups establish hierarchies and at least rudimentary bureaucratic procedures. One of the reasons the Italian authorities were successful in defeating the Red Brigades was that most of its ''columns'' had ''librarians'' whose responsibility it was to keep detailed records concerning the group's operations. When the police broke into a BR hideout, they seized these documents and then used them in subsequent prosecutions.

As with other organizations with complicated tasks to perform, large-sized terrorist groups produce a division of labor and a specialization of function. Thus, at one time the Montoneros had a national leadership committee that directed platoons and militias (for the fighting) along with subsidiary units for trade unionists, women, youth, and electoral politics. It even had a ''press secretariat'' for public relations purposes.[59] These complicated arrangements are not all that unusual; other examples could be brought to bear. Instead of thinking of these terrorist groups as small gangs of desperadoes, we should consider some of them as approximating the form of small political parties.

Like political parties, terrorist organizations exhibit differences concerning the degree of control exercised by a central leadership over the activities of subsidiary units. Some organizations, like the Italian BR, are strongly centralized with a national committee providing clearly defined instructions to local branches over when and how they should carry out specific operations and other tasks. Other groups bear some resemblance to decentralized political parties prevalent in some Western democracies in that the local units make basic decisions over when, where, and how to attack their targets.

An interpretation which stresses the similarities between terrorist and political party organizations is strengthened by the fact that on occasion terrorist groups *are* political parties or at least sections thereof. In some instances, as with the PIRA in Northern Ireland, a terrorist organization will advance its cause by developing an above-ground political party to compete at elections and achieve representation in public assemblies. In this case, the reference is to the Sinn Fein. But in other circumstances the relationship is reversed; and it is the above-ground political party, e.g., the Social Revolutionaries in czarist Russia, that creates a combat organization to pursue its overall goals by terrorist means.

Autonomy

It seems to be a truism that all organizations seek to achieve a degree of independence or autonomy from other forces in their environment.[60]

This rule seems to apply in the case of terrorist groups as well. And as is true in other instances, some organizations succeed while others fail. The issue of autonomy so far as terrorism is concerned often presents something of a dilemma.

One way of understanding terrorist groups in a comparative perspective is to divide them into the rich and the poor. There is a kind of class system at work. Poor groups, such as the South Moluccan one active in the Netherlands during the 1970s, achieve autonomy because they are unable to find patrons willing to sponsor their activities. But poverty often inhibits their effectiveness. Contemporary terrorism can be an expensive undertaking.

The real problem arises for terrorist groups whose operations win them support from wealthy patrons, such as the PLO or PLO-related groups in the Middle East. Large cash contributions enhance their ability to recruit new members and carry out complex operations. But there is usually a price to be paid by terrorist organizations that become the clients of wealthy sponsors. The group's reputation may be harmed among segments of the population whose support it seeks. Nationalist-separatist groups that are revealed to be in the pay of a foreign power will have questions raised about the authenticity of their commitments. Sponsoring states or patrons may want the terrorist group to carry out attacks which advance its interests rather than those of the organization it is funding. Often this leads terrorist organizations toward an effort to achieve autonomy by developing their own sources of financial support. In the case of PIRA and the Ulster Defense Association (UDA) in Northern Ireland and the Armed Revolutionary Forces of Colombia (FARC) this has meant participation in organized crime activities. Running a protection racket in Belfast or offering security services to drug dealers in Bogotá are effective ways of earning money for the cause.[61] In the case of groups under the PLO umbrella, the quest for autonomy has involved a combination of legal and illegal business endeavors. These ventures may enhance the terrorist group's autonomy, but they carry with them certain negative consequences.

Given normal human impulses, concerns about business management, investment decisions, and the consumptive possibilities of affluence may distract the organization, particularly its leaders, from its original purpose. For example: "Members of the Baader-Meinhof gang have described how they engaged in the same *Dolce Vita,* complete with champagne and delicacies, that had disgusted them in bourgeois society; and Baumann states that once money came rolling in, some of his colleagues displayed a penchant for velvet suits and similar luxuries, until they looked 'fresh out of *Playboy.*'"[62] Also not to be forgotten is the possibility that by engaging in organized criminal pursuits in the quest for autonomy and political effectiveness terrorist groups will deteriorate into criminal gangs whose political rhetoric simply offers a cover for the more pecuniary motivation.

Duration

Terrorist organizations also vary in the length of time they are in existence. Some small, ephemeral bands, whose members are caught up in the emotions of the moment, commit a handful of violent acts before dissolving, their members having other interests to pursue. These groups rarely last long enough to be included in the various directories and handbooks of such organizations that have become available in recent years. One recent study clusters seventy-six contemporary terrorist groups that managed to achieve inclusion in these compendia. Their duration is noted in Table 4-5. According to these data, a clear majority of contemporary terrorist groups has been able to sustain itself for over a decade, an impressive accomplishment given the nature of the activities in which such groups are engaged. If we measure the success or failure of these organizations by their duration, are there any attributes that distinguish the successful from the unsuccessful?

All the ten short-lived groups (in existence from one to five years) had their bases of operation located inside the countries in which their terrorist activities were conducted. These nations were either democracies (France, West Germany, Israel, and the United States) or military dictatorships (Brazil, Argentina). The groups themselves had goals that were either revolutionary or reactionary (but not of the religious kind discussed earlier). No nationalist-separatist organizations were included.

This was not true for the longer-lasting organizations (those in existence for over a decade). By our standards fourteen of the forty-two successful organizations had a nationalist-separatist objective as their announced goal. This figure is of some note, but it hardly justifies a conclusion that nationalist-separatist terrorists in general are able to sus-

TABLE 4-5
THE DURATION OF SEVENTY-SIX CONTEMPORARY TERRORIST ORGANIZATIONS

Duration of existence	Number	Percent
1 to 5 years	10	13
5 to 10 years	24	32
Over 10 years	<u>42</u>	<u>55</u>
	76	100%

Source: Martha Crenshaw, "How Terrorism Ends" (a paper presented at the annual meeting of the American Political Science Association, Chicago, Sept. 3–6, 1987), pp. 39–42.

tain themselves over a longer period of time than others because of the popularity they enjoy among populations whose aspirations for independence they seek to champion. The majority of the successful groups had goals similar to those of the unsuccessful ones. Clearly, then, there are other factors at work. Among them, two in particular should be mentioned. First, a number of the successful organizations, those active in the Philippines, Colombia, Venezuela, and other Latin American countries, were part of rural guerrilla insurgencies, organizations that combined operations in the countryside with terrorist attacks in the cities. Second, included among the long-enduring organizations were ones, largely from the Middle East, whose bases of operation were outside the country that was the target for their violence. It may be the case then that the success or failure, as defined by duration, of terrorist groups is predicted more by their ability to find safe havens in rural areas or in other countries than by their goals. It is simply harder for the authorities to repress them.

Group Dynamics

The kind of "craziness" frequently ascribed to terrorist behavior—i.e., the taking of extreme risks, insensitivity to human life, persistence in the use of violence without much hope that it will produce the desired political goals—may be less associated with the psychopathologies of individuals who become terrorists than with the characteristics of the groups with which they become affiliated. It may be the nature of the group, not the type of people who join it, that produces the effect. The literature on this subject derives from evidence based on the behavior of primary groups in general and ones subject to isolation and extreme danger in particular.[63] This body of writing emphasizes the strong pressures toward conformity and cohesion brought on by the development of strong emotional bonds among members of groups living in precarious situations and sharing common fates. What consequences do these conditions have on the behavior of the group?

One contention has it that over time the persistence of a group as an organized entity becomes more important as a goal than its original political purpose. Its members become more concerned about pleasing each other than they are about the group's ostensible political aims. One result is for the group's violence to continue irrespective of the political realities in the outside world. Furthermore, perceptions of the outside world become progressively more distorted. Communications from it are filtered through the group in such a way as to magnify the group's importance and exaggerate its prospects. Also, as we noted in connection with the process of terrorist group formation, members of primary groups that prize conformity are willing to make riskier decisions and take more chances than the same individuals acting alone.

Still other contentions concerning the impact of the primary group on terrorist behavior have been advanced. For one, belonging to a group with a shared outlook on the world may have the effect of absolving the individual member of the guilt he or she may feel as the result of taking human life. For another, repeated acts of violence in the group context may desensitize the perpetrators of such acts by rendering them indispensable in the framework of the group's ideology.[64]

In our judgment these observations make a good deal of sense. But they hardly are applicable to all terrorist organizations. The histories of such organizations abound with examples of group fragmentation, individual betrayal, and even the abandonment of violence. How are these phenomena to be explained? The answers may have to do with both the organizations themselves and the environments in which they operate.

To begin, not all terrorist organizations are the self-contained primary groups to which the above observations are intended to apply. The larger ones exhibit divisions of labor and specializations of function, and while primary groups may promote cohesion and conformity, large, complex organizations will often give rise to factional disputes; the political perspectives of members are influenced by their particular places in the organization. Furthermore, external reality may be distorted, but it cannot be completely kept out. For example, if the terrorist group begins to experience one arrest after another, it is usually inevitable that a few members will reach the conclusion that something is wrong. They may react by voicing their dissent, by looking for ways out before they too are apprehended, or by forming their own group to carry on the struggle under different auspices.

Finally, a terrorist group may not enjoy a monopoly. As in some Western European political party systems with three or four different parties seeking to represent the left (communists, socialists, social democrats), so too in the case of terrorism there may be several organizations sharing similar goals active simultaneously. Italy's Red Brigades shared the field with Front Line and several smaller aggregations. Likewise, the PLO is composed of a variety of competing groups. In these situations it is possible for dissenters within one group to switch groups without abandoning terrorism.

TRANSFORMATION AND THE END OF TERRORISM

We prefer to reserve the general discussion of the ends of terrorist groups until the concluding chapter of this book. At this point it seems sufficient to point out that not all terrorist organizations come to an end when their structures are destroyed and their members are either killed or captured by the authorities. In some cases, the organizations remain, perhaps in modified form, but the methods they employ no longer involve terrorism. As we noted earlier, the origins of some terrorist groups are to be found in political parties or factions thereof. Some continue to retain ties to such parties even while they practice terrorism. Is it possible for these groups to end as they began?

The Irgun in mandatory Palestine, begun in the 1930s as a branch of revisionist Zionism, after the achievement of Israeli independence was transformed into a political party whose leader, Menachem Begin, later became prime minister. With the restoration of Uruguayan democracy several years ago, the Tupamaros have begun to run slates of candidates at parliamentary elections, albeit without much success so far. And thanks to the Spanish government's policy of "Social Reinsertion," one faction of the ETA, the political-military wing, has become demilitarized. Many of its former cadres now participate in democratic politics in the Basque country as members of a regional political party.[65] The history of the struggles of Catholics in Ireland and Basques in Spain suggests that these struggles have taken different forms at different periods of time, sometimes peaceful, sometimes violent. It may very well be that, in general, terrorism as a strategy can be put away or picked up again by the same organization as the need arises and as conditions dictate. In this connection, it is interesting to note that George Habash, leader of the rejectionist Popular Front for the Liberation of Palestine, has recently been reported as saying that strikes at "imperialist" targets have become detrimental to the Palestinian cause.[66] Habash is, after all, the same man who initiated such strikes back in the 1960s.

A FINAL OBSERVATION

Stories that appear on television or in the newspapers frequently emphasize the bizarre or unusual elements in contemporary terrorism. The individuals and groups that carry out acts of terrorist violence are often depicted in ways which stress their abnormality. Given the nature of the acts and the needs of the mass media, this result is, perhaps, inevitable.

The evidence reported in this chapter, with respect to both the kinds of individuals who become terrorists and the types of organizations they join, requires a different assessment. Instead of the peculiar, the pictures of terrorists and their groups that emerge are ones that seem familiar. In general, terrorists appear as relatively normal people whose groups bear some resemblance to other political organizations. The exotic may make headlines, but the reality is something different.

KEY TERMS

"dolce vita" social reinsertion
homofighters xenofighters
Sabra and Shatilla camps

NOTES

1 See, for example, Jerrold Post, "Group and Organizational Dynamics of Political Terrorism" (a paper presented at the annual scientific meeting of the International Society of Political Psychology, Amsterdam, July 1986).
2 For a biography, see Colin Smith, *Carlos: Portrait of a Terrorist* (New York: Holt, Rinehart and Winston, 1976).
3 Allesandro Silj, *Never Again without a Rifle* (New York: Karz Publishers, 1979), pp. 71–82.
4 Christopher Dobson and Ronald Payne, *The Never Ending War* (New York: Facts on File, 1987), pp. 229–230; Yossi Melman, *The Master Terrorist: The True Story of Abu Nidal* (New York: Avon Books, 1987).
5. Jillian Becker, *Hitler's Children* (Philadelphia: J. B. Lippincott Company, 1977), pp. 109–204.
6 Claire Sterling, *The Time of the Assassins* (New York: Holt, Rinehart and Winston, 1983), pp. 38–52.
7 L. J. Davis, "Ballad of an American Terrorist," *Harper's* (July 1986), pp. 53–62.
8 Richard Rubenstein, *Alchemists of Revolution* (New York: Basic Books, 1987), p. 234.
9 Walter Laqueur, *The Age of Terrorism*, rev. ed. (Boston: Little, Brown and Company, 1987), pp. 72–95.
10 See, for example, Samuel Barnes, Max Kaase, et al., *Political Action* (Beverly Hills, Ca.: Sage Publications, 1979), pp. 97–112.
11 Thomas H. Greene, *Comparative Revolutionary Movements* (Englewood Cliffs, N.J.: Prentice-Hall, Inc., 1974), p. 17.
12 Marco Revelli, "Italy," in Detlef Muhlberger (ed.), *The Social Basis of European Fascist Movements* (London: Croom Helm, 1987), p. 11.
13 Detlef Muhlberger, "Germany," in ibid., pp. 58–59.
14 Charles A. Russell and Bowman Miller, "Profile of a Terrorist," in Lawrence Freedman and Yonah Alexander (eds.), *Perspective on Terrorism* (Wilmington, Del.: Scholarly Resources, 1983), pp. 45–60.
15 Leonard Weinberg, "The Radical Right and Varieties of Right-Wing Politics in the United States" (a paper presented at the annual scientific meeting of the International Society of Political Psychology, San Francisco, July 1987), pp. 25–26.
16 Bruce Hoffman, *Right-Wing Terrorism in Europe* (Santa Monica, Ca.: Rand Corporation, 1982), p. 15.
17 See, for example, Michael Corbett, *Political Tolerance in America* (New York: Longmann, 1982), pp. 123–162.
18 Robin Wright, *Sacred Rage* (New York: Simon and Schuster, 1986), pp. 69–110.

19 See, for example, Leonard Weinberg and William Eubank, "Italian Women Terrorists," *Terrorism*, 9:3 (1987), pp. 241–262.
20 See Daniel E. Georges-Abesie, "Women as Terrorists," in Freedman and Alexander (eds.), op. cit., pp. 71–84.
21 Eva Kolinsky, "Terrorism in West Germany," in Juliet Lodge (ed.), *The Threat of Terrorism* (Boulder, Col.: Westview Press, 1988), pp. 75–76.
22 Russell and Miller, op. cit., p. 55.
23 Sabri Sayari, *Generational Changes in Terrorist Movements: The Turkish Case* (Santa Monica, Ca.: The Rand Corporation, 1985), pp. 10–11.
24 Leonard Weinberg and William Eubank, "Recruitment of Italian Political Terrorists," in Martin Slann and William Schectermann (eds.), *Multidimensional Terrorism* (Boulder, Col.: Lynne Rienner, 1987), pp. 81–94.
25 Quoted in Leonard Weinberg and William Eubank, *The Rise and Fall of Italian Terrorism* (Boulder, Col.: Westview Press, 1987), p. 37.
26 Frederick Hacker, *Crusaders, Criminals, Crazies* (New York: W. W. Norton & Company, Inc., 1976), pp. 35–44.
27 Konrad Kellen, *Terrorists—What Are They Like?* (Santa Monica, Ca.: The Rand Corporation, 1979), p. 27.
28 "Northern Ireland: Brotherly Hate," *The Economist* (June 25, 1988), pp. 19–22.
29 Frederick Hacker, "Dialectical Interrelationships of Personal and Political Factors in Terrorism," in Freedman and Alexander (eds.), op. cit., pp. 24–25.
30 Kellen, op. cit., p. 39.
31 Viola Bernard, Perry Ottenberg, and Fritz Redl, "Dehumanization," in Nevitt Sanford and Craig Comstock (eds.), *Sanctions for Evil* (San Francisco: Jossey-Bass, 1971), pp. 102–124.
32 This literature is summarized in Martha Crenshaw, "The Psychology of Political Terrorism," in Margaret Hermann (ed.), *Political Psychology* (San Francisco: Jossey-Bass, 1986), pp. 384–390.
33 John W. Crayton, "Terrorism and the Psychology of the Self," in Freedman and Alexander (eds.), op. cit., pp. 33–41.
34 Ibid., p. 37.
35 See, especially, Crenshaw, op. cit., pp. 390–395; and Erik Erikson, *Identity: Youth and Crisis* (New York: W. W. Norton & Company, 1968).
36 Crenshaw, op. cit., p. 392.
37 "Northern Ireland: Brotherly Hate," *The Economist* (June 25, 1988), pp. 19–22.
38 On this theme see Peter Merkl, "Approaches to the Study of Political Violence," in Peter Merkl (ed.), *Political Violence and Terror* (Berkeley: University of California Press, 1986), pp. 48–53; and Franco Ferracuti and Francesco Bruno, "Psychiatric Aspects of Terrorism in Italy," in C. R. Huff and I. L. Barak (eds.), *The Mad, the Bad and the Different* (Lexington, Mass.: Lexington Books, 1981), pp. 199–213.
39 Crenshaw, op. cit., pp. 388–389.
40 This work is based on the writings of James Q. Wilson, *Political Organizations* (New York: Basic Books, 1973), pp. 30–51.
41 *San Francisco Chronicle* (Oct. 15, 1987), p. 21.

42 Martha Crenshaw, "An Organizational Approach to the Analysis of Political Terrorism" (a paper presented at the World Congress of the International Political Science Association, Paris, July 1985), p. 8.
43 Connor Cruise O'Brien, "Bloody Business," *The New Republic* (Dec. 2, 1985), p. 36.
44 Ayatollah Taleghani, *Society and Economics in Islam* (Tehran: n.d.), p. 100.
45 Quoted in Claire Sterling, *The Terror Network* (New York: Holt, Rinehart and Winston, 1981), p. 113.
46 Laqueur, op. cit., p. 8.
47 Russell and Miller, op. cit., pp. 57–58.
48 Klaus Wasmund, "The Political Socialization of Terrorist Groups in West Germany," *Journal of Political and Military Sociology,* 2:2 (1983), p. 227.
49 Kellen, op. cit., pp. 12–13.
50 Crenshaw, "An Organizational Approach to the Analysis of Political Terrorism," op. cit., pp. 9–10.
51 Irving Janis, *Victims of Groupthink* (Boston: Houghton Mifflin Company, 1972), p. 13.
52 Ariel Merari, "A Classification of Terrorist Groups," *Terrorism,* 1:3, 4 (1978), pp. 331–346.
53 Bonnie Cordes et al., *A Conceptual Framework for the Analysis of Terrorist Groups* (Santa Monica, Ca.: Rand Corporation, 1985).
54 Helena Cobban, *The Palestinian Liberation Organization* (Cambridge, Mass.: Cambridge University Press, 1984), pp. 36–57.
55 William Quandt et al., *The Politics of Palestinian Nationalism* (Berkeley: University of California Press, 1973), p. 66.
56 Kent Layne Oots, *A Political Organization Approach to Transnational Terrorism* (New York: Greenwood Press, 1986), p. 40.
57 Ibid., p. 125.
58 J. K. Zawodny, "Infrastructures of Terrorist Organizations," in Freedman and Alexander (eds.), op. cit., p. 63.
59 Richard Gillespie, *Soldiers of Peron* (Oxford: Clarendon Press, 1982), p. 278.
60 See, for example, Anthony Downs, *Inside Bureaucracy* (Boston: Little, Brown and Company, 1966), pp. 7–10.
61 James Adams, *The Financing of Terror* (New York: Simon and Schuster, 1986), pp. 156–184.
62 Kellen, op. cit., p. 38.
63 See, especially, Sidney Verba, *Small Groups and Political Behavior* (Princeton, N.J.: Princeton University Press, 1961).
64 Crenshaw, "The Psychology of Political Terrorism," in Hermann (ed.), op. cit., pp. 395–400.
65 Benny Pollack and Graham Hunter, "Dictatorship, Democracy and Terrorism in Spain" in Lodge (ed.), *The Threat of Terrorism*, op. cit. (see note 20), pp. 135–137.
66 Cited in Martha Crenshaw, "How Terrorism Ends" (a paper presented at the annual meeting of the American Political Science Association, Chicago, September 1987), p. 11.

CHAPTER 5

THE EFFECTS OF TERRORIST OPERATIONS

The concern of this chapter is with the impact of contemporary terrorism. The best way to begin an evaluation of its effects is by recalling the ingredients out of which acts of terrorism are composed. As will be remembered, for acts of political violence to be defined as terroristic there must be a victim, the attack on whom is intended to send a message to a broader audience whose behavior, in turn, is to be modified in some fashion. Given this understanding, we intend to review the effects of terrorism by first assessing the damage terrorist groups have inflicted on their immediate victims. Next, we will examine the impact they have had on the mass media, the means these groups use to transmit their messages, and on public opinion, their presumed audience. Finally, we will provide the reader with some assessment of contemporary terrorism's social and political effects. To what extent have terrorist groups been successful in achieving their long-run goals? To what extent have they failed?

VICTIMS

In recent years various studies, carried out by both public and private organizations, have attempted to assess the damage caused by terrorist operations. These endeavors may be divided into those that have reported data on acts of international terrorism and ones whose concerns are domestic, focused on terrorist attacks within one country (see Chapter 1 for the distinction). To our knowledge, no effort has yet been made to compile overall casualty figures for each nation to have experienced separate episodes of domestic terrorism, India plus Northern Ireland plus Turkey, and so on, although some single-country investigations are available. There is then some problem in calculating the human toll of domestic terrorist events. Another problem in measuring the impact terrorism has had on its victims involves making a decision over when a terrorist episode stops and when some wider form of violence has begun. Lebanon, for instance, has been the site of terrorist violence that escalated into a full-scale civil war, in the context of which additional acts of terrorism have been committed. The same might be said in connection with recent developments in Sri Lanka. Should we regard as the victims of terrorism all those killed or injured as the result of these conflicts? If not, where should the line be drawn?

This is not to say that these problems are insuperable or that the questions cannot be answered. It is to suggest, however, that it may be somewhat easier to treat the effects of international terrorism. Indeed, several worthwhile studies are available on this subject.[1]

According to figures compiled by the Central Intelligence Agency and the U.S. State Department, there were a total of 10,326 international terrorist events between 1968 and 1986. Over these years 6444 people were killed and another 14,169 wounded as a result of the events.[2] Neither the victims of these attacks nor the places where they occurred were randomly distributed around the world. The principal victims of international terrorism in these years have been North Americans and citizens of Western European countries. They are followed by citizens of Middle Eastern and Latin American nations. In addition, the victims do not represent a cross section of the population when their sources of employment or social backgrounds are introduced into the calculations. Although the most horrifying terrorist events are ones in which the victims are randomly targeted bystanders, e.g., passersby at an airport, this circumstance prevails somewhat less frequently than might be supposed. The data recorded in Table 5-1 are restricted to American targets from 1968 through 1980, but the pattern they reflect applies to victims of other nationalities as well.[3] For the most part the targets have not been ordinary citizens chosen at random. The central tendency has been for the terrorists to pick out specific targets: business executives, diplomats and other government officials, military officers and personnel, and the facilities in which they are located. What meaning should be assigned to this information?

Some discussions of terrorism have stressed the irrationality of its perpetrators. But the data compiled by the U.S. government sources reveal a very different picture, at least so far as international terrorism is concerned. These data suggest that the most frequent victims of attack have been members of the elites of Western and especially American societies.

TABLE 5-1
INTERNATIONAL TERRORIST ATTACKS ON U.S. CITIZENS OR PROPERTY,
1968–1980, BY CATEGORY

Category	Number	Percent
Diplomatic officials or property	805	28.1
Military officials or property	456	15.9
Other U.S. government officials or property	344	12.0
Business facilities or executives	901	31.5
Private citizens	357	12.5
	2863	100 %

Source: Patterns of International Terrorism 1980 (Washington, D.C.: National Foreign Assessment Center, June 1981), p. 4.

This targeting pattern appears to indicate a high degree of rationality on the part of the terrorists. First, attacks on Americans and Western Europeans ensure a high level of coverage by the mass media, a prime terrorist objective, given Western domination of the major channels of mass communication around the world. And, second, for many of the groups practicing international terrorism, the targets—American and European business, political, and military elites—represent their real enemies, the forces at work in the world with which they are at war. Since many of the perpetrators have been from the Third World, Latin America, and the Middle East in particular, international terrorist attacks appear as perfectly logical extensions of the terrorists' opposition to capitalism, imperialism, Zionism, and Western influence in general.

The location of international terrorist attacks in the period from 1968 to 1985 is displayed in Table 5-2. As may be seen, the major sites for these events have been Western Europe, Latin America, and the Middle East. Despite the fact that Americans have been the most frequent victims, relatively few terrorist attacks occurred within the United States. It is when Americans live or travel abroad that they appear to be most susceptible to the violence. The overall pattern that emerges, combining both who and where, is that of attacks on members of Western elites resident in Western Europe or Latin America and the Middle East. And, to date, it has not been the Third World in general but only the latter two regions of it where these events have tended to occur.

We have made an effort to compile casualty figures for victims of recent episodes of domestic terrorism. The results are hardly complete, but at least they take into consideration countries whose terrorist experiences can be disentangled from broader forms of political violence.

Despite the fragmentary nature of the figures reported in Table 5-3, it is apparent that domestic terrorism has been far more lethal than the in-

TABLE 5-2
GEOGRAPHIC DISTRIBUTION OF INTERNATIONAL TERRORIST
INCIDENTS, 1968–1985

Region	Number	Percent
North America	754	7.9
Latin America	1977	20.7
Western Europe	3309	34.6
U.S.S.R., Eastern Europe	79	1.0
Sub-Saharan Africa	359	4.0
Middle East and North Africa	2199	23.0
Asia, Pacific states	699	7.3
Other	176	1.8
	9552	100 %

Source: Patterns of International Terrorism 1980 (Washington, D.C.: National Foreign Assessment Center, June 1981), p. 2; U.S. Department of State, Patterns of Global Terrorism 1985 (October 1986), p. 30.

ternational variety. Without taking into consideration terrorist-caused fatalities in such countries as Sri Lanka, India, or Colombia, the number of individuals killed in just those countries we have included well exceeds the international figure. We do not wish to leave the reader with a false sense of precision. What we can say with some certainty is that a mini-

TABLE 5-3
DEATHS CAUSED BY DOMESTIC TERRORISM IN SELECTED NATIONS

Nation	Number of deaths
Argentina (1969–1979)	1504
Italy (1969–1982)	350
Northern Ireland (1969–1982)	2204
Spain (1968–1981)	667
Turkey (1977–1980)	4500
United States (1969–1986)	51
West Germany (1969–1979)	25
	9301

Source: Robert Cox, "Total Terrorism: Argentina, 1969 to 1979," in Martha Crenshaw (ed.), Terrorism, Legitimacy, and Power (Middletown, Conn.: Wesleyan University Press, 1983), pp. 130–131; Sabri Sayari, Generational Changes in Terrorist Movements: The Turkish Case (Santa Monica, Ca.: The Rand Corporation, 1985), p. 1; Jeffrey Ross and Ted Gurr, "Why Terrorism Subsides: A Comparative Study of Trends and Groups in Terrorism in Canada and the United States" (a paper presented at the annual meeting of the American Political Science Association, Chicago, September 1987), pp. 11–13; Leonard Weinberg and William Eubank, The Rise and Fall of Italian Terrorism (Boulder, Col.: Westview Press, 1987), p. 110; Peter Merkl (ed.), Political Violence and Terror (Berkeley: University of California Press, 1986), pp. 103, 192; Berry Pollack and Graham Hunter, "Dictatorship, Democracy and Terrorism in Spain," in Juliet Lodge (ed.), The Threat of Terrorism (Boulder, Col.: Westview Press, 1988), p. 119.

mum of approximately 16,000 people have lost their lives since 1968 as the result of terrorism, both domestic and international. If it were available, the real figure would be substantially higher.

What should we make of this calculation? Does the fact that more than 16,000 people have been killed mean that contemporary terrorism has been a particularly deadly form of political violence? Or, alternatively, does it mean that a mountain has been made out of a molehill and the effects of terrorism vastly exaggerated? If its effects are measured simply by the number of lives it has claimed, the appropriate answer is one which would emphasize the molehill more than the mountain. Far more people have been killed over the same period by various Latin American or Southeast Asian governments in their efforts to repress their opponents than have been murdered by all the world's terrorist organizations taken together.[4] Another comparison: one analyst has estimated that 750,000 people worldwide lost their lives as the result of internal wars from 1961 through 1965.[5] Of course, any unnecessary loss of life is a tragedy, but compared with such a figure deaths due to terrorism seem of diminished significance.

In addition to being killed or physically wounded people may be harmed in other ways as the result of terrorist attacks. One of the common forms of terrorist violence involves hostage taking and kidnapping. A number of distinctions may be introduced here.[6] For one, victims may be held at the site where they have been taken captive, e.g., inside an embassy, or they may be moved from this location to some hidden place, as were American journalists in Beirut. Second, there is obviously variation in the kinds of people who are victimized. They range from prominent political and business leaders to individuals unlucky enough to have been at the wrong place at the wrong time when the airliner was skyjacked. Also, there are differences in the immediate aims the terrorists wish to achieve as the result of these operations. In addition to publicity for their cause, they may seek ransom or an exchange of prisoners, for example, the liberation of other members of their band held by the authorities for the freedom of their hostages. Yet despite these differences hostages all share the experience of captivity by abductors who threaten their lives while talks usually go on with those in authority.

A number of analyses have been done on not only the frequency but also the outcomes of terrorist kidnappings and hostage-taking events.[7] In a high proportion of these incidents investigators report that the victims have been set free. Unsurprisingly, deaths are most likely to occur when the authorities make an attempt to liberate the captives by force. The cold-blooded execution of hostages is relatively rare.

Yet when it is reported that hostages have been released unharmed the reference is to their physical condition. Clearly, there are other ways of harming people, and the experience of being held captive may result in emotional wounds. What sorts of feelings are unleashed when someone is taken captive by terrorists?

In a few cases where prominent persons have been kidnapped they reported having premonitions that such an event might take place. Sir Geoffrey Jackson, the British ambassador to Uruguay, who was kidnapped by the Tupamaros in 1971, experienced such forewarnings. Before his abduction he sensed that things were not quite right in his environment. He had an eerie feeling of being spied upon and noticed certain curious anomalies in his surroundings. For example, he saw the same young people sunning themselves in the park directly across the street from his embassy each day for a month. The same motor scooter habitually passed his official car as it approached his residence.[8] Similarly, the late Aldo Moro reportedly told his wife he felt a sense of foreboding some weeks before he was kidnapped and later killed by the Red Brigades. The American General James Dozier, also kidnapped by the Red Brigades, apparently experienced such apprehensions before he was taken captive.

It is unclear how common these premonitions are. It seems likely, however, that they would be felt by individuals who had some reason to suspect they might make attractive targets for terrorist groups and who were sufficiently sensitive to notice subtle changes in their surroundings.

Whether or not the victims develop these feelings before the event, the experience of being taken captive by terrorists yields a relatively common set of circumstances. Previously independent individuals going about their daily lives are suddenly confronted by a totally new situation. They are no longer free to come and go as they please. When or if they eat, sleep, go to the bathroom, or move from one place to another is now determined by others. In addition, the others usually possess weapons and threaten with immediate death all those in their control who do not follow their instructions. To make matters still worse, the decision over whether the hostage lives or dies is now outside his or her control. Often it will depend on the captors obtaining certain things from authorities whose reactions to the event may appear as unfathomable as that of the captors. To put it mildly, this is a stress-inducing situation.

Human reactions to stress induced by terrorist captivity are both physical and psychological. The former affects the autonomic nervous system: the heart rate increases, the pupil of the eye dilates, adrenaline production increases as the body prepares itself for a fight or flight reaction to a life-threatening situation.[9] But under the conditions described above, either a fight or flight response by a captive at the initial stages of a terrorist seizure is usually the most dangerous reaction a hostage can make; it is the one most likely to cause death. One psychiatrist concerned about the reactions of victims to terrorist captivity has placed the array of possible psychological responses under the general concept of adaptation. "Adaptation includes all the responses and strategies a hostage may make or use in order to reduce stress and maximize his chances of survival."[10] Subsumed under this concept are two sorts of reactions: defense mechanisms and coping. The former refers to the largely unconscious or almost automatic adjustments the individual makes to a stressful, anxiety-producing situation. Particular defense mechanisms will often reflect the captive's underlying personality characteristics. Coping, on the other hand, refers to conscious, often innovative, strategies people devise in order to adjust to difficult situations.

Either type of adaptation will be influenced by the captive's personality and prior life experiences, what he or she brings to the situation. But the situation itself—the duration of the captivity, the attitude of the terrorists toward their victim—also will affect the response. In short, there will be considerable variability in the way people adapt.

One commonly observed defense mechanism is denial, a refusal to believe that the event is actually taking place. In the early stages of a kidnapping or hostage taking, the victim who responds by denying the reality of the situation in the short run may be doing more to save his or her life than someone who manifests a heroic or "macho" response.

Denial, though, is hardly the only unconscious reaction victims have displayed. Among the others analysts have noticed are "intellectualization" and "creative elaboration," or fantasy.[11] In the case of intellectualization, stress is reduced by draining the situation of its emotional content and making it more a puzzle to be solved or a problem whose resolution can give rise to speculation. In one instance, in the Netherlands, hostages speculated over whether or not they would receive compensation from the Dutch government for the inconveniences they were forced to experience. The objects of victims' fantasies or creative elaborations are frequently food and freedom. Victims will often imagine, in great detail, the meals they will consume and the activities in which they will participate after their ordeal is over.

The most widely discussed form of adaptation to terrorist kidnapping and hostage taking is the Stockholm syndrome. First observed in the aftermath of a nonpolitical bank robbery and hostage-barricade situation in Sweden in 1973, the Stockholm syndrome refers to the propensity of some victims to develop friendly feelings toward or even, in some cases, an identification with their captors.[12] In one case after another, observers have been amazed to discover that immediately after their liberation some victims have reported how well disposed they felt toward their former captors. Sometimes they have expressed sympathy for the terrorists' political cause as well as warm feelings for the humane treatment they received during their captivity. The obvious question to ask concerning the Stockholm syndrome is why anyone would have such positive feelings toward individuals who had recently threatened to kill them for little apparent reason.

Explanations for the syndrome's roots have focused on both their psychological and situational causes. Some analysts have maintained that the syndrome is a form of "identification with the aggressor," a type of regressive childlike behavior noticed with concentration camp inmates, among others. The logic is that victims are so stunned by the life-threatening situation in which they find themselves, and so overwhelmed by the fact that captors have taken control over their lives, they begin to view their captors much in the way young children view their parents, even ones who are abusive toward them.

Other observers have contended that the syndrome is largely brought on by the nature of the situation in which the hostages find themselves. Over time they become aware of the fact that they share a state of mutual isolation with their captors. Both hostage and hostage taker are cut off from the outside world in an extremely precarious situation, one in which any violent response by the authorities could lead to the deaths of all concerned. In other words, they may share a common fate and a mutual interest so far as the outcome is concerned. Under these conditions, if the terrorists and their victims begin to interact in a relatively normal way, they may develop sympathetic feelings toward one another and a joint hope that the authorities will meet the terrorists' demands.

Evidence to support this interpretation is based on the fact that the syndrome does not manifest itself when the victims belong to a group their captors regard with intense hostility. There are, for example, no instances of Israelis displaying such symptoms after they have been taken captive by Arab terrorists.[13] Likewise, when members of the Hanafi Muslim sect seized hostages at the headquarters of the B'nai B'rith organization in Washington, D.C., in 1977, the victims, when interviewed after their release, showed no signs of the Stockholm syndrome. On the other hand, when captives are neutral or, in a few cases, sympathetic to the terrorists' political cause, the possibility exists for captors and captives to develop a more human interaction. And when this occurs, the prospects for the growth of sympathetic feelings are heightened.

To this point we have discussed the formation of sympathetic feelings of the victims toward the terrorists, but the literature also makes reference to the emotion flowing the other way: from the captors to their hostages. Here analysts emphasize the desirability of victims deliberately behaving in such a way as to elicit such feelings from the terrorists as a device to enhance their chances of survival. One of the best ways of coping when taken captive is for the hostage to do and say things that will persuade the terrorists of his or her humanity. In 1975 a Dutch journalist in imminent danger of execution by his Moluccan captors was saved when they overheard him discuss his intimate family problems with another hostage.[14] He appeared so human to them that they simply could not kill him.

The establishment of positive contacts with the terrorists is not the only coping strategy available to hostages. Other techniques that will reduce stress and improve the captive's chances of survival include focusing on some future goal or purpose and establishing group ties with other hostages.[15] William Niehous, an American business executive working in Venezuela, was kidnapped in Caracas in 1976 and held captive for almost three years. After his rescue he recorded some of the things that helped him survive:

> I set individual goals. I would live until a specific date, whether it was my son's graduation, or my wife's birthday, or Christmas. As the date came and went, with my release not imminent, I did become despondent; however, I then set another goal for life sometime in the future. I kept telling myself that those holding me surely would release me by the date of my next goal.[16]

In this case the specific purpose provided the victim with some hope not only that he would have a future but that it would involve pleasant experiences as well.

While Mr. Niehous was held in isolation, many kidnapping and hostage-taking situations are ones in which numbers of people are taken captive. In these circumstances an effective means of coping with stress involves the development of group bonds among the victims. At the beginning of the experience, passengers on board a skyjacked plane may be as anonymous to one another as they are to the terrorists. If they are able to establish contact with each other and form a group, they are likely to offer one another the comfort of communicating their feelings to sympathetic listeners. In these settings, the possibility also exists that one or two captives will emerge as leaders of the group. When this happens these individuals can strengthen the resolve of the other captives by providing some independence of will against the terrorists.

The impact of captivity often does not end when the hostages are released. The particular kinds of aftereffects victims experience are influenced by the duration and severity of the experience itself and the particular types of people they were before it began. Some kidnapping victims, General Dozier, for example, resume their previous duties with few apparent long-term consequences. Other ex-captives have written books or taken to the lecture circuit as a way of relating their experiences to others. But a high proportion of victims suffer some psychological aftereffects. The literature here refers especially to sleep disorders and the formation of certain phobias.[17] For example, employees of B'nai B'rith who were taken hostage by the Hanafi Muslims reported having great difficulty getting into taxicabs in Washington, D.C., long after their release. This phobic reaction derived from their belief that Hanafi followers often were cab drivers in that city. The ex-captives feared that if they entered the taxi they would again be taken hostage. Other consequences of the experience included depression, prolonged irritability, and a diminished capacity to concentrate.

We should not conclude our discussion of the effects terrorism has had on its victims without mentioning the damage caused to property and some of the other costs involved. Attaching a dollar amount to the effects of terrorist operations is no easy feat. Buildings have been bombed. Metal detectors and other devices have had to be installed at airports and elsewhere to deter would-be skyjackers. In 1986 alone, airlines spent more that $200 million to upgrade their security.[18] Embassies have been reconstructed or reinforced to better protect them against attack. In the wake of the 1985 skyjacking of TWA flight 847 and other terrorist events many Americans were deterred from spending their vacations in Europe out of fear they too would become the targets of terrorist attacks. The tourist business suffered. Millions have been paid in ransom for the release of hostages by business firms whose executives have been kidnapped and by families whose relatives have been taken captive. The list could go on, but all told it seems likely that the cost of contemporary terrorism has been several billion dollars.

THE MASS MEDIA AND PUBLIC OPINION

The purpose of all this violence—the killings, kidnappings, bombings, and so on—is to send a message. We ought then to pay particular attention to the effect that terrorism has had on the means by which this message is communicated and with the audience to which it is addressed.

What comes to mind immediately when we think about the message-sending purpose of terrorism is the role played by the mass media, television especially. Yet before we bring it under discussion, we should point out that in some cases terrorist groups and organizations sympathetic to them have developed their own independent channels for communicating with the public, not trusting the largely Western-controlled mass media to get the story straight.

Often this will involve more than simply the distribution of handbills and pamphlets which describe a group's political aims. The PLO has its own radio station, the Voice of Palestine. During Italy's recent terrorist episode, Radio Sherwood (named after Robin Hood's base of operations) and other professedly revolutionary stations made announcements on behalf of the leftist terrorist groups. There were also newspapers and other widely circulated publications with links to the New Left movements that performed a similar task in acting as sources of "counterinformation."[19]

Terrorists have explored other means of circumventing the editorial judgments of professional journalists. On occasion terrorist groups have simply taken control of radio and television stations and had their own spokespersons deliver their communiqués over the air. They have also taken advantage of the new videocassette recorder (VCR) technology by conducting their own interviews with hostages and then distributing these productions in cassette form to interested television stations. In the United States, groups tied to the Aryan Nations movement have created a computer network that permits users with the appropriate log-in number to receive their violently anti-Semitic messages on their computer terminals.

It is clear, however, that the principal means by which terrorists communicate with their audiences is through the mass media, channels of communication not under their direct control. The obvious questions to be posed concern the coverage the mass media extend to terrorist activities. Why is so much attention paid? And what effect does such coverage have on both the terrorists themselves and on the audiences exposed to it?

So far as the former question is concerned, the first response is that stories about terrorist events are newsworthy. According to one observer, for any event to meet this criterion, it should be timely and out of the ordinary, contain an element of adventure, possess some entertainment value, and somehow affect the lives of those exposed to the account.[20] If these are the standards, it is no wonder that acts of terrorism, particularly if they are directed at people like ourselves or prominent individuals, attract our attention in ways that developments of greater long-term importance, such as budget deficits or complex arms negotiations, do not.

Terrorism, as the saying goes, sells papers. Sometimes this is literally the case. Immediately after Aldo Moro was kidnapped by the Red Brigades in 1978, the circulations of the major Italian dailies increased sharply as the public became engaged by the event.[21] Furthermore, acts of terrorism offer the possibility of commercial spin-offs. Films, television series, and popular novels have all been done in order to exploit the popular fascination with the subject. Given the competitive environment in which the Western mass media operate, with money to be made and the careers of individual journalists to be advanced, different newspapers and radio and television stations compete with one another to present terrorist events in the most dramatic fashion possible. In this context, appeals from the authorities and other interested parties for self-restraint often fall on deaf ears. To be fair, it should be noted that in the United States and Great Britain some newspapers and television stations have exercised self-restraint by limiting their coverage of hostage seizures when there is reason to believe victims' lives would be endangered. And in Britain as well as other democracies where television is a public enterprise, the government has exerted pressure to censor the coverage of terrorist events.[22]

If the newsworthy quality of terrorist activities is not sufficient to gain their perpetrators access to the mass media, they also have other means at their disposal, notably blackmail and physical intimidation. Not uncommonly terrorists will insist that their political messages be printed in certain newspapers or read verbatim over television channels as a precondition for the release of hostages whose lives they are threatening. They also have used the blackmail technique of privileged access to ensure themselves of suitable coverage. A journalist and his or her employer will be offered an opportunity to interview the member of a terrorist group or a person it is holding captive. If the resulting account does not meet the terrorists' expectations, the journalist will be denied additional opportunities to scoop competitors. Access will be denied and the opportunity for more inside stories will later be made available to other journalists.

As recent events in Beirut illustrate, journalists themselves are not immune to terrorist violence; some have been killed, others injured or taken hostage. This physical intimidation of journalists has certain effects. Fearful for their personal safety, these journalists may exercise a kind of self-censorship over the way they report the operations of various terrorist groups.[23] Moreover, knowing that one of their colleagues has been attacked may make it more likely journalists will cover a terrorist event in greater depth than if the same type of attack were carried out against individuals from other backgrounds.

The Western mass media have had multiple effects on the development of contemporary terrorism. Naturally, the opinions of journalists and their critics often conflict on this subject. The former are inclined to argue that all they do is report events as they occur, be they natural disasters or acts of terrorist violence. In both instances the journalists are simply the bearers of bad news. And just as we would not hold the mass media responsible for an earthquake, so too we should not blame them for terrorist activity.[24] But unlike earthquakes or other natural disasters, whose causes are not subject to influence by the media, terrorist acts are human-made and, consequently, may recur or not depending upon the reception they receive by reporters, editors, and news directors.

Some have maintained that the mass media have helped to legitimize terrorist groups by affording their spokespersons opportunities to appear on television or have their views printed in mass circulation newspapers alongside those of other political figures. The television screen, for example, will show a reporter eliciting the views of a terrorist group's spokesperson in about the same way as it will display the responses of a prominent public official to the questions of the same reporter. The visual effect then is to place the terrorist and the official on the same level, with the assumption that the views of both are worth the equal attention of the viewer because the format for their rendition will be identical.[25]

Through their appearances on television and other channels of mass communication, terrorists are able to obtain publicity for their various causes which would not have been possible without the dramatic use of violence. Small groups with previously obscure political concerns appear in the spotlight thanks to the attention brought to them by the media. How many of us would have been aware of the situation of South Moluccans living in the Netherlands in the absence of the attention it received as the result of terrorism?

Among the most widely discussed consequences of the mass media in relation to terrorism is the contagion effect.[26] This notion really has several components. First, the coverage of terrorist acts, air piracy for example, promotes the emulation of such acts by others. Individuals or groups in the audience will be aroused to commit similar deeds by virtue of their observation of the initial one. In this way the mass media help to spread the disease. Second, by publicizing the activities of terrorist groups, the media perform a recruitment function. Some individuals in the audience will be so moved by these activities that they may become disposed to join a terrorist organization. This was apparently the case for later generations of Red Brigadists in Italy. And, in the United States, why did the leaders of a Chicago-based youth gang volunteer their services to Colonel Ghaddafi, if not as the result of messages about his financial support for terrorism they perceived through the mass media? Third, terrorist groups may refine and improve their techniques as the result of mass media coverage. They may be able to improve techniques that will create the widest effect and abandon others that have the least impact by evaluating how the mass media have depicted their exploits.

We should not forget that, compared with other types of armed conflict where media attention is incidental to the event, contemporary terrorism is often aimed at acquiring exposure on television. Insurgent guerrillas will launch an attack on a government outpost to achieve a military victory. Whatever coverage the media accord the event is secondary to this purpose. But, for contemporary terrorists, often the victory is the coverage itself. Holding children hostage in an elementary school will not weaken the armed forces of their opponents. It will, however, win considerable publicity for the group that has seized them. In this way, the mass media cause terrorist events to occur that would not have happened in the absence of media coverage.[27]

In kidnap and hostage-taking situations the mass media have, on occasion, endangered the captives' lives. For example, during the Hanafi seizure of B'nai B'rith headquarters in Washington, a reporter for a local radio station phoned the Hanafi leader inside the building and asked him when he planned to execute the first hostage. The leader had not had any such scheme in mind until the reporter made the suggestion to him. Fortunately, in this instance no one was killed. But there have been other events.

A similar case apparently took place earlier, in November 1974, when a British Airways plane traveling from Dubai to Libya was hijacked. Demands were made for the release of thirteen terrorists incarcerated in Egypt. An aircraft supposedly carrying the thirteen terrorists arrived from Cairo. Suddenly a local reporter broadcasted that the operation was a ruse and that there were no freed terrorists on board the Cairo aircraft. In retaliation a German banker was selected among the hostages and executed.[28]

Another way in which media coverage has threatened victims involves the live reporting of the actions of their would-be rescuers. In some circumstances, live television stories have been done showing military or police units moving into position to storm a building in which terrorists were holding hostages. The terrorists inside the building had access to television sets so they could observe the preparation being made and take the steps they believed necessary to defend themselves.[29] During the 1985 skyjacking of TWA flight 847, one American television network showed live pictures taken on board a U.S. naval vessel in the Mediterranean in which military personnel identified as belonging to the Delta Force were seen engaged in preparation for a rescue attempt. There even have been occasions when reporters have misinformed the public and the terrorists by disclosing the imminence of a rescue attempt when the authorities had no such plan in mind.

The issue of live, on-the-scene coverage of terrorist events was the subject of an opinion survey in the United States. In 1977 the views of chiefs of police in the country's thirty largest cities were solicited. Their reactions were then compared with those of TV news directors. The results reflected a wide divergence of opinion in the predictable direction. Ninety-three percent of the police chiefs believed that live coverage of terrorist events served to encourage further terrorism. The comparable figure for the TV news directors was 35 percent. And when asked to assess the threat to hostage safety caused by live coverage, nearly one half (46 percent) of the police chiefs but only 3 percent of the news directors indicated it represented a great threat.[30] In other words, individuals with tactical responsibility for overseeing the immediate response to terrorist events were worried about the role of television, while those responsible for determining what gets on the air did not seem to share this concern, at least not to the same extent.

There is some evidence that American television presents the public with a distorted picture of terrorism. Claims that all television news accounts do is report the reality of terrorist activity have been challenged by recent findings.[31] Researchers have systematically compared the incidence of international terrorist events as they were recorded in one data collection (ITERATE) from 1969 through 1980 with the coverage of these events as they appeared on the ABC, NBC, and CBS evening news programs over the same time period. The investigators discovered, first, that the amount of coverage the networks provided bore little relationship to the actual frequency of terrorist events. In some years when there was little terrorism there was extensive coverage of a few incidents. In other years in which there was a high number of events there was relatively little reporting of them. If a role for the mass media is to inform the public and decision makers of the severity of the terrorist threat, they did not perform it very well. The news programs exaggerated it in some years and underestimated it in others.

Second, American television accounts distorted the geography of international terrorism. In relation to the frequency of the occurrence of terrorist attacks in the Middle East, the networks substantially overreported terrorist attacks in that region. On the other side of the ledger, they underreported, often dramatically, the incidence of terrorism in Latin America. Under the assumption that both regions of the world are of great importance to the United States, viewers were left with distorted images concerning the location of terrorist events. Third, the type of terrorist attack influenced the amount of coverage it received. Bombings, the most common acts of terrorism, were underreported, while incidents of hostage taking and air piracy were extended too much coverage in relation to the frequency with which they happened.

Finally, the network news programs misinformed their audiences over who the victims of international terrorism were, at least insofar as Americans were concerned. Attacks on private American citizens, such as tourists, were the least frequent occurrences, while they received the most extensive coverage on television. American businesspeople were the most common targets of terrorist violence; yet these events were the least likely to be reported on the nightly news. One obvious effect of this practice was to exaggerate the danger posed to ordinary Americans. As a consequence, the latter were made to appear far more threatened than they actually were.

Not only have the mass media presented American audiences with a distorted picture of terrorist events, but, on occasion, they have also reported the occurrence of events that never took place. They have participated in the distribution of misinformation. During the 1970s in the United States, a Chicago newspaper reported that the authorities had killed a large number of Black Panther activists in the years preceding the account. A subsequent investigation revealed that most of those allegedly killed were still alive. The reporter who wrote the original story had relied on a member of the Black Panthers for his information. The latter was interested in portraying his organization as the victim of governmental repression, and the invention helped build and publicize his case.[32] In the Middle East various PLO groups have claimed and been given credit by the media for attacks on Israeli targets that never occurred. In some cases the misinformation has come from government sources with their own political axes to grind. Not too long ago the Egyptian government staged a bogus "assassination" of a leading Libyan exile politician in order to embarrass the regime in Tripoli. Another example involved the bombing of the National Agricultural Bank in Milan in December 1969. This event actually took place. Sixteen bank customers died in the explosion. But the local police officials announced that the bombing was the work of a left-wing anarchist group and proceeded to arrest two members of it. The press reported the story based on what they had been told by the authorities. A few years later, it was disclosed that the bombing had been done by a neo-Fascist organization, with links to the police officials involved, interested in mobilizing public opinion against leftist movements in Italy.[33] The misinformation conveyed in these cases is the result of the media's dependence upon sources with strong incentives to manipulate the public in the impressions received of political terrorism and those responsible for its repression.

At this stage of our analysis the reader likely will have drawn the conclusion that the mass media in democratic societies, and television especially, have been used by terrorist groups to promote their political objectives. There is, however, another side to the story. We should keep in mind that publicity is one thing, sympathy something else. It does not follow that the enormous attention American television showers on illegal drug use and dramatic acts of violent crime is intended to stimulate popular support for the purveyors of cocaine or serial killers: far from it.

By focusing on a dramatic terrorist event for a minute or two on the nightly news programs, the impression television often conveys is of senseless violence inflicted on totally innocent victims.[34] In many cases the terrorists' political messages become detached from the visual presentation of the deed. And if any political meaning is assigned to the event, it is often done through background interviews with spokespersons for the very government against which the terrorist group is waging its campaign of violence. On those occasions, when the terrorists do get an opportunity to make their case, not infrequently they respond by a barrage of rhetoric so obscure or threatening as to bewilder or antagonize most members of the audience. Further, there is some evidence that people who acquire their knowledge of terrorist events exclusively by watching television accounts differ from those who also obtain information by reading about such events in newspapers and magazines. The viewers tend to attribute responsibility for the events to different sources. Readers are more inclined to interpret the events by reference to broad social and political background factors, while viewers understand the same events largely in terms of their perpetrators' immediate motivations, without focusing on the wider context.[35]

Like other individuals who are accorded great attention by the mass media, terrorists may develop an exaggerated sense of their own importance. As with actors and actresses so too with terrorists; the ego-inflating publicity may enhance their career prospects. On the other hand, members of terrorist groups may come to believe they are more powerful and menacing than is really the case. This may lead them to the conclusion that they pose a serious military threat to the government. In turn, when they stage operations on the basis of this misperception, the outcomes are likely to prove disastrous from their point of view. Certainly, the fact that PLO leaders were persuaded their organization represented a serious military challenge to the Israelis led to significant defeats in Lebanon and elsewhere.[36] The same effect will be achieved if the authorities gather an exaggerated impression of the terrorists' power and respond accordingly.

While it is true that the media's coverage of terrorist events may help inflate the perpetrators' perceptions of themselves, it may have the same effect on their victims. Until he was kidnapped by the Red Brigades, Aldo Moro was the object of intense criticism by the Italian press for the way he had led the scandal-ridden Italian government. But his abduction and subsequent murder at the hands of terrorists transformed the presentation of his character by the mass media. From a conventional Christian Democratic party politician, he was, through his martyrdom, made into a near saint. Italian cities now have streets that have been renamed in his honor.[37] The more recent assassination of Swedish Prime Minister Olof Palme by still unidentified gunmen may have a similar posthumous effect.

If the point of all this media coverage is to influence public opinion, the logical question to ask is: What reactions does the public have to the images of terrorist violence to which it has been exposed? Surprisingly there are few studies that attempt to address this question in a systematic way. Before we report some of the partial findings of public opinion surveys, there are several matters that need to be clarified.

First, there are numerous polls which report public views about aspects of contemporary terrorism. But we cannot be sure about the extent to which these reactions were caused by the mass media. Other factors, such as personal experience, may play an independent role in influencing the formation of opinion.[38] It is true that in the United States few people have had a direct experience with terrorism, although many have been the victims of criminal violence, such as muggings and robberies, to which terrorist events bear some resemblance and from which they may draw conclusions.

Second, opinions about political phenomena may be classified in a number of ways. There is the question of salience. How important or serious do members of the public consider the matter to be? In this case the question is: How significant a problem does the public regard political terrorism? Next, opinions about politics may vary in direction. Do people respond positively or negatively to the political issue or occurrence under consideration? Or are they neutral about it? Are public opinions favorable or unfavorable to the terrorists and their various causes? Also, depending upon the particular issue, opinions will show variation in their intensity. Are the views of the public, be they positive or negative, strongly held or not?[39]

Third, in the case of political terrorism we are dealing with public reactions not in one country but in many. There are different national audiences whose reactions should be considered. In this connection we would expect differences to emerge in the salience, direction, and intensity of public opinion about terrorism on the basis of the particular public's relationship to terrorist groups. These organizations must deal with three types of audiences for their operations: friends, enemies, and neutrals. Friends are populations whose political causes terrorist groups wish to advance. The public reactions a terrorist group wants to stimulate among friends are the mobilization of mass support for the cause and for the particular group waging the terrorist campaign on its behalf, in an environment in which there may be other organizations competing for their favor. The terrorist group's impact on its enemies should be one of arousing fear in such a way that they will become disoriented, and consequently will behave in self-destructive ways which, unintentionally, will aid the terrorist cause. Initially neutral audiences should be made aware, through the violence, of the terrorist group's cause; and, at least in the long run, the neutrals should be transformed into sympathizers.

Differences in the audiences for terrorist operations vary not only among nations but also within nations. Terrorist groups will treat as friends, enemies, and neutrals different social classes and ethnic groups within the same country and expect to evoke different reactions from each according to these perceptions.

Ideally a study of the effects of terrorism on public opinion should take all these elements into consideration. Unfortunately no such study presently exists. As a result, our own account will be rather fragmentary.

In April 1986 the Gallup organization asked a random sample of Americans whether they would be willing to travel abroad that summer given the threat posed by terrorism. Close to 80 percent of those persons asked indicated they would decline the opportunity.[40] We may infer from this reaction that terrorism was a highly salient concern for Americans at that time. But the question was asked in the wake of a series of highly publicized terrorist attacks against Americans in Europe and after U.S. forces had carried out bombing raids on Libyan targets in retaliation.

In 1978 polling organizations in Great Britain and West Germany, as well as the United States, asked citizens how serious a problem they considered terrorism to be. Substantial majorities of Britons, Germans, and Americans responded by indicating they regarded the violence to be very serious.[41]

In 1984 the results of an Italian opinion survey were published. Its respondents had been asked to identify what future historians would regard as the most important event or events in the previous fifty years of Italian history. In this case a substantial plurality chose the country's recent terrorist episodes.[42] Fascism and its collapse during World War II finished a distant second. Similar surveys done in the late 1970s found that Israelis considered terrorism to be a substantial threat to their society.[43]

The impression left by these findings is that the public in those countries surveyed regarded terrorism as a highly salient phenomenon. The problem with these responses, though, is that they were based on snapshots taken at single points in time. The questions were usually asked during or just after a particularly dramatic terrorist event or events, that is, at a time when the public was most likely to be aroused by the violence and where media coverage was likely to have been of the crisis variety, as in the case of the seizure of American Embassy personnel in Tehran. It seems likely that the salience of terrorism for the public will display wide variation from high to low depending upon the immediacy of a media-enhanced terrorist event, rather like responses to the issue of nuclear power generation after the Chernobyl and Three Mile Island disasters as against reactions at other times when such power plants are operating smoothly.

Survey data drawn from several Western democracies concerning the direction of the public reaction to terrorism suggest it is negative, and usually overwhelmingly so. This generalization applies to both the activity itself and the organizations perpetrating it. To illustrate:

A series of polls conducted in Western European countries between February 1970 and November 1977, a period of growing terrorism, shows a steady erosion of support for the statement that "our society must be gradually improved by reform," and growing support for the statement, "our present society must be valiantly defended against all subversive forces."[44]

Of course, these findings do not show that opposition to terrorism was the exclusive cause of the conservative swing in public opinion. Yet given the years in which the surveys were conducted it would be hard to deny that an aversion to terrorism was not a contributing factor. At least in one instance the negative appraisal was even retrospective. In 1979 in France only 5 percent of a national sample expressed approval of the terrorist campaign carried out by the Secret Army Organization at the end of the Algerian war in the early 1960s.[45]

In Great Britain, at about the same time the French survey was conducted, a vast majority of citizens responding to a poll question refused to regard people who committed acts of violence against civilians as freedom fighters. Most Britons preferred to think of them instead as terrorists whose behavior they never considered justified.[46] In the United States citizens were asked for their appraisal of the PLO during the 1982 Israeli attack in Lebanon. At a time when that organization might have evoked some sympathy as its fighters were besieged in Beirut in the midst of Palestinian civilians, close to 80 percent of Americans expressed disapproval.[47]

Perhaps better measures of the Western public's reaction to terrorism, in both direction and intensity, may be obtained by examining the methods it approves to combat it. The generalization that emerges is that the citizens of democratic countries often endorse the use of extraordinary means when the elimination of terrorism is the end. Rather than becoming sympathetic or terrified, the public seems to react in anger. For example, close to two-thirds of the Dutch public was willing to support placing South Moluccans (in 1977) under strict surveillance "even though our country might then resemble a police state."[48] About the same percentage of West Germans (in 1978) favored the strengthening of police powers in order to fight terrorism despite the fact this might involve increased surveillance, house searches, and other limitations on their personal freedoms.[49] Three-quarters of Britons, as well as substantial majorities of Italians and West Germans, have supported the use of the death penalty for convicted terrorists even though these three countries have abolished capital punishment. The figure for Israeli support of the death penalty approximated the British one.[50]

What these survey results suggest is that to the extent terrorism poses a threat to the democracies that threat does not stem from the support its practitioners receive from the public. Rather it derives from the willingness of the people to see limitations placed on the exercise of their civil liberties as part of the effort to eliminate the violence and in their support for a reversal of the decades-long trend toward the abolition of the death penalty in the Western world.

Despite this overall pattern, there is some evidence that there are small pockets of support for terrorism within the Western democracies. This support comes from members of ethnic groups, for example, some people of Irish background in the United States, who see the terrorists as acting in self-defense or as expressing the legitimate historical grievances of their communities.[51] In the Middle East, the PLO's use of terrorism has won it massive support among wide segments of the public on the occupied West Bank. A 1985 poll found that a large majority of Palestinians living under Israeli control approved the continued use of terrorism against civilians. And their endorsement of Arafat and the PLO was overwhelming.[52] On the other side of the conflict, close to a plurality of Israelis (47 percent) have supported the establishment of an "unofficial group" to engage in "counterterror" against their Arab enemies.[53]

SOCIAL EFFECTS OF TERRORISM

In general, the social effects of terrorism depend upon the severity of the experience. In some places terrorism has had a very limited impact on the domestic environment, whereas in others the threat is a fact of daily life, something that many people must worry about as they go about their business. Since the onset of the "troubles" in Northern Ireland, for example, there has been an 81 percent increase in alcohol-related problems leading to admissions to mental hospitals in that region.[54] In Israel citizens are warned to alert the authorities when they notice any unattended parcels or packages in public places out of fear they may contain bombs. Clearly, these are societies where the threat of terrorism is pervasive and where the possibility of attack is something about which people are highly conscious. Norwegians or Swedes, on the other hand, need not have such worries.

For societies in which terrorist campaigns pit one ethnic group against another, Palestinians versus Israelis in the Middle East or Catholics against Protestants in Northern Ireland, one effect is to sharpen group differences. All members of the opposing ethnic group come to be seen as belonging to the enemy camp. Members of each group seek to put as much distance, physical and psychological, as possible between themselves and the other group. As in a conventional war between nations, primitive stereotypes of the "enemy" are erected. David Shipler describes this process at work in the Middle East in his Pulitzer prize–winning book *Arab and Jew: Wounded Spirits in a Promised Land*. Members of each community have come to regard the other as brutal, violent, cowardly, etc.[55] As a consequence, social interactions are reduced as the atmosphere of mutual fear and mistrust builds. In cases where these tendencies already exist, terrorist campaigns will likely reinforce them.

If terrorism tends to widen differences between ethnic groups, its effect among members of the same group often is to narrow them.[56] Natural differences within the group based on wealth, status, place of residence, etc., decline as a siege mentality sets in. We would expect this pattern to be especially pronounced in cases where terrorist groups, as during the Algerian conflict of the mid-1950s to early 1960s, carry out indiscriminate attacks on members of the "enemy" population. In these polarized conditions, appeals for compromise and moderation coming from within either of the affected populations are likely to be regarded as acts of treason or betrayal, their advocates treated as pariahs.

Growing up in a society which is the site of a protracted terrorist campaign may affect the development of children. One study done in Belfast found that the moral development of Catholic and Protestant children had been severely impaired as the result of their having lived in such a stressful environment during their early years.[57] By their adolescence many children were prepared to use the same violent tactics that they saw adults use in their surroundings. The study also reported that the fantasy lives of these Northern Irish young people were full of images of death and destruction. It does not seem necessary to conduct a comparable study in Beirut to speculate that young Lebanese are likely to have been harmed in analogous ways. Furthermore, most people, young or old, do not derive much satisfaction from living in areas where terrorist attacks are a daily occurrence. As a result, such cities as Belfast and Beirut have experienced significant waves of emigration since the advent of their troubles.

As anyone who has recently walked through an airport can attest, the fear of terrorism has had some impact on the lives of people far removed from the major centers of terrorist activity. Subjecting passengers and their luggage to electronic and physical scrutiny represents an intrusion into people's lives that has become commonplace. In fact, it may be argued that the concern about terrorism has become so pervasive that people living in open democracies are now more tolerant of various invasions of their privacy than they used to be.

The threat of terrorist attack also may be a disruptive influence on the lives of persons who believe themselves to be likely targets. Socially or politically prominent individuals and their families have to be careful about when and where they go: shopping in stores, eating at restaurants, going to school or to the office, and other daily activities often must be arranged to take account of the potential dangers of kidnapping and assassination. In

America, members of Congress were warned against traveling abroad during the summer of 1986 because of the terrorist threat. Providing advice to and personal security for individuals in these exposed positions has even become a minor growth industry in recent years.

POLITICAL EFFECTS OF TERRORISM

Terrorism catches our attention. It creates disruption. In certain circumstances it influences the lives of many people. But what are its political effects? How important a factor is contemporary terrorism in influencing the political arena? Some observers have maintained that it is much ado about nothing, an attempt to create the illusion of strength in the absence of its reality.[58] The logic is that since many terrorist groups are small they cannot pose serious military challenges to modern states willing to defend themselves. This is usually true, but true by definition. The hope of terrorists and the fear of their opponents is that David will slay Goliath if he can locate a place where the giant is particularly vulnerable. If a group can evolve into a mass movement or a guerrilla army, the organization may no longer be a terrorist band, but it will have achieved its purpose. And, as we have seen, on occasion terrorism has been used by already existing mass movements and guerrilla armies as one of a repertoire of devices with which to attack their enemies. Does the technique help the cause or is it symptomatic of its weakness?

A fundamental problem in evaluating terrorism's political effects concerns the criteria that are applied in measuring them. What standards should we use in determining the political impact of terrorist activities?

A sensible way by which to address the latter question is by specifying the following criteria for judging its effects. First, there is the domain of terrorism's influence. According to Robert Dahl, "The domain of an actor's influence consists of the other actors influenced by him."[59] Translating this abstract formulation for our purposes, we think it desirable to distinguish between the effects of terrorism within nations, its domestic influence, and that between nations, its international consequences. Next, there is the notion of *scope* to be considered. This idea refers to the range of terrorism's influence on different policies and political developments.[60] Does terrorism affect a wide or narrow range of political occurrences? Also, terrorism may have certain political effects, but these need not be ones either anticipated or desired by its perpetrators. Thus we should ask ourselves if the political effects are ones desired by the terrorists or their opponents. Finally, we may at least speculate about the *amount* of influence terrorism has exerted. We could, for instance, perform a rain dance in the hope that our gyrations would cause the sky to darken and the water to fall from it. But if it did, few meteorologists would confirm our claims that we had caused the event to occur. In the case of terrorism, some political developments may take place whether or not there were a terrorist group around to promote them. The fact that a terrorist organization wanted such an event to happen does not mean that the group caused the event to happen.

In the domain of domestic politics, the most far-reaching effects of terrorism involve changes in the incumbent political regime. In the post-World War II era the British withdrawal from Palestine, Aden, Kenya, and Cyprus was probably accelerated as the result of terrorist campaigns waged against their colonial presence. The same should be said about the National Liberation Front's operations in Algerian cities in persuading the French to give up their control of that country. In these cases terrorism, along with other forces such as mass mobilization and guerrilla warfare, led to the achievement of goals—national independence—those committing the violence had in mind when they initiated it.[61]

In a few countries, Spain and the Philippines recently, right-wing groups have used terrorism in order to prevent the transition from authoritarian to democratic rule from taking place. Supporters of the Franco and Marcos dictatorships used terrorist violence to create a general atmosphere of turmoil in the hope that elements in the military would veto the installation of democratic governments. In these cases, however, they we_e not successful.

Terrorist organizations also have influenced changes in the character of political regimes they did not expect or wish to take place. As discussed earlier, the military's seizure of power in Uruguay and Argentina was a reaction against the inability of civilian governments to cope with terrorist activities in these countries. If the terrorists hoped that military intervention would in the long run serve their purposes by disclosing to the general population the repressive nature of state power, this hypothesis was not confirmed by subsequent developments. The amount of influence terrorism exerted in producing these largely unanticipated changes seems to have been far higher than in those situations where the terrorists achieved their goals.

Terrorism has played a role in affecting the structure of the state. Here we have in mind both the formation and dissolution of subnational regional governments. During the 1960s a section of northern Italy with a significant German-speaking population, Trentino-Alto Adige, was granted special powers of self-administration in part as the result of a terrorist campaign waged by a small number of that region's inhabitants and their Austrian sympathizers. The operations of the ETA influenced the Spanish government's decision to establish a Basque autonomous community.[62] In Sri Lanka, the Tamils are in the process of winning their own right to local self-government in large part because of terrorist activities and the near civil war they have stimulated. The decomposition of Lebanon into small ethnic enclaves led by rival warlords is the result of a civil war which, in turn, was the product of a mounting wave of terrorism. On the other hand, Northern Ireland lost its regional government for a while in 1972 when the British imposed direct rule from London because of that area's troubles.

Another of terrorism's domestic effects concerns not the structure but the leadership of government. There are the obvious cases of political leaders falling victim to terrorist assassination in recent years—Sadat, Moro, Palme, Gemayal, Gandhi, the prime minister of revolutionary Iran along with dozens of members of that country's parliament—but there have been others who have lost their jobs rather than their lives in connection with terrorist episodes. The American President Jimmy Carter was defeated in his 1980 reelection bid in part because of his inability to win freedom for American hostages in Iran. The administration of his successor, Ronald Reagan, was shaken as a result of the scandal stemming from its unsuccessful efforts to win the release of American captives in Lebanon by providing weapons to the revolutionary Iranian regime. Some of Reagan's principal national security advisers were forced to resign over this "Iranscam" episode. Nor have these terrorism-induced leadership problems been confined to the United States. Cabinet members and other political notables have been forced to resign their offices or had their careers disrupted in Italy, Brazil, and various other nations.

Post-Duvalier Haiti offers an example of another way in which terrorism has influenced domestic political developments. In this case it is the electoral process. In Haiti and elsewhere in Latin America, political groups have employed terrorist violence to intimidate prospective voters and keep them away from the polls. This has been done in order to reduce the overall level of political participation in the country as well as to challenge the legitimacy of the whole process.

In democratic countries with relatively cohesive populations, a terrorist campaign directed against the government by a small group may have the effect of strengthening its popular support.[63] The same might be said about operations carried out against it from abroad. The West German, Italian, and Israeli governments apparently have been the inadvertent beneficiaries of popular backlash against the terrorists. Furthermore, the violence may enable governments to discredit their opponents by labeling them as having facilitated the terrorists' work through their criticisms of those in power. In Italy, the Christian Democrats were able to play this game, with some success, against the Communists; the former's West German counterparts have done the same with their left-wing critics.

But democratic governments whose popular support has been raised by terrorist attacks may find it lowered if they do not pursue vigorous policies to repress the terrorists. The appearance of weakness and vacillation, as the Carter administration discovered, will reduce its standing with the public. In turn, democratic governments may overreact to the terrorist threat by their leaders' uttering statements and implementing hard-line policies aimed more at satisfying public opinion than at actually eliminating the phenomenon. Another danger is that in the process of responding to popular pressure to stop terrorism a democratic government will attempt to erode the very constitutional principles it is seeking to protect.[64] Such measures as trial without jury and preventive detention used by the British government in Northern Ireland are a case in point. The effects of terrorism on political regimes whose populations are divided along ethnic or racial lines may be more severe. If the terrorism grows out of these social divisions, rather than benefiting from increases in popular support, governments may find themselves confronted by a polarization of public opinion. In these circumstances, appeals for moderation and efforts to reach political compromises may be greeted with the hostility of whichever ethnic group views itself as disadvantaged by the proposals. The reactions of Protestants in Northern Ireland, Christians in Lebanon, and Sinhalese in Sri Lanka provide examples.

Given the variety of countries subject to terrorist campaigns in recent decades and the differences in the severity of the violence within these nations, the effort to generalize about the scope, intentionality, and amount of political influence they exerted is not easy. On the whole, though, the following observations seem to make some sense. The weaker the regime, the greater and the wider in scope the political effects of terrorism. This generalization applies both to influences that the terrorist groups intended and to effects they did not anticipate or want. In these cases, terrorism had its greatest impact when there were other forces at work that served to weaken the political fabric of these countries.

For the strong industrialized democracies, the scope and amount of influence exerted by terrorist groups have been far more limited. It would not be fair to say that the influence was exclusively inadvertent. There were some instances where the terrorists were able to create some of the effects they had wanted. Nonetheless, terrorism in these nations came to be viewed in approximately the same way as drug trafficking and other forms of organized criminal pursuits. Its political effects have tended to be unanticipated by its perpetrators, unless we are willing to believe that the terrorists wanted to unleash popular demands on governments for their own liquidation.

In addition to its domestic influence, terrorist activity has had some effects in the domain of international politics. In this case the most far-reaching of political effects concerns the eruption of wars and other forms of armed conflict.[65]

The one event here most clearly traceable to terrorism was the American attack on Libya in 1986.[66] The announced purpose of the bombing raid on Tripoli and Benghazi was to retaliate against Libyan-sponsored terrorist acts against the United States in West Germany and elsewhere. Aside from this limited action, a terrorist event, the attempted assassination of the Israeli ambassador to Great Britain, was used as a justification by his government to launch an invasion of Lebanon in 1982. But this operation evidently had been planned for some time, and the event itself simply provided an excuse. Iraq's decision to invade Iran in 1980 was based in part on the latter's support of terrorist attacks intended to undermine the Baghdad regime.

Terrorism also has been used in efforts to influence the outcomes of wars that are already under way. For example, terrorists with links to the Soviet-supported regime in Afghanistan have carried out attacks inside Pakistan aimed at reducing that government's willingness to permit its territory to be used as a base of supply for the insurgent groups with which it is at war. Further, in the Middle East in 1978 PLO-related groups staged terrorist attacks on Israeli targets in an effort to disrupt peace negotiations with Egypt whose direction they opposed.[67] Terrorist operations were more successful, however, in persuading the American-led multinational peacekeeping force to leave Lebanon in 1984 in the wake of the bombing of the Marine Corps barracks in Beirut.[68]

Contemporary terrorism has had other impacts on relationships between different nations. Some have been immediate and direct, while others belong in the realm of atmospherics.

There have been a number of instances in which terrorism has led directly to the rupture of diplomatic relations. The finding in a criminal court that the Syrian embassy had been involved in a plan to blow up an El Al 747 after its departure from Heathrow Airport led the British government to break relations with Damascus. Likewise, the Libyan People's Bureau in London was closed not long after an English policewoman was killed by a shot fired from one of its windows as part of an effort to disrupt an anti-Ghaddafi demonstration. American relations with Iran were broken off as the result of the hostage-taking incident in Tehran. French diplomatic ties with Iran were broken because of the latter government's refusal to permit a member of its embassy staff in Paris to be questioned in connection with a wave of terrorist attacks in that city. Recently Iranian diplomats in West Germany and other European nations have been expelled because of suspicions concerning their involvement in planning terrorist operations.

There is another side to the story. The PLO has been accorded observer status at the United Nations and has been extended diplomatic recognition by many nations around the world. It is not clear, though, whether these accomplishments were the result of its terrorist operations or the product of other factors, such as the strategic interests of different nations, genuine sympathy for its cause, and the wealth of its supporters in the Arab world.[69]

In various ways contemporary terrorism has strained relations among different countries, as evidenced by the diversity of their responses to the phenomenon. This has been true both for the relationships between countries belonging to the Western alliance and for their relationships to Third World and Communist bloc nations.

We propose to discuss the steps the Western democracies have taken toward greater cooperation in their efforts to combat terrorism in the next chapter. At this stage of our analysis we want to pay some attention to conditions where terrorism has produced disharmony.

Relations between the United States and Italy were strained as the result of the *Achille Lauro* incident. In this case an American SEAL (sea-air-land) unit apprehended the members of a Palestinian group headed by Abu Abbas in Sicily after they had seized an Italian cruise ship in the Mediterranean and killed an American passenger. The Americans turned their captives over to the Italian authorities for prosecution. But the latter released Abbas shortly afterward. Italian Defense Minister Giovanni Spadolini resigned in protest against his government's decision, thereby toppling the ruling coalition. The United States expressed its displeasure with Italy's decision to release the individual it regarded as the mastermind of the operation.

The raid on Libya in 1986 also had negative effects on America's relations with a number of its allies. France, in particular, refused to permit its air space to be used by American fighter-bombers on their way to attack Libyan targets. While the American public was highly supportive of the raid, opinion polls in some European nations showed public opposition to the attack, and this sentiment was reflected in the positions taken by various governments.[70]

Problems also have arisen in connection with the extradition of accused terrorists. The Italian government has voiced displeasure at France's reluctance to return Red Brigades' suspects for trial. The British have expressed concern over what they perceived as the slowness of the Americans to extradite citizens of Northern Ireland wanted in connection with PIRA activities.

In themselves none of these problems seems to be particularly serious or long-lasting. The Atlantic alliance is certainly resilient enough to withstand such pinpricks. On the other hand, they may have some cumulative effects by reinforcing existing stereotypes of, for example, the American government being too trigger-happy in dealing with its adversaries and of the Europeans being too soft.

Although issues similar to those cited have arisen in connection with the influence of terrorism on the relations between the industrialized democracies and Third World nations as well as with the Soviet Union and its allies, the underlying problem in these circumstances concerns what one analyst has referred to as the ideological-moral pluralism of the present world order.[71] From the point of view of many Third World and communist governments the behavior defined as terrorism by the democracies represents the legitimate actions of national liberation movements and other progressive forces. As a result, appeals from the former for assistance in combating terrorism have not uncommonly been met by hostility at the United Nations and other international forums. Opposition to terrorism gets redefined as a thinly disguised defense of the international status quo by those governments that are dissatisfied with the current distribution of power. In this way, the issue of terrorism and what, if anything, to do about it has helped to widen divisions between the wealthy democracies and the Third World or portions thereof.

A similar judgment may be reached about the relationship between the Soviet Union and the United States. Despite repeated condemnations of contemporary terrorism, the Soviets and some of their Warsaw Pact allies have provided help to a variety of terrorist organizations.[72] The perhaps exaggerated role of the Soviets in promoting terrorism helped revive Cold War sentiment in the United States in the early 1980s. Former Secretary of State Alexander Haig and other foreign policy spokespersons issued statements to the effect that the Russians were sponsoring terrorism in order to destabilize the West and that this form of low-intensity conflict constituted a new type of warfare. Whether justified or not, the rhetoric gave the impression that the Soviets had launched a worldwide campaign to undermine America's vital interests for which appropriate military responses were needed.

The state support of terrorism and the reaction against it, rhetorical and otherwise, by the United States has also played a part in inflating the international status of Libya and its president. A country with less than 3 million citizens whose armed forces have been unable to withstand an offensive by the army of Chad has come to be viewed as a major factor in international politics by virtue of Colonel Ghaddafi's encouragement of various terrorist groups. One effect of this inflated perception of Libya as a menace to the security of various governments has been the latter's efforts to return the compliment by seeking to undermine Ghaddafi's regime.

It is probably too soon to reach any fundamental conclusions about the long-term impact of contemporary terrorism on international politics. Compared with its domestic consequences, there have been no basic changes in the distribution of power, deliberate or inadvertent. The already volatile relations between North and South Korea have not been improved by disclosures concerning the former's terrorist operations against its southern neighbor. But these have not sparked an open conflict to date. On the other hand, the accepted rules governing the conduct of diplomatic representatives stationed abroad, in terms of both their expected behavior and the treatment they are accorded, have clearly been eroded. Terrorism has added additional sources of friction to the relations between different governments, but, for the most part, the context already was one of underlying antagonism or mistrust. The scope of terrorism's effect in this domain may be wide, but the amount of its influence so far has been limited.

A final question that needs to be addressed concerns the extent to which terrorist groups have gotten what they wanted. Have they won or lost? It is clear that there have been both victories and defeats. In general, terrorist groups in Western Europe and Latin America whose ultimate aims were ideological and revolutionary have been defeated.[73] But right-wing bands of the death-squad variety seem to have had better luck; their successes in the repression of their opponents seem to have been derived more from the covert support they received from Latin American governments rather than from the violence itself.

The major success stories are to be found among groups acting on behalf of ethnic groups for nationalist-separatist causes. The Tamils, Basques, Catholics in Northern Ireland, and, arguably, the Palestinians come to mind. These have been cases where the relevant groups have been able to win popular support among the populations whose cause they sought to lead. They also have been cases where the relevant groups were able to receive help from sympathetic elements outside the immediate area of conflict. Finally, terrorism seems most effective when it has been used for a limited time and in conjunction with other means of protest and popular mobilization.

A SUMMARY OBSERVATION

This chapter has sought to evaluate the impact of contemporary terrorism on its various victims and targets, ranging from single individuals to whole societies. In reviewing the effects of terrorism it is important to bear in mind that some analysts maintain that the vast attention paid to the phenomenon has been out of proportion to its real and relatively meager consequences. Measured by the total number of deaths and injuries caused by terrorist acts, compared with that by other forms of political violence, this conclusion is appropriate. But it also misses the point. Either by itself or in conjunction with other means of political activity, terrorism clearly has had a significant impact on recent political developments, both domestic and international. In essence, that is the message conveyed in this chapter. One way of judging the seriousness of the terrorist problem is by examining the measures governments have taken to overcome it. This is the subject to be considered in the next chapter.

KEY TERMS

adaptation

contagion effect

coping

creative elaboration (fantasy)

defense mechanisms

hostage taking

intellectualization

kidnapping

Stockholm syndrome

NOTES

1 See, for example, Edward Mickolus, "Statistical Approaches to the Study of Terrorism," in Yonah Alexander and Seymour Finger (eds.), *Terrorism: Interdisciplinary Perspectives* (New York: John Jay Press, 1977), pp. 209–269; Bowman Miller and Charles Russell, "The Evolution of Revolutionary Warfare," in Robert Kupperman and Darrell Trent (eds.), *Terrorism: Threat, Reality, Response* (Stanford: The Hoover Institution, 1979), pp. 185–199; Bonnie Cordes et al., *Trends in International Terrorism* (Santa Monica, Ca.: The Rand Corporation, 1984); Edward Heyman and Edward Mickolus, "Iterate: Monitoring Transnational Terrorism," in Yonah Alexander and John Gleason (eds.), *Behavioral and Quantitive Perspectives on Terrorism* (New York: Pergamon Press, 1981), pp. 153–174.

2 National Foreign Assessment Center, *Patterns of International Terrorism: 1980*, PA81-1-162U (June 1981); U.S. Department of State, *Patterns of Global Terrorism: 1984* (November 1985), *Patterns of Global Terrorism: 1985* (October 1986), and *Patterns of Global Terrorism: 1986* (January 1988).

3 U.S. Department of State, *Patterns of Global Terrorism: 1985* (October 1986), p. 3.

4 See, for example, John Sloan, "State Repression and Enforcement Terrorism in Latin America," in Michael Stohl and George Lopez (eds.), *The State as Terrorist* (Westport, Conn.: Greenwood Press, 1984), pp. 89–90.

5 Ted Robert Gurr, "A Comparative Study of Civil Strife," in Hugh Graham and Ted Robert Gurr (eds.), *Violence in America* (New York: New American Library, 1969), p. 565.

6 Donald Crelinsten and Denis Szabo, *Hostage-Taking* (Lexington, Mass.: Lexington Books, 1979), pp. 13–16.

7 See, for example, Clive Aston, "Political Hostage Taking in Western Europe," in Lawrence Freedman and Yonah Alexander (eds.), *Perspectives on Terrorism* (Wilmington, Del.: Scholarly Resources, 1983), pp. 99–130.

8 Sir Geoffrey Jackson, "Premonitions and Forewarnings," in Martin Herz (ed.), *Diplomats and Terrorists: What Works, What Doesn't* (Washington, D.C.: Institute for the Study of Diplomacy, 1982), pp. 22–23.

9 Walton Roth, "The Meaning of Stress," in Frank Ochberg and David Soskis (eds.), *Victims of Terrorism* (Boulder, Col.: Westview Press, 1982), pp. 37–57.

10 Jared Tinklenberg, "Coping with Terrorist Victimization," in Ochberg and Soskis (eds.), ibid., pp. 59–60.

11 Ibid., pp. 65–66.

12 Thomas Strentz, "The Stockholm Syndrome: Law Enforcement Policy and Hostage Behavior," in Ochberg and Soskis (eds.), ibid., pp. 149–163.

13 Abraham Miller, *Terrorism and Hostage Negotiations* (Boulder, Col.: Westview Press, 1980), p. 50.

14 Frank Ochberg, "A Case Study: Gerard Vaders," in Ochberg and Soskis (eds.), op. cit., pp. 29–32.

15 Tinklenberg, op. cit., pp. 68–71.

16 William Niehous, "How to Survive as a Hostage," in Herz (ed.), op. cit., p. 34.

17 Robert Hauben, "Hostage-Taking: The Dutch Experience," in Freedman and Alexander (eds.), op. cit., pp. 135–140; Leo Eitinger, "The Effects of Captivity," in Ochberg and Soskis (eds.), op. cit., pp. 73–91.

18 Maura Christopher, "Terrorism's Brutal Impact—In Dollars and Cents," *Scholastic Update* (May 16, 1986), p. 23.

19 Robin Erica Wagner-Pacifici, *The Moro Morality Play* (Chicago: University of Chicago Press, 1986), pp. 56–57.

20 Bernard Johnpoll, "Terrorism and the Mass Media in the United States," in Alexander and Finger (eds.), op. cit. (see note 1), pp. 157–163.

21 Alex Schmid and Janny de Graaf, *Violence as Communication* (Beverly Hills, Ca.: Sage Publications, 1982), p. 68.

22 James Hodge, "The Media and Terrorism," and Walter Jaehnig, "Terrorism in Britain: On the Limits of Free Expression," both in Abraham Miller (ed.), *Terrorism, the Media and the Law* (Dobbs Ferry, N.Y.: Transnational Publishers, 1982), pp. 89–105, 106–122.

23 Ze'ev Chafets, *Double Vision* (New York: William Morrow, 1985), pp. 49–110.

24 For a discussion from the journalist's point of view see James Hodge, "The Media and Terrorism," in Abraham Miller (ed.), *Terrorism, the Media and the Law* (Dobbs Ferry, N.Y.: Transnational Publishers, 1982), pp. 89–105.

25 Schmid and de Graaf, op. cit., pp. 33–42.

26 M. Cherif Bassiouni, "Problems in Media Coverage of Nonstate-Sponsored Terror-Violence Incidents," in Freedman and Alexander (eds.), op. cit., pp. 177–200.

27 Charles Krauthammer, "Partners in Crime," in Benjamin Netanyahu (ed.), *Terrorism: How the West Can Win* (New York: Farrar, Straus & Giroux, 1986), pp. 111–113.

28 Abraham Miller, "Terrorism, the Media and the Law: A Discussion of the Issues," in Miller (ed.), op. cit., p. 30.

29 Ibid., p. 29.

30 Ibid., pp. 177–179.

31 Michael Delli Caprini and Bruce Williams, "Television and Terrorism: Patterns of Presentation and Occurrence, 1969 to 1980," *The Western Political*

Quarterly, 40:1 (1987), pp. 45–64. There is some evidence that this distortion is not limited to television but includes newspaper coverage as well, nor is it restricted to the United States. See Michael Kelly and Thomas Mitchell, "Transnational Terrorism and the Western Elite Press," in Doris Graber (ed.), *Media Power in Politics* (Washington, D.C.: Congressional Quarterly, 1984), pp. 282–289.

32 Schmid and de Graaf, op. cit., pp. 89–90.

33 Leonard Weinberg, "The Violent Life: An Analysis of Left and Right-Wing Terrorism in Italy," in Peter Merkl (ed.), *Political Violence and Terror* (Berkeley: University of California Press, 1986), p. 145.

34 Schmid and de Graaf, op. cit., p. 84.

35 Michael Milburn, Brian Cistuli, and Marjorie Garr, "Survey and Experimental Studies of the Effect of Television News on Individuals' Attributions about Terrorism" (a paper presented at the Annual Scientific Meeting of the International Society of Political Psychology, New York, July 1–5, 1988).

36 Yonah Alexander, "Terrorism and the Media in the Middle East," in Alexander and Finger (eds.), op. cit., pp. 166–206.

37 Wagner-Pacifici, op. cit. (see note 19), pp. 220–230.

38 Doris Graber, *Mass Media and American Politics,* 2d ed. (Washington, D.C.: Congressional Quarterly, 1984), pp. 169–170.

39 For a discussion, see Dan Nimmo and Charles Bonjean (ed.), *Political Attitudes and Public Opinion* (New York: David McKay, 1972), pp. 5–6.

40 *The Gallup Report,* 247 (April 1986), p. 12.

41 Connie de Boer, "The Polls: Terrorism and Hijacking," *Public Opinion Quarterly,* 43 (1979), p. 412.

42 Leonard Weinberg and William Eubank, *The Rise and Fall of Italian Terrorism* (Boulder, Col.: Westview Press, 1987), p. 5.

43 Martha Crenshaw, "The Psychology of Political Terrorism," in Margaret Hermann (ed.), *Political Psychology* (San Francisco: Jossey-Bass, 1986), p. 401.

44 "Revolution, Reform and Subversion in West European Countries," *World Opinion Update,* 2:5 (1978), pp. 114–117.

45 Elizabeth Hastings and Philip Hastings (eds.), *Index to International Public Opinion 1979–1980* (Westport, Conn.: Greenwood Press, 1980), p. 228.

46 De Boer, op. cit., p. 412.

47 *The Gallup Report,* 204 (September 1982), p. 28.

48 De Boer, op. cit., p. 415.

49 Elizabeth Hastings and Philip Hastings (eds.), *Index to International Public Opinion 1978–1979* (Westport, Conn.: Greenwood Press, 1980), p. 124.

50 George Gallup (ed.), *The Gallup International Public Opinion Polls: Great Britain* (New York: Random House, 1975), vol. 2, p. 1280; Hastings and Hastings (eds.), *Index to International Public Opinion 1978–1979,* op. cit., p. 123; De Boer, op. cit., p. 415.

51 See, for example, William Ascher, "The Moralism of Attitudes Supporting Intergroup Violence," *Political Psychology,* 7:3 (1986), pp. 403–425.

52 Thomas Friedman, "Poll in West Bank Finds Palestinians Favor Arafat," *The New York Times* (September 9, 1986), p. 6.

53 Hastings and Hastings (eds.), *Index to International Public Opinion 1978–1979,* op. cit., p. 53.

54 Rona Fields, "Research on the Victims of Terrorism," in Ochberg and Soskis (eds.), op. cit., p. 143.

55 David Shipler, *Arab and Jew: Wounded Spirits in a Promised Land* (New York: Penguin Books, 1986), pp. 181–264.

56 On the general subject, see Lewis Coser, *The Functions of Social Conflict* (New York: The Free Press, 1956).

57 Fields, op. cit., pp. 143–145.

58 See, for example, Walter Laqueur, "Reflections on Terrorism," *Foreign Affairs* (Fall 1986), pp. 86–100.

59 Robert Dahl, *Modern Political Analysis,* 3d ed. (Englewood Cliffs, N.J.: Prentice-Hall, Inc., 1976), p. 33.

60 Ibid., p. 33.

61 Martha Crenshaw (ed.), *Terrorism, Legitimacy and Power* (Middletown, Conn.: Wesleyan University Press, 1983), pp. 7–9.

62 Robert Clark, "The Question of Regional Autonomy in Spain's Democratic Transition," in Robert Clark and Michael Haltzel (eds.), *Spain in the 1980s* (Cambridge, Mass.: Ballinger Books, 1987), pp. 139–156.

63 Yehezkel Dror, "Terrorism as a Challenge to the Democratic Capacity to Govern," in Crenshaw (ed.), op. cit., pp. 79–80.

64 Paul Wilkinson, *Terrorism and the Liberal State* (New York: New York University Press, 1979), pp. 114–132.

65 J. Bowyer Bell, "Terrorism and the Eruption of Wars," in Ariel Marari (ed.), *On Terrorism and Combating Terrorism* (Frederick, Md.: University Publications of America, 1985), pp. 41–51.

66 Robert Oakley, "International Terrorism," *Foreign Affairs,* 65:3 (1987), pp. 611–629; Seymour Hersh, "Target Quaddafi," *The New York Times Magazine* (February 22, 1987), pp. 16–26.

67 Connor Cruise O'Brien, *The Siege* (New York: Simon and Schuster, 1986), pp. 583–584.

68 Brian Jenkins, "The American Response to State-Sponsored Terrorism," in Steven Spiegel, Mark Heller, and Jacob Goldberg (eds.), *The Soviet-American Competition in the Middle East* (Lexington, Mass.: D. C. Heath and Company, 1988), pp. 183–200.

69 Helena Cobban, *The Palestinian Liberation Organization* (Cambridge: Cambridge University Press, 1984), pp. 228–231.

70 Oakley, op. cit., pp. 618–619.

71 Noemi Gal-Or, *International Cooperation to Suppress Terrorism* (New York: St. Martin's Press, 1985), p. 61.

72 For a discussion, see Walter Laqueur, *The Age of Terrorism,* rev. ed. (Boston: Little, Brown and Company, 1987), pp. 270–280.

73 See Irving Louis Horowitz, "The Routinization of Terrorism and Its Unanticipated Consequences," in Crenshaw (ed.), op. cit., pp. 38–51.

CHAPTER 6

EFFORTS TO COMBAT TERRORISM

Before examining the measures governments and various international organizations have taken in opposition to contemporary terrorism, we should identify both the nature of the problem it represents and the types of regimes to whom it is posed. To begin, let us try to clarify the nature of the problem.

Most observers regard terrorism as a form of criminality, a type of warfare, or a manifestation of underlying social and political problems. The kind of effort mounted against it often reflects these different perceptions. According to the first view, the kinds of violent acts in which terrorists engage—bombing, kidnapping, killing—represent crimes under the laws of almost all civilized societies.[1] The fact that the crimes are politically motivated or that their perpetrators claim to be acting on behalf of a just cause does not exempt them from criminal responsibility for their deeds. In this context, we should bear in mind that terrorists often will go to considerable lengths to distinguish themselves from ordinary criminals. Imprisoned PIRA members in Northern Ireland have been willing to stage hunger strikes rather than be treated like common criminals by the British authorities. Often a terrorist group will adopt a name, such as "liberation army," and assign its leader a title, such as "commander," intended to convey the impression it is waging war, not engaged in a crime spree. Also, not infrequently terrorist groups have sought to turn the issue upside down by creating their own system of justice. Thus, hostages will be confined in "people's prisons" and be tried before "people's tribunals."

For those who do not accept the self-serving (and propagandistic) procedures, terrorist acts are common crimes; their investigation and the apprehension of their perpetrators should be the task of the relevant police forces. Local criminal courts applying the normal criminal code should be used to determine the guilt or innocence of those individuals accused of having committed particular criminal acts.[2]

Placing contemporary terrorism under the rubric of crime makes considerable sense if we identify the violence with such groups as the Symbionese Liberation Army and Aryan Brotherhood in the United States, the Angry Brigade in Great Britain, and Direct Action in France. But does this definition of the situation conform to the realities of state-sponsored terrorism? The U.S. State Department has compiled an extensive list of assassinations, embassy bombings, and acts of air piracy carried out over the past several years by groups supported or directed by the revolutionary regime in Iran.[3] Does it make sense to place these activities within the frameworks of American, French, or Kuwaiti criminal law?

In light of these developments, there has been a growing tendency to regard contemporary terrorism as a form of warfare.[4] Because large-scale military conflicts have become increasingly costly and hazardous undertakings, various nations have found it advantageous to pursue their interests by the encouragement or sponsorship of terrorist attacks on their enemies. Viewing terrorism in this way is, in effect, to acknowledge the claims of some terrorist organizations that they indeed are engaged in wars against government authorities rather than being practitioners of common criminality. For those governments that regard themselves as the targets of warlike acts carried out by the surrogates of other nations, it follows that their responses likely will not be confined to the application of their domestic criminal justice apparatus to individual wrongdoers. Different rules and techniques come into play. For example, military planners in the Pentagon make a distinction between forms of warfare based on the level of their intensity: low, medium, and high. Terrorism has come to be regarded as a type of low-intensity conflict.[5] From this perspective, terrorism should be opposed by military units prepared to carry out special operations and by intelligence agencies skilled in the use of covert measures.

While the first two views of terrorism focus on reactions to its overt manifestations, the third emphasizes its root causes, domestic and international. From this perspective terrorism, rather like urban crime, is the outgrowth of certain underlying social conditions. On the international scene, it is used by movements seeking to free their nations from colonial domination and alien occupation. Domestically, racism (as in South Africa), high levels of youth unemployment, major disparities of wealth and privilege, and discriminatory practices directed against ethnic minorities represent the root causes of contemporary terrorism.[6] Unless and until actions are undertaken to ameliorate the aforementioned conditions, terrorist activity will persist.

There seem to be elements of truth in each of these three views. Further, they need not be mutually exclusive. Terrorism may, at times, have root causes; it does involve acts of criminality; and, on occasion, it does display the attributes of low-intensity warfare. Which view predominates and how different governments respond to terrorism will depend upon the nature of the particular challenges with which they are confronted.

Given these views, for what types of political regimes does contemporary terrorism constitute a serious problem? This question should be addressed in the context of the widespread impression that the effort to combat terrorism is exceptionally difficult, one requiring great subtlety, skill, and imagination. In view of the vulnerabilities of modern societies, the anonymity provided by vast urban areas, and the existence of safe havens abroad, the appropriate formula for defeating terrorist groups is complicated with many unknowns. This impression though is rather misleading.

Communist regimes have been largely immune from significant terrorist episodes. On occasion, Soviet, Cuban, and Yugoslav diplomats and other personnel have been the victims of terrorist attacks by Armenian, Jewish, Croatian, anti-Castro Cuban, and Arab organizations, but only when these individuals were stationed abroad. During the 1950s and 1960s small groups of citizens from Warsaw Pact nations as well as Cuba skyjacked planes and compelled their pilots to fly them to the West. Asylum, not political propaganda, was their goal. Despite these incidents, the generalization holds. Why? The obvious answer is that, irrespective of root causes, these regimes are capable of denying potential terrorists access to weapons with which to stage attacks and to the mass media with which to publicize them. Even assuming that interested individuals would be able to evade the available surveillance techniques, the audience for propaganda by deed would be a limited one.

Some nations in the Middle East and Latin America that have been confronted by significant terrorist challenges were able to overcome them without much difficulty. In Syria, the authoritarian regime of Hafez al-Asad was challenged by a surge of terrorist violence launched by the fundamentalist Muslim Brothers from 1977 forward (see Chapter 3). It responded by making membership in the latter punishable by death. In 1982 when the Brotherhood attempted to take control of the city of Hama, killing some 250 government supporters in the process, military forces were called in and reacted by killing thousands of Brothers along with totally uninvolved residents. Whole neighborhoods were destroyed.

Since this massive act of repression, the Brotherhood's terrorist activities have subsided.[7]

The new revolutionary regime of the Ayatollah Khomeini in Iran was confronted by a terrorist threat in 1981. Attacks were launched by the Mujahedeen, a left-wing group dissatisfied by the course the nation's clerical leadership was following. Over a few months Mujahedeen members killed the prime minister, leaders of the ruling political party, cabinet officers, and dozens of members of the national parliament.

> Perhaps never before had a terrorist onslaught been so successful. Yet within another three months, the terrorists either were dead or had escaped abroad. The government acted with great brutality; it extracted information by means of torture; it refused as a matter of principle to extend medical help to injured terrorists. And it broke the back of the terrorist movement.[8]

In Turkey, Uruguay, and Argentina, once democratic regimes were displaced by military dictatorships, terrorist problems were resolved rapidly by the raw use of brutal means. If terrorism is the overriding concern, then the evidence in these cases is persuasive that an uninhibited government willing to employ torture, mass roundups of suspects, and summary executions will be able to eliminate the problem or, at a minimum, reduce it to an inconsequential level. Repression works. But by the standards of civilized conduct this solution is far worse than the problem to which it is addressed. Terrorism then represents a challenge only to those regimes unwilling or unable to use the coercive techniques.

THE DEMOCRATIC RESPONSE

What guiding rules or principles should constitutional democracies follow in their efforts to combat terrorist violence? At a minimum, they should be ones that permit affected governments to retain their democratic character but not leave them helpless in the face of terrorist attacks.

According to the British political scientist Paul Wilkinson, foremost consideration must be given to the preservation of the law.[9] This commitment carries with it a variety of consequences. The first is that violations of the law should be punished. For both practical (it encourages more of the same) and moral reasons, democratic governments should not permit themselves to comply with the demands of terrorist groups. Yet, it also follows from the same rule-of-law principle that criminal behavior—violations of law—involves the actions of particular individuals. Accordingly, the antiterrorist policies of the liberal democracies should not involve reprisals against segments of the population thought to be sympathetic to the terrorists. Again both practical and moral considerations come into play. If democratic governments react to terrorist attacks by using indiscriminate violence against an ethnic community on whose behalf the terrorists claim to be acting, they are engaging in precisely the same sort of practice as the terrorists. Also, if governments behave in this way, they may build rather than weaken whatever support the terrorist group enjoys among members of the relevant population.

Democratic governments should be expected to behave in accordance with their own constitutions and laws. Among other things, this means that they should avoid declarations of martial law and the type of emergency measures that usually follow them. When such actions are taken, it creates the obvious impression among the public that a crisis is at hand, often precisely the reaction that terrorist organizations wish to convey. Furthermore, democratic governments must take care that security services and other police or military units given the task of combating terrorism operate within the framework of the law to whose defense they are committed. This means that civilian control must be retained over their activities through legislative oversight and judicial constraints. If it is not:

> The terrorists and their fellow-travellers can make enormous propaganda capital out of violations of the law by members of the security services and use these as additional justification for their own campaigns. Thus they conveniently divert the public's gaze away from the violations of the law and outrages stemming from their own petty tyranny, and attempt to portray the incumbent authorities as monstrous blood-soaked oppressors.[10]

The rule-of-law principle and applications to antiterrorist policies Wilkinson deduces from it are largely directed at the control of domestic terrorism, with the understanding that the latter is a form of criminality. But what of those views which emphasize the international warlike quality of terrorism and its roots in various social, economic, and political problems? Are there any principles, comparable to the rule of law, that are appropriate as guides to democratic governments which view terrorism from these two perspectives?

At least for those democracies whose traditions derive from Western civilization, the answer is affirmative. In the matter of war, medieval philosophers and theologians made a distinction between the justice *of* war and justice *in* war.[11] Often the two concepts were considered separable. Wars could be fought for just or unjust causes, and different scholars attempted to list the attributes of each. But whatever the causes, wars could be waged in either a just or unjust way according to not why but *how* they were fought. Justice or injustice in warfare referred to the weapons or implements that were used and to the treatment accorded participants and nonparticipants in the conflict.

Historically the doctrine of the justice or injustice of a state's cause took precedence, and served to heighten the severity of warfare, because if its cause were just, the government viewed itself as acting in the name of God. In this situation, the destruction of the enemy could be defined as in conformity with divine intent, particularly if the battle were waged against unbelievers and no mercy shown the enemy.

By the seventeenth century (the Peace of Westphalia in 1648) the just-cause doctrine began to be superseded by the justice-in-war concept. "The emphasis shifted from the justification for war to the means for its regulation."[12] Over the next centuries a number of international agreements were reached aimed at ameliorating the effects of war. These conventions focused on limiting the types of weapons that could be used, the status of neutrals, the treatment of prisoners of war, and the recognition of a distinction between combatants and noncombatants in conflicts between states.

The twentieth century has not been kind to the justice-in-war doctrine. Weapons of mass destruction have been used that would have been inconceivable in earlier centuries. Noncombatants have been the victims of mass bombings, acts of genocide, and numerous other atrocities. Despite these occurrences, the principle of justice in war has found repeated expression in international law. The concept of war crimes was introduced by the prosecution at the Nuremberg trial of the Nazi leadership after World War II; the United Nations has adopted a convention on genocide; the 1949 Geneva Convention put forth a guideline for the protection of the victims of war. Although often violated or unenforced, the principle of justice in war continues to be recognized in international law and in the domestic legislation of many nations.

This century also has seen manifestations of the just-war doctrine. According to the United Nations' Charter, states are obliged to refrain from the threat or use of warfare to endanger the territorial integrity and national independence of other nations. Under provisions of the same document, wars may be undertaken for reasons of self-defense or under the sanction of the UN Security Council.

The legal doctrines of just war and justice in war have two broad applications insofar as the issue of terrorism is concerned.[13] First, to the extent democratic governments have been the victims of state-sponsored terrorist attacks, they have just cause for retaliation. But the just-cause principle does not exempt them from the justice-in-war rule. As with the principle of the rule of law in a consideration of terrorism as criminality, so, too, in this instance, indiscriminate reprisals against civilian populations or noncombatants are incompatible with the principle. And as a practical matter, the same logic also applies. Indiscriminate reprisals against segments of a population thought to be sympathetic to the terrorists' cause may enhance rather than diminish the popularity of the terrorists. The consequences of Israeli air strikes against PLO targets in Lebanon and Tunisia may serve as a case in point.

There is another side to the argument. Some states have justified their support for terrorist groups on the basis of the just-cause contention. Specifically, they have maintained that these groups are engaged in wars of national liberation, and that their pursuit of this goal constitutes just cause for their violent operations and for the support they receive from sympathetic states. Whether or not democratic governments recognize the justice of the state-supported terrorists' cause, they should not, by so doing, absolve the terrorists from responsibility. Terrorism, by its nature, is a violation of the justice-in-war principle. To believe and behave otherwise would be to leave the citizens of democratic states helpless in the face of indiscriminate terrorist attacks and deny their governments the most elementary rights of self-defense. The justice or injustice of the cause should be disentangled from the means used to pursue it.

EARLY RESPONSES

Since 1968 democratic governments have sought to respond by various means to the terrorist threats, both domestic and international, with which they were confronted. Their reactions over this time have varied according to the severity of the threat and to different perceptions of national interest. The early responses tended to be largely piecemeal and uncoordinated.

At first, Israel was the most threatened and consequently reacted the most vigorously. Attempts to hijack its El Al planes coupled with the Lod Airport and Munich Olympic Games massacres in 1972 were the events that sparked its response. As a result of these attacks, security measures were taken to better protect its embassies, consular offices, and commercial airliners. In situations where Israeli citizens were taken hostage, the government's reaction was not to grant concessions to those holding them even if the decision resulted in the loss of life.

But the Israeli response was not confined to these defensive practices. In addition, it included retaliatory strikes against the terrorists. A special unit, the Wrath of God, was created in the aftermath of the Munich massacre. It proceeded to wage a campaign of assassination against PLO figures in Western Europe and Lebanon.[14] The most spectacular success Israel achieved during this early phase of its counterterrorist operations was the raid at the Entebbe Airport in Uganda in 1976. After an Air France plane had been diverted to that location by a mixed Palestinian and German terrorist band, the latter demanded that Palestinian prisoners in Israel be released in exchange for the lives of the flight's Jewish passengers. Instead, while "negotiations" were under way, an Israeli commando unit flew to Entebbe, liberated the hostages, and killed most of their captors. The story became headline news around the world.

The Lod and Munich incidents also provided the background for the initial American reactions to terrorism. At the end of September 1972 the Nixon administration formed a cabinet committee, chaired by the secretary of state, to formulate the American response. More specifically, the committee was requested to coordinate the work of various agencies in the effort to prevent terrorism and devise detailed measures and general policies to this purpose.[15] The committee was assisted by a working group, composed of representatives from those agencies whose work bore some relationship to matters of terrorism, headed by a special assistant to the secretary of state. This apparatus was later criticized for a number of reasons, but it at least conveyed the impression to a concerned public that the government was doing something about the problem.

There were other American initiatives. In 1972 the United States submitted to the United Nations a draft convention on international terrorism which encouraged member nations to either extradite or prosecute individuals accused of terrorist acts of international significance (these were spelled out in some detail). This proposal ran into a barrage of opposition in the UN General Assembly on the grounds that it failed to address the root causes of terrorism. A more successful bilateral agreement was reached with Cuba in 1973. It required each country to either punish or return skyjackers for prosecution in their country of origin. This arrangement had the effect of reducing dramatically the number of acts of air piracy between the two nations. Although the Castro regime formally abrogated the agreement several years later, after an attack on a Cuban airliner, it continues to abide by its provisions.

It was also in this period that the American government first adopted an overall policy with respect to hostage taking and kidnapping.[16] As articulated by both President Nixon and his national security adviser, Henry Kissinger, that policy was to be one of no negotiations and no concessions. Their reasoning was that concessions made to terrorists aimed at saving the lives of one group of hostages would have the long-run effect of condemning many more Americans to similar attacks because the terrorists would develop the expectation that they would receive something in exchange for their captives. The objective was deterrence by denial.

Despite the steps taken by Israel, the United States, and other democracies in the early years of the terrorist age, most terrorists were able to avoid punishment. One study of sixty-three major hostage-taking cases between 1968 and 1974 reported that 79 percent of all the terrorists involved escaped death or punishment for their deeds.[17] In other words, the cost of terrorism for its perpetrators was low, while the impact of publicity was high. For the most part, the terrorists were getting away with it. Why?

There was, for one thing, the phenomenon of the "poisoned pawn." In France, West Germany, Italy, and other European democracies, governments became aware that holding captured terrorists in prison was an invitation to additional attacks, ones committed by groups out to liberate their imprisoned comrades in exchange for new captives. Illustratively, two members of Black September skyjacked a Lufthansa airliner in October 1972 and held its passengers hostage until the West German government agreed to free other members of the band it was holding in connection with the Munich massacre. According to one estimate, 141 of the 150 Middle Eastern terrorists arrested in Western Europe over the next five years were released without trial.[18]

Another factor facilitating international terrorist operations in the democracies was the willingness of some governments to develop tacit understandings with terrorist groups. Italy and France, for example, were willing to overlook the presence of these organizations on their territory so long as they carried out their attacks elsewhere. Sometimes associated with this policy was the legal concept of the political crime. Among the democracies, the laws concerning the extradition of accused criminals to their countries of origin often contained exemptions based on the political character of the act involved. If the offense was committed to achieve a political goal, its perpetrators would not be extradited to the site of the crime for prosecution.[19] The original objective of the political exemption provisions was to prevent the victims of political persecution from being denied asylum in the democracies for acts they had committed against repressive authoritarian regimes. But it came to be applied in cases where other democracies were seeking to obtain criminal jurisdiction over individuals accused of terrorist acts.

There were also genuine humanitarian considerations at work when hostages' lives were at stake. Few leaders in the democracies wished to be responsible for the deaths of innocent hostages. It was better to save their lives than save face. Thus, in 1970 Canadian Prime Minister Pierre Trudeau was willing to permit the flight of Quebec separatists rather than have them murder the British trade minister whom they had kidnapped. Other such decisions could be mentioned.

There were other factors that worked against an effective and coordinated democratic response during this early phase. For example, Interpol, the international police agency headquartered in France, was unwilling to consider requests for information in terrorist cases on the grounds they were political crimes and therefore outside its jurisdiction.[20] Intelligence agencies in Italy and the United States were the objects of public scrutiny as the result of scandals growing out of their illegal activities, e.g., maintaining surveillance over peaceful political dissidents at home. No doubt the public concern over such activities was a healthy democratic reaction to the abuses, but the effect was to make it somewhat more difficult for these agencies to gather intelligence on the operations of terrorist groups. In some countries there were lengthy debates over the appropriate organizational response to the terrorists. Was it a problem better left to the police forces, and, if so, which ones, or should the military play a role? Was there a need for special emergency legislation to cope with the problem or was the existing body of law sufficient to do the job? If changes in the law were needed, to what extent would they threaten existing safeguards of personal liberty?[21] If states were promoting or sponsoring terrorism, what steps, if any, should be taken to discourage them? These questions aroused widespread discussion in the democracies. The answers are best reviewed within the context of the particular measures the democracies have taken against terrorism since the early stages of its existence.

ORGANIZATIONAL RESPONSES

Since the initial shock, the democracies have become better organized to respond to terrorist threats, both domestic and international. On the international level, few new organizations have been created, but preexisting ones have come to be used for antiterrorist purposes. The Summit Seven, Great Britain, France, Canada, Japan, Italy, West Germany, and the United States, those seven democracies with the strongest economies whose leaders meet on an annual basis, have repeatedly placed the issue of terrorism on their agenda. A committee of experts was formed and now meets from time to time to make recommendations to the leaders. The results have been mixed. The 1978 meeting in Bonn resolved that the seven would cease all commercial flights to and from any state which refused to extradite or prosecute those individuals responsible for acts of air piracy. And the June 1987 summit in Venice resulted in a declaration affirming that no concessions ought to be made to terrorists.[22] While these and other principles have been agreed upon, they have not always been put into practice. Afghanistan, for example, is the only country whose airline industry has been affected by the Bonn declaration. Conflicting perceptions of national interest have limited the implementation of these broad statements of purpose.

NATO is another organization that has been encouraged to play a role in combating terrorism. Its standing committee on counterintelligence began to consider terrorism-related matters in the 1985–1986 period, and there are now bilateral exchanges of information within this framework.[23]

Members of the European Community (EC) and a few other interested nations (Switzerland, Israel) have formed the TREVI group (for terrorism, radicalism, and violence international). It is not a policymaking body, but since 1977 it has provided an opportunity for interior ministers, chiefs of police, and other relevant officials to exchange information and coordinate their investigations of terrorist groups active in Western Europe.[24] TREVI activities were intensified after the stepup of Middle East–based terrorism in the mid-1980s. A blacklist of terrorists, assassins, and arms dealers has been compiled. It is circulated, along with other pertinent information, to all twelve EC members through a secure "action link."

Despite opposition from the Greek government, the EC member states have sought to address the problem of state-sponsored terrorism. Libya, Syria, Iran, and Iraq were identified as sponsors. Restrictions have been imposed on the freedom of movement of their diplomatic and consular personnel. Tighter visa requirements were imposed on individuals seeking to enter EC nations from these countries. And in the wake of Libyan threats following the 1986 American air raid, the EC foreign ministers agreed to an arms embargo against the regime in Tripoli.[25]

On a broader front, the 142 nations belonging to the Interpol network changed that organization's policy concerning acts of terrorism. Since 1985 these acts have been reclassified as crimes and, therefore, suitable subjects for Interpol involvement. Between January 1985 and June 1986 the United States sent or received 114 notices through the Interpol network dealing with terrorist activities. Here are three examples:

Message from Interpol secretary general requesting information on a commando group concerning a planned hijacking.

Foreign country requested international search and arrest of subject wanted for hijacking an aircraft, unlawful imprisonment of persons for terroristic aims, and unlawful possession of firearms and explosives.

FBI requested information on the hijackers of TWA flight 847.[26]

Other international organizations, including the Council of Europe, the International Civil Aviation Organization (ICAO), and the International Maritime Organization (IMO), among others, have become involved. But the form this involvement has taken concerns the drafting of legal agreements covering acts of terrorist violence. And this subject is best left for a discussion of legislative measures against terrorism.

While it is true that few new international organizations have been formed explicitly to deal with the terrorist threat, the situation within the democracies has been different. At this domestic level, a variety of new agencies has been created, ones often designed for the use of force against terrorist groups at home and abroad.

The basic problem to which many of these new organizations are a response concerns the appropriate level of force to be employed in confrontations with terrorists. To the extent that the national police bodies in such European countries as France and Italy have intervened in politics over the years, their role has characteristically involved riot control and other types of mass protest. Conventional military forces, on the other hand, have been equipped and organized to fight opposing armies. Terrorism is typically covertly planned and executed small-group violence against which neither sort of organization may be entirely suitable. The recognition of this gap between the nature of the threat and the structure of existing forces to combat the threat has led a number of democracies to form new small-scale units to deal with situations involving terrorism.

The four major European democracies have found it necessary to create such units. The British have their Special Air Services (SAS) regiment, several members of which recently killed members of a PIRA active service unit as they were preparing to detonate a bomb in Gibraltar. The SAS also attracted considerable publicity in 1980 after it liberated the Iranian Embassy in London from opponents of the Ayatollah Khomeini who had seized it and held its occupants hostage. In West Germany the failure of the Bavarian state police to prevent the 1972 Munich Olympics massacre led to the formation of the Grenschutz Gruppe 9 (GSG 9), whose most famous exploit was the rescue of passengers aboard a hijacked Lufthansa airliner at Mogadishu, Somalia, in 1977. The Italian government reorganized its two principal national police forces in its effort to overcome the major domestic terrorist episodes with which it was confronted from the mid-1970s to the early 1980s. In 1978 the *carabinieri* formed a special unit, under the direction of the late Carlo Alberto Della Chiesa, specifically to defeat the Red Brigades; and the National Police formed a Division for General Investigations and Special Operations (DIGOS) to combat the terrorist groups and organized crime. Both these investigatory organizations created their own small intervention teams, one of which (the "leatherheads") broke into an apartment in Padua in 1982 and freed the American General James Dozier from his Red Brigades' captors. The equivalent role in France is played by the National Gendarmerie Intervention Team (GIGN), part of the Gendarmerie Nationale and under the control of the defense ministry. In 1980 members of GIGN stormed a hotel on Corsica and freed residents held hostage by a separatist group.[27]

Within the United States, the lead agencies assigned the responsibility for countering domestic terrorism are the Federal Bureau of Investigation (FBI) and the Federal Aviation Administration (FAA). The latter's role involves antiskyjacking activities.[28] In addition to the Special Weapons and Tactics (SWAT) squads present at each of the FBI's fifty-nine field offices, the agency has created a hostage rescue team capable of intervening in the event of major terrorist events. Now help is also provided to local law enforcement agencies if and when they need assistance in dealing with terrorist events falling within their jurisdictions.

The failure of the helicopter-based effort to rescue hostages at the U.S. Embassy in Tehran in 1980 along with the success the United States enjoyed in capturing those responsible for murdering an elderly American passenger on the cruise liner *Achille Lauro* in 1985 drew attention to the role of the American military in international antiterrorist operations.[29]

Each branch of the U.S. military now has Special Operations Forces (SOF) prepared for use in low-intensity conflicts likely to occur in the Third World. Some of these units have been prepared to fight in guerrilla warfare situations, others to assist and train foreign groups to do the fighting; those part of the Army and Navy have been assigned counterterrorism tasks. Ostensibly secret but nonetheless the most publicized of these groups (the subject of a motion picture) is the Delta Force, an army unit. It is flown to and from missions by a group of specially trained helicopter pilots identified collectively as Task Force 160 and nicknamed "the Night Stalkers."[30] In recent years, Night Stalker–aided Delta Force teams were reportedly sent to Cyprus to prepare for a rescue of passengers aboard TWA flight 847 in Beirut. Other accounts have reported their presence in the Sudan, Venezuela, and Kuwait in connection with other incidents of air piracy and hostage taking.

The Navy has its sea-air-land troops, or SEALs, intended for special warfare missions. SEAL Team 6, formed in 1980, is trained for counterterrorism operations. It was a SEAL unit that was responsible for the apprehension of the Abu Abbas group in Sicily in the aftermath of the *Achille Lauro* incident in 1985.

These special operations forces, including their antiterrorism components, have been plagued by a variety of problems. One recent episode involved the Delta Force and concerned the misuse of funds and equipment by some of its officers. Another problem has involved the overall coordination and command of these forces. Interservice rivalries and the low priority SOF received from military leaders in the Pentagon, whose principal concern is conventional warfare, combined to create an atmosphere of confused authority and divided command responsibilities.[31] An effort to remedy this problem has been made through the formation of a Joint Special Operations Command to integrate and control the activities of the different SOF units. This step may solve the problem of coordination, but another one remains unresolved, that of democratic accountability. If and when Delta or SEAL units are used, at what stage does the U.S. Congress exercise responsibilities toward overseeing such operations?

The United States and the four large Western European democracies have not been the only countries to have formed small groups to rescue hostages and intervene in terrorist situations. According to one account, since the late 1970s Australia, Belgium, Denmark, the Netherlands, Norway, Switzerland, Austria, Egypt, and Indonesia have organized similar units.[32] There is also a rumor that the Soviet Union, a country not usually identified with antiterrorism, has launched its own group. When four Soviet diplomats were kidnapped in Beirut in 1985 by Islamic Jihad, a persistent report alleged that a specially trained KGB team was sent to Lebanon, which then killed a relative of one of the captors in an act of retaliation.[33]

The policy of deploying these special organizations for use against terrorists has not been without its critics.[34] It has been argued, for example, that these counterterrorist groups blur the distinction between police and military functions when they are used to intervene in essentially domestic situations. Also, it has been maintained that once in existence, they may be used for purposes other than counterterrorism, for example, in industrial disputes or for protecting Third World dictatorships. For democracies these are troubling possibilities. But some things may be said in their defense. For one, they represent a response proportionate to the threat for which they were created. They offer decision makers an alternative to a massive show or use of force, as exemplified by the American air raid on Libya or the Israeli air force's attack on PLO headquarters in Tunis. Innocent civilians are, therefore, less likely to be killed. Second, in the democracies the use of these forces may be regulated by law. When they are not, embarrassing public scandals can ensue, as happened after a French unit sank a ship, the *Rainbow Warrior,* that was preparing to sail in protest against French nuclear tests in the South Pacific. Third, particularly in the case of hostage rescue situations, it seems desirable to have units specially trained in the appropriate techniques for negotiation and rapid intervention rather than attempt to deal with these cases on an ad hoc basis.

Although probably the most prominent, the creation of special operations forces is by no means the only organizational innovation related to the age of terrorism. The West German authorities have developed an elaborate computer-based data file, nicknamed "the Kommisar," which contains an enormous volume of information on the backgrounds, methods of operation, etc., of different terrorists and terrorist groups.[35] Italy as well as West Germany has constructed new maximum security prisons in which to confine convicted terrorists, ones whose colleagues on the outside have been willing in the past to go to considerable lengths to free them. In some countries, the public bureaucracy has been modified to take account of the terrorist threat. In the United States, for instance, the Department of State now has an office for counterterrorism and emergency planning. Terrorism clearly has accelerated a trend toward the centralization of police authority in West Germany and elsewhere. For observers concerned about the protection of civil liberties, these organizational developments should be a source of concern. They represent, nonetheless, some of the major means by which the democracies have attempted to cope with the problem of terrorism.

LEGISLATIVE RESPONSES

At first glance it seems unlikely that the passage of new legislation, international and domestic, would deter terrorists from committing acts of violence. Almost by their very nature terrorists are opposed to the law and hold little regard for its principles. Furthermore, most of their deeds are already recognized as crimes within the democracies to whom they have posed the greatest challenge. What, then, is the purpose of new laws?

One function is clearly symbolic.[36] In some of the democracies antiterrorist legislation has been enacted whose purpose appears to have been to persuade a disturbed public that the government is taking steps to stop the violence, irrespective of the concrete effects these measures would likely have on the volume of terrorist incidents. Symbolically, the public has been reassured that the government is not helpless but, instead, is bringing the full weight of the law to bear against the perpetrators of the violence. Declaring membership in armed bands, ones that are already underground and committing acts of mayhem, a criminal offense may not do much to convince their adherents to abandon the struggle, but it may persuade the public of the vigor with which its representatives are addressing the problem.

Efforts to combat terrorism through international law have had an analogous symbolic meaning. Having various international organizations draft conventions and issue declarations identifying terrorists as "international outlaws" gives the impression that the entire world community is outraged by their activities. Oftentimes, however, these forums, the United Nations especially, have been the sites for conflicting symbolic crusades, with representatives of various Third World regimes attempting to legitimize terrorist groups by seeking to have them identified as "freedom fighters" engaged in "wars of national liberation."

But the use of law to combat terrorism has had practical consequences as well. Some measures, to be discussed, have had tangible effects in making terrorist operations more hazardous undertakings than they previously were.

International Law

The subject of political terrorism is not new to international law. The murders of King Alexander of Yugoslavia and French Foreign Minister

Barthou in Marseilles in 1934, by Croatian separatists, and the assassination of Austrian Prime Minister Dolfuss, by Nazis, during the same year prompted the League of Nations to take the matter under consideration. The results of its deliberations, held in Geneva, were two draft conventions, dating from November 1937, on the prevention and punishment of terrorism and for the creation of an international criminal court.[37] The former proposed making it a crime under international law to commit acts of terror by attempting to murder the heads of state, members of their families, other public officials, and, indeed, members of the general public. Criminal liability was invested in individuals, and states were prohibited from protecting or granting asylum to such persons. Furthermore, the second draft convention proposed the creation of an international criminal court to hear cases involving violations of the first document's provisions. But neither convention was ratified by enough states (only thirteen did so) to enter into force by the time World War II broke out. Then, as now, it was the democracies that were the strongest advocates of these proposals.

Even prior to the failed League of Nations' undertaking an important issue related to the question of terrorism had arisen in international law. The issue concerned extradition, and the question revolved around what exemptions individuals should be granted from it. Extradition is normally a judicial procedure whereby a state removes a person from its jurisdiction for purposes of criminal prosecution in another state. The modern practice dates from treaties European nations agreed to in the eighteenth and nineteenth centuries. If a person who commits a crime in one state then flees to another, the state in which the offense was committed will seek to have the perpetrator of the crime extradited for purposes of prosecution. But what if the crime is of a political character? Should an individual who spoke out against a repressive dictatorship or participated in a failed rebellion against it be extradited from the state in which he or she is seeking asylum in order to be punished by the dictatorial regime? In light of these questions, the practice developed of exempting such political crimes from coverage under the domestic laws and bilateral treaties of certain states. In 1833 the Belgian government enacted a law exempting political offenses from extradition, and the following year this principle was incorporated in a treaty between France and Belgium.[38] The issue, though, hinges around what exactly constitutes a political offense and how it can be distinguished from acts of ordinary criminality.

Beginning in 1855 with the failed attempt by Corsini on the life of the French emperor, extradition treaties were modified to exclude political assassination attempts from the political offense protection. British practice came to be governed by two landmark court decisions: *In Re Castioni* (1890) and *In Re Meunier* (1894). In the former case, the court ruled that to constitute a political offense the act in question had to occur during a general political revolt and to have been related to this uprising. It was decided in the latter decision that anarchists who committed isolated acts of politically motivated violence were not to be covered by the political exclusion rule. Over the years different states have applied a variety of standards in defining the concept of political offense. The reason it has been discussed at some length here is that recent efforts to combat international terrorism often have involved the issue of extradition and whether or not acts of terrorism represent political offenses.

It is also worth calling the reader's attention to the fact that conventional international law has for centuries recognized piracy, the seizure of ships on the high seas by private individuals and groups, as a crime. In these cases the operative principle has been that of universal jurisdiction. That is, any state able to apprehend pirates is authorized to prosecute them for their crime.

To this point, the discussion has focused on acts of individuals and how they should be treated under international law. Most international law, though, is the law of nations and has been intended to regulate the conduct not of persons but of sovereign states in their dealings with one another. Some international laws, recognized either by customary practice or by written convention, have a bearing on the matters at hand and were in place before the advent of the terrorist age. It is a general rule that the forces of one state may not enter the territory of another without obtaining the latter's consent. Further, international law prohibits the use of force against another country's territorial integrity or political independence. But these principles are qualified by the long recognized right of self-defense, so long as the exercise of this right is proportionate to the threat posed.[39] If an armed band located within the territory of one sovereign state enters that of another, there is precedent for the latter to respond with force if the former is unable or unwilling to do so. For example, in 1916 the United States sent troops into Mexico in pursuit of Pancho Villa and his followers after they had raided communities in Texas and New Mexico. With these facts in mind, let us turn our attention to contemporary developments.

To date the few successful efforts to use international law as a means to combat terrorism have involved relatively specific applications against individual terrorists rather than cases of state sponsorship. In legal terms the latter remains a no-man's-land where attempts at legal proscription mix with diplomatic initiatives, economic sanctions, and the occasional use of force.

Some bilateral agreements have had an impact. The memorandum of understanding between the United States and Cuba in 1973, which included an extradition provision, brought an end to the wave of skyjackings of American aircraft to Havana. The United States has recently (1986) revised its extradition treaty with Great Britain in order to eliminate the political offense exemption for serious crimes of violence.[40]

There have been two significant efforts to deal with the terrorist problem on a regional basis. In 1971 members of the Organization of American States (OAS) agreed to a Convention to Prevent and Punish the Acts of Terrorism Taking the Form of Crimes against Persons and Related Extortions That Are of International Significance. And in 1977 the Council of Europe, composed of almost all the Western European democracies, enacted a Convention on the Suppression of Terrorism.[41] Both agreements are built around the principle of "extradite or prosecute"; states are obligated either to extradite individuals accused of certain terrorist acts to the nation in which they were committed or to prosecute the offenders themselves. The OAS convention clearly reflected a concern with the wave of murders and kidnappings of ambassadors and other diplomatic representatives carried out by terrorist groups in Latin America during the late 1960s and early 1970s. Article 1 refers to attacks on persons "whom the state has the duty according to international law to give special protection." Assaults on such persons are to be regarded as of international significance and also to be treated as crimes, not covered by the political offense exemption.[42]

While the OAS convention is confined to acts of terrorism directed against diplomats, the Council of Europe's convention is a wider, more ambitious undertaking. Not only does it refer to attacks on "internationally protected persons," but it also covers (Article 1) acts of air piracy and other offenses involving kidnapping, hostage taking, bombings, and other threats to the life and liberty of all citizens. The perpetrators of such attacks are not to be covered by the political offense exclusions of existing extradition treaties; and, as with the OAS document, the parties to the convention agree to extradite or prosecute those suspected of committing these crimes.[43]

Both conventions suffer from a number of obvious defects, not least of which has been the refusal of some of the states to ratify them. Further, because the tradition of granting political asylum is regarded with such importance by most members of each organization, the conventions reserve to the various states party to them their own right to determine which particular deeds are to be excluded from the political offense protection and thus serve as the basis for an extradition proceeding. In reality this escape technique permits governments to adjust their interpretations of the conventions to suit their own foreign policy interests. France, for example, neither prosecuted nor extradited Abu Daoud, alleged to be responsible for planning the massacre at the Munich Olympics, despite a request for extradition from the West German authorities.

The principle of extradite or prosecute has been adopted in connection with acts of sabotage and hijacking of civilian aircraft. Under the auspices of the International Civil Aviation Organization (ICAO), conventions were approved at the Hague in 1970 and in Montreal the following year.[44] The need for such measures is not hard to understand. In the two years preceding the Hague convention (1968–1969), there were a total of 120 attempts to seize commercial flights affecting over 5000 passengers.[45] The Hague Convention for the Suppression of the Unlawful Seizure of Aircraft is directed against acts of air piracy while the Montreal treaty seeks to expand the notion to include those who attempt to sabotage or destroy planes that are still on the ground. In both cases the general obligation for those states adhering to the conventions is to extradite or try those responsible for such attacks. But, as with the OAS and Council of Europe agreements, these conventions permit each state to make its own decision with respect to the political offense exemption. Furthermore, there are no mechanisms for enforcement, no means for applying sanctions to states that ignore their obligations. Since these conventions came into force, some of the democracies have made efforts to strengthen them by refusing landing rights to airlines from nations that do not comply, and a private organization, the International Federation of Airline Pilots, has threatened boycotts against nations on the same basis. However, judged by the number of acts of sabotage and air piracy that have occurred since the Hague and Montreal agreements came into force, their effectiveness has been very limited.

Beginning in 1972 with the submission of a proposal by its then secretary general, Kurt Waldheim, the United Nations has been the site of acrimonious debates over the question of terrorism. In general, these arguments have followed the tabling of draft conventions and the submission of proposed Security Council and General Assembly resolutions directed against terrorism or particular manifestations of it. Representatives from various Third World and Warsaw Pact countries often have reacted by insisting that action against terrorism be considered only in conjunction with its, for them, underlying causes. Further, whatever the antiterrorist measure under consideration, these representatives have emphasized that no action be taken that would jeopardize the rights of people engaged in struggles of national liberation "against colonial and racist regimes or other forms of alien domination."[46] The medieval concept of the just war has been applied in the contemporary debate.

Against this background, two international conventions have emerged from the UN General Assembly's deliberations. In December 1973 the Convention on the Prevention and Punishment of Crimes against Internationally Protected Persons, Including Diplomats, was approved and opened for accession by the member states. It seeks to cover all internationally protected persons, meaning heads of state, diplomats, and representatives of international organizations from murder, kidnapping, and other types of violent attack. To accomplish this protection, states are requested to adopt domestic legislation in conformity with this goal and be prepared to prosecute or extradite offenders.[47]

One would think that at a minimum UN diplomats would have been particularly vigorous in seeking, in effect, to protect themselves. But this was not the case. The convention was qualified by a General Assembly resolution adopted at the same time that provided an interpretation of its meaning. Paragraph 4 of this document stipulates that nothing in the convention should be understood to prejudice the rights of peoples seeking independence from "colonialism, alien domination, foreign occupation, racial discrimination and apartheid" from continuing their struggles. Presumably then, so far as international law is concerned, diplomats representing states exhibiting any of the traits mentioned in the resolution continue to be fair game for terrorist groups. By 1986 over sixty UN members had approved the convention, including the United States.

The second convention, approved by the General Assembly in 1979, seeks to criminalize the taking of hostages under international law when these acts involve the citizens or territory of more than one country. It includes an extradite or prosecute provision. However, at the urging of Soviet bloc and Third World representatives the final wording insists that a distinction be made between terrorist groups and national liberation movements. Under Article 12(1) the latter are permitted to seize hostages as part of their struggles.[48] Furthermore, another provision permits states to deny extradition of suspects if, in their judgment, they are likely to receive unfair treatment when returned to the country requesting it.

To say that these measures appear weak would be something of an understatement. They do have the virtue, though, of having been taken with the object in mind of limiting two types of terrorist activity. Recently there have been efforts to use international law as a way to encourage the use of terrorism.

Modern international law on piracy has altered and limited the customary understanding. The 1982 UN convention on the law of the sea defines piracy as an "illegal act of violence, detention or depredation against a ship for private ends."[49] While the principle of universal jurisdiction has been retained, and the convention encourages states to cooperate in the suppression of piracy, acts of piracy carried out for political purposes are excluded from these restrictions.

Parts of modern international law governing the conduct of warfare have been changed to protect terrorists and limit the ability of nations to defend themselves against terrorist attacks. The context for these modifications was a conference held in Geneva between 1974 and 1977 under the sponsorship of the International Red Cross. The meeting's purpose was to improve the laws of war contained in the 1949 Geneva convention on the treatment of prisoners of war.[50] Article 3 of this document recognized armed conflicts "not of an international character," that is, insurgencies confined within the territory of one nation as well as conventional wars between states. But having made this recognition, Article 3 went on to prescribe certain legal standards that were intended to bind the conduct of the participants in these conflicts. Most important, the provision emphasized the distinction between combatants and noncombatants: "Persons taking no active part in the hostilities...shall in all circumstances be treated humanely." Based on this imperative Article 3 went on to prohibit the taking of hostages, acts of torture and humiliation, murder, etc. Noncombatants, including not only civilians but also members of the warring parties who were wounded or who had laid down their weapons, were to be protected against these forms of violence. In short, this section of the 1949 convention recognized acts of terrorism as prohibited criminal conduct.

Article 4 defined prisoner-of-war status and the humane treatment that was to be accorded persons falling within this category. In general, prisoners of war were identified as members of the armed forces or insurgent groups party to the conflict who had fallen under the control of their enemies. They were distinguishable in certain ways: if they were under the command of a superior officer, wore fixed and distinctive signs or uniforms recognizable at a distance, carried arms openly, and conducted "their operations in accordance with the laws and customs of war." Thus Article 4 excluded terrorists, who almost by definition do not meet these standards, from being treated as prisoners of war.

Dominated by Afro-Asian regimes, those from the Middle East in particular, the Geneva Conference approved protocols that modified the 1949 convention. And, as one analyst noted:

> At the Diplomatic Conference, however, traditional considerations of the rights and interests of individuals...conflicted with the conception of humanitarian law dominant among the Socialist/Third World majority. In that conception, humanitarian law is not about individuals, but causes. If a rule that protects innocent bystanders impedes the success of a humanitarian cause— one aimed at liberating a territory from "colonialists," "aliens," or "racists"—it is not humanitarian law.[51]

The new agreement extends prisoner-of-war status to members of groups which claim to be engaged in struggles against "colonial domination, alien occupation or a racist regime." The members of such groups are not to be regarded as criminals, even if they ignore all the requirements noted in the 1949 convention, including those concerning openly carrying weapons, wearing uniforms, or abiding by the rules of war. As against the 1949 convention, a group that routinely carries out attacks on noncombatants, seizes hostages, murders civilians, or commits acts of torture does not, by so doing, lose its status as a legally protected belligerent so long as its self-proclaimed purposes are an end to colonial domination, alien occupation, or a racist regime. In the name of these principles, the protocols withdraw the 1949 international legal protections from civilian noncombatants while extending them to their attackers.[52]

Not only in this instance but in general it seems clear that international law has provided few legal remedies for the problem of contemporary terrorism. The democracies must look elsewhere.

Domestic Legislation

The democracies do not confront the same type of opposition to countering terrorism through law at home as they do in the international realm. To the extent that the democracies are responsive to public opinion their governments have typically found permissive majorities of citizens angered by terrorist activities who wish them to do something about the problem. In these instances the boundaries are set not by other nations with competing outlooks but by their own legal traditions. Given this more supportive environment, what have the democracies done?

Antiterrorism laws may best be reviewed by dividing them into those that are substantive, often ones that create new crimes, and measures that are procedural, intended to enhance the ability of the authorities to investigate and prosecute crimes associated with terrorism.[53]

In terms of substantive measures, a number of democracies have responded to the threat of domestic terrorism by making it a crime to organize or belong to a terrorist group. In these cases it is not only the particular acts in which members of the group engage but membership itself that has been made into a crime. In a few countries constitutions and penal codes already contained provisions against membership in organizations opposed to the democratic order, as with Fascist groups in Italy, for example. These provisions were expanded or modified to take account of the new post-1968 situation. In other democracies, it was a matter of starting from scratch.

Among the democracies whose legal systems are based on the common law tradition, both the Republic of Ireland and Great Britain have amended previously existing legislation. The Irish Offenses against the State Act of 1939, that, among other things, proscribed membership in the IRA, was changed in 1972 and again in 1976 to make it easier to convict people for membership in the IRA and other, new terrorist organizations.[54] The equivalent precedent under British law was the Prevention of Violence (Temporary Provisions) Act, also dating from 1939. In the aftermath of a series of bombings, Parliament adopted new legislation in 1974 which was later revised in 1976, 1979, and 1984. Substantively these measures proscribed the IRA and the Irish National Liberation Army, and criminalized not only membership but also the solicitation of funds on their behalf and public displays of support for them.[55] The latter restriction has been used, for example, to prevent PIRA advocates from appearing on television.

In the United States court interpretations of the First Amendment presently restrain Congress and the state legislatures from making membership in a political group a crime in itself, despite earlier attempts along these lines in the eras following the First and Second World Wars.[56] However, the First Amendment does not prohibit prosecutions of participants in criminal conspiracies, ones planned to achieve their purposes through violence. Accordingly, federal laws originally designed to fight organized crime have been used in the prosecution of leaders of such right-wing groups as the Aryan Nations and the Ku Klux Klan. Furthermore, a number of the states, as well as the federal government, have created new crimes related to terrorism.

Legislatures in Arkansas, California, Delaware, Hawaii, Iowa, and Kansas, among other states, have enacted laws that make it an offense to practice the "terroristic threatening" of others if these threats are linked to the use of violence.[57] At the federal level the concern has been with both domestic and international terrorism. So far as the former is concerned, it is now a federal crime to threaten or commit acts of violence against high-ranking officials and members of their immediate families, including all members of Congress, the heads of executive agencies, and federal judges. Skyjacking an aircraft is also a federal crime. And since 1984 the law now makes it an offense to commit an act of violence against any airline passenger within the United States, or any American passenger if the act occurs outside the borders of the United States.[58]

Several laws have been passed in response to the problem of international terrorism. One that is most directly concerned with state sponsorship dates from 1984. This omnibus legislation, Public Law 98-533, bars economic and military assistance to any nation that the president has determined grants sanctuary to or provides support for terrorist groups. Furthermore, the president, in consultation with Congress, may prohibit the importation of goods and services from such countries. Also, the president is authorized to request that other governments impose similar sanctions.[59]

The democracies of continental Europe whose legal systems derive from the civil law tradition have also enacted new substantive measures to combat terrorism. Because of their pre-World War II experiences with Nazism and Fascism, the Federal Republic of Germany and Italy have been particularly sensitive to the problem. The sensitivity stems from two considerations. First, lawmakers in these countries were aware of the fact that the Nazi and Fascist movements had risen to power where weak democratic regimes proved unwilling or incapable of using the law to eliminate the paramilitary-based violence of these antidemocratic forces. But, second, they were also aware that once in power the Hitler and Mussolini dictatorships used the coercive instruments of the state to repress all forms of dissent. The German and Italian dilemma was how to avoid the earlier results without resorting to the latter techniques.

In the West German case the answer provided for modifications in the criminal code through a series of amendments passed between 1974 and 1978. In particular, the new crime of forming a terrorist association was established. Those found guilty of organizing, recruiting for, or joining such a group were subjected to certain penalties, including imprisonment; they were also barred from holding public office. In addition, the Anti-Constitutional Advocacy Act was changed to criminalize certain types of political expression. Prison sentences of up to three years were imposed on persons found guilty of publishing, distributing, or publicizing material supportive of violent acts against the democratic system. The glorification of violence and the public approval of criminal acts were also made criminal offenses.[60] Thus the West German government has used the law not only against members of terrorist groups but also against all those who publicly display support and sympathy for them.

The Italian criminal code, like its West German equivalent, already contained provisions on political crimes of an antidemocratic character when the terrorist era began. The advocacy and promotion of Fascism were banned, as was the formation of neo-Fascist groups. Membership in "subversive associations," ones that advocated the use of violence to achieve the dictatorship of one class over another, was proscribed. Still another provision criminalized participation in "armed bands," groups whose purpose was the violent overthrow of the Italian state. Equipped with such legislation, new antiterrorism laws seemed rather redundant.

Nonetheless, in the period immediately following the kidnapping of Aldo Moro in 1978 the government issued emergency decrees, which were later enacted into law by Parliament, that amended the criminal code. The new crime of terrorism or subversion of the democratic order was created. Kidnapping for terroristic and subversive purposes was criminalized; later the concept of terrorism and subversion of the democratic order was expanded to include membership in and promotion of groups whose ends were so defined.[61]

Though perhaps the most dramatic examples, West Germany and Italy were not the only European democracies to pass legislation outlawing terrorist groups and criminalizing membership in them; France, the Netherlands, and Greece, for example, have taken similar steps. The problem, aside from the matter of their utility, is their impact on the right of free association and the distinction between political advocacy and criminal conspiracy. The issue that is unresolved concerns the extent to which legal measures against the latter have damaged the former.

The legislative response to terrorism in the democracies has been the most far-reaching in the area of procedure, the measures authorities may use in the prevention of terrorist acts and in the investigation and prosecution of those who seek to commit them. The generalization is that the rules governing such elements of due process as arrest, detention, search and seizure, and fair trial have been changed to make it easier for those responsible for the repression of terrorism to do their jobs.

Some democracies where terrorist acts have been committed by foreign nationals, France, Britain, and Sweden, for example, have tightened their visa requirements for admission to these countries. In the United States the law now requires that a license be granted before any citizen may train a foreign national in the use of weapons on a specified list.[62] Italy has strengthened its laws governing the importation of firearms and munitions. Practically all the democracies have taken steps to strengthen security procedures at airports.

In a number of countries legislation has been passed permitting preventive detention, the apprehension and confinement of terrorist suspects without a formal charge being brought against them. The length of time involved varies. In Northern Ireland the practice of internment, detention without trial, was revived in 1972. The emergency law permitted a suspected terrorist to be held in custody up to twenty-eight days on the basis of an administrative order, not a judicial finding. And after a police hearing, the period of detention could stretch on almost indefinitely. However, because of protests from civil libertarians and Northern Irish Catholics, who felt justifiably that the application of the law was discriminatory, the practice was phased out beginning in 1975. At present, in Great Britain suspected terrorists may be held for seven days without being formally charged with a crime.[63] In Italy suspects may be detained up to forty-eight hours before a judge must be informed, and once this is done another week may elapse before the suspect is formally charged with a crime.[64] Furthermore, being charged with a crime need not lead to freedom pending a trial. The emergency laws of 1979 to 1980 permitted suspected terrorists to be imprisoned for over three years before their cases went to trial.

Access to defense attorneys has been restricted. In West Germany the law was changed to provide police scrutiny of written communications between suspects and defense lawyers. In 1977 a contact ban was imposed, according to which defendants could not meet with their counsel if such contacts were likely to threaten the lives of civilians, that is, if the police had reason to believe the lawyer would pass on a terrorist suspect's messages to colleagues on the outside. It also became possible to exclude defense lawyers from the trials themselves when they were thought likely to "endanger the security of the state." In Italy the police acquired the right to interrogate suspects without the presence of an attorney. The trials may be held in courtrooms constructed especially for the purpose of hearing terrorism-based cases. And if and when they are convicted, terrorists in West Germany and Italy also can expect to serve their sentences in new high-security prisons or in isolation from other inmates.

It is not uncommon for terrorist groups to attempt the intimidation of judges, jurors, and witnesses involved in the trials of their cohorts. In Italy a Red Brigades unit even assassinated a defense lawyer whom those members of the organization on trial did not wish to represent them. In different democracies a great number of judges, jurors, and witnesses, particularly former members of groups who agreed to testify against their erstwhile colleagues, have been killed. Among the various actions taken in response has been the suspension of the right to trial by jury in Northern Ireland. Instead of the customary practice, so-called Diplock courts, ones in which a single judge makes the decision of guilt or innocence, have been used to try terrorist suspects since 1973.

Other due process restraints have been loosened. Democracies ranging from the Swedish to the Italian have made it easier for the police to tap telephones and open personal correspondence (the letter bomb has been a widely used terrorist device). In West Germany and Italy the police acquired the ability to stop people on the street for questioning (and to arrest them if they refused to provide identification) and search their automobiles and places of residence without warrants in ways that would not have been lawful before the beginning of the terrorist era. In Italy whole neighborhoods in the major cities became subject to warrantless searches when the police had reason to believe that terrorists were hiding in them.

From a civil libertarian point of view these are all distressing practices. If the objective of fighting terrorism is the preservation of the rule of law, do not these measures violate the principle? The fact they threaten it seems indisputable. But before concluding that they should be condemned, it should be pointed out that many of the laws that made them possible were enacted on an emergency basis and require periodic review by the relevant national parliaments for their continuation. As the threat of terrorism subsides, the special measures can be eliminated. Some countries already have taken this step.

Among the democracies most affected, the tendency has been to stiffen the penalties imposed on individuals found guilty of violent crimes committed for terroristic purposes. Instead of the political offense exemption in international law, the domestic practice, in general, has been to punish more severely persons who commit crimes for political as opposed to private reasons. There are a few instances, however, where the carrot as well as the stick has been used.

In Northern Ireland since 1981 the British have made use of "supergrasses." Imprisoned members of the terrorist groups willing to provide the authorities with information and testify against their former associates at their trials have been rewarded by reduced sentences or complete freedom and a new identity.[65] Italian legislation on the disassociation from terrorism created a category of "repentants."[66] Terrorists wishing to abandon the struggle and furnish information about the operations of their groups have been accorded treatment similar to Northern Ireland's supergrasses. In both instances, the incentive yielded a bonanza of terrorist arrests and convictions. And in the Italian case, the repentants enabled the police to break the back of the major organizations.

The former president of Colombia, Belisario Betancur, offered amnesty to members of that nation's guerrilla and terrorist bands along with an opportunity for them to reenter the democratic political arena. But the results of this initiative have been mixed. Many who took advantage of the opportunity were later assassinated by the military and right-wing death squads.[67]

COUNTERTERRORIST POLICIES

The policies pursued by the democracies in their efforts to defeat terrorism represent a combination of organizational and legal practices as well as executive actions and administrative decisions. These policies may be directed at domestic and international varieties of terrorism. They also vary in terms of their scope. Some are "macro" policies, focused on overall or strategic considerations, while others are "micro" policies concerned with such narrow practices as hostage-taking negotiations. This section of the chapter reviews some of these policies and makes an attempt to evaluate their effectiveness.

One option always available to policymakers is to do nothing. Since the number of casualties caused by terrorist activities is limited and the activities themselves inside the democracies appear to do little to arouse popular sympathy for the causes of their practitioners, a case can be made for doing little beyond having the police conduct their normal investigations in cases involving the commission of violent crimes. Likewise, at the international level, terrorism may be regarded as simply a cost of doing business. Japan and the European democracies have strong incentives—oil imports, commercial exports—for maintaining amicable relations with countries in the Middle East that apparently support terrorism. Similarly, the United States may have a national interest in reducing tensions with the Soviet Union that takes precedence over the latter's assistance to selected national liberation movements.

All of this may be true, but if the goal of policy is the reduction in the level of terrorist violence, there is evidence that doing nothing will not work. In 1969 Catholic sections of Northern Ireland were declared "No Go" areas by the IRA. The local constabulary plus the British Army agreed to stay out of these places for several years, believing their presence would make matters worse. Instead, the volume of terrorist violence actually increased during this period.[68] At the international level, the willingness of the French and Italian governments to look the otl.er way when terrorist groups from the Middle East used their nations as staging areas for attacks elsewhere did not insulate their own citizens from subsequent assaults, as events in Paris during 1986 illustrated.

If something is to be done, what should it be? One possibility that a few democracies have explored is pursuing a truce and conducting peace negotiations with terrorist groups. At various times governments in Colombia, Northern Ireland, and Spain have entered into such arrangements with their adversaries. For politicians operating in democratic contexts this is an appealing choice. It is believed that no one will be killed while an effort is under way to arrive at a compromise solution. The record, though, is not encouraging.

For one thing, a ceasefire coupled with negotiations may unleash factional disagreements within the terrorist groups over the desirability of dealing with their enemies. Some factions may break away to form their own units and proceed to break the truce. For another, terrorists are usually extremists who view compromise and the normal give and take of democratic politics as forms of betrayal. Thus, the negotiations are unlikely to give the terrorists all of what they want. The available evidence suggests that truces are successful in the sense that the volume of violence is reduced while they are in force. But once they are over, the terrorist attacks quickly resume and the number of attacks may exceed levels that existed prior to the ceasefire.[69]

Practically all the democracies have responded to terrorism by a strategy of hardening the targets, by taking precautions which make it more difficult for terrorists to carry out their attacks.[70] A whole range of procedures belong under this heading, but most of them entail providing better personal security for individuals likely to be subject to attack and physical security at installations—airports, embassies, government buildings, power stations—terrorist groups find tempting targets. These defensive measures make good sense given the fact that terrorist groups have not expanded their repertoire much over the years. Ninety-five percent of all terrorist incidents involve six tactics: bombings, assassinations, armed assaults, kidnappings, hostage taking, and skyjacking.[71] Vast sums have been spent in the improvement of embassy security by the United States and other democracies, to a point where many of these structures now look more like high-technology fortresses than diplomatic offices. But the investments apparently have been worth it. According to figures compiled by the Rand Corporation, the number of attacks on embassies has declined in the 1980s compared with the frequency of such assaults during the previous decade.[72]

The overall effect of these defensive preparations appears to be one of compelling terrorist groups to shift their attacks from the more to the less protected targets. Thus, if security is improved at Heathrow Airport in London and Charles de Gaulle Airport in Paris, targets in Rome and Athens become more attractive possibilities. The better protected high-ranking officials become, the more likely terrorist groups will attack members of the general public. Of course, it is impossible to protect everything and everybody, but over time logic suggests that security will then be improved at the more vulnerable targets as well.

The practice of deterring terrorist attacks by hardening the targets has an additional advantage. If there is no attack, there are no poisoned pawns for the authorities to take into custody and no fallen martyrs in whose names terrorist groups will justify further operations or build popular support.

There are many who advocate the defeat of terrorism by addressing its root causes, such as high unemployment, depressed economic conditions, ethnic grievances, racial and religious discrimination, etc. Unless democratic governments take steps to improve these background conditions, terrorism will persist no matter how many targets are hardened. If terrorists thrive in conditions of social and political polarization in which societies are divided along lines of economic class or social group affiliation, it follows that democratic governments should pursue policies aimed at improving these conditions and depolarizing the situation.

It is intrinsically desirable for democracies to adopt policies with the above objectives in mind. But the evidence is decidedly mixed when it comes to the impact of these policies on reducing the level of terrorism. In the Netherlands, the government has had some success in the case of South Moluccan terrorism through the establishment of a permanent joint Dutch–South Moluccan committee to hear grievances and explore alternative solutions plus increased public expenditures to improve the living conditions for South Moluccans living in the Netherlands.[73] But these policies were developed simultaneously with the use of stronger police and legal measures against the terrorists.

So far as efforts to improve economic conditions are concerned, one recent study actually reports negative conclusions. In the case of Northern Ireland, the British government succeeded in reducing the unemployment rate somewhat by a combination of public and private investment strategies. But this study reports a negative correlation between the unemployment rate and the incidence of terrorism: the lower the unemployment the greater the number of terrorist attacks.[74] Terrorism in the Basque region of Spain escalated despite the fact that the region was the most prosperous in the country. The conditions of the Basque economy were so good that it drew workers from other parts of Spain, thereby making young Basques more rather than less sensitive to their cultural differences with the rest of the population. In Italy, those regions in the northern part of the country with high rates of unemployment also tended to be the sites of high levels of terrorist violence. But the government managed to dramatically reduce the latter without doing much to improve the former.[75]

In the cases of Spain and Northern Ireland, it makes sense to believe that the root causes of terrorism are not economic but ethnic, and the appropriate policies for democratic governments to employ are ones aimed at reducing the grievances of the affected communities. Of course, in some cases it is beyond the power of government to make such changes. For example, the Dutch government, no matter how much it might have wished to do so, could not establish an independent state of South Molucca, now part of Indonesia. On the other hand, both the Spanish and British governments undertook a series of reforms that eliminated many of the cultural and political disabilities suffered by the Basque and Catholic populations. Regional autonomy was extended to the Basques, and the Anglo-Irish agreement of 1985 gave the Dublin government some role in the affairs of Ulster.

The impact of these reforms has been complex. Their public announcement was followed by an increase in the level of terrorist violence. But after they were implemented, there was a decline in terrorist activity.[76] At present, the picture remains clouded, but in both regions terrorism remains a major problem. For reasons discussed in Chapter 4, terrorist groups often seem to take on a life of their own as their original goals are displaced by ones having to do with their own persistence. If this is true, then we should expect that whatever impact the reforms would have would be long-range. In theory at least, the existing members of terrorist groups would not abandon the struggle, but over time they would experience increased difficulty in recruiting new members as the original grievances become less salient to the ethnic communities from which the terrorist bands have drawn their adherents. At present, though, this is a hope rather than a reality. Not to be forgotten is the fact that in some cases satisfying the demands of one ethnic group may antagonize another. In Northern Ireland, extremist Protestants have reacted to Catholic advances by stepping up their own terrorist operations.

Some democracies, including the British and West German ones, have sought to reduce the level of terrorism by denying its practitioners access to the mass media. The assumption, of course, is that terrorist groups seek publicity for their causes. If their representatives are prohibited from appearing on television, they will be less likely to commit acts of violence in order to obtain access to the media. The Dutch government has made the same assumption but pursued a very different policy. In the Netherlands, advocates of all causes, no matter how extreme, are able to gain free access to television in order to make their views known to the public. Further, dissident groups are able to receive government subsidies without great difficulty. This policy of co-optation, or killing them with kindness, is aimed at channeling political protest groups along peaceful lines before their members give serious consideration to the terrorist alternative. And, aside from the relatively brief South Moluccan episode, the Netherlands has not experienced much terrorist violence.[77]

The strongest generalization to emerge from a recent study of domestic terrorism in five nations is a seemingly circular one. Specifically, the largest reduction in the rate of terrorist violence is achieved when the highest number of terrorists are in prison.[78] Apparently the pool of individuals willing to join terrorist groups is not inexhaustible. It is reduced when potential recruits become aware that they are likely to wind up in prison as a consequence of their exertions. The fewer people there are at large who are already engaged in terrorism, the fewer the number of terrorist incidents there will be. This finding bears some resemblance to the repeat-offender phenomenon and the crime rate in American cities. According to this analysis, a high proportion of crimes, e.g., burglary, is committed by a relatively small number of habitual criminals. The rate of crime is reduced substantially when the police are successful in arresting and imprisoning these repeat offenders. In the case of terrorism the repeat offenders are clustered together in bands. If the authorities are successful in apprehending one or two members of a terrorist group, the impact is likely to be far-reaching, since those arrested presumably will be able to supply the authorities with information about other members of their organization. If this is true, the question becomes, what policies will be most effective in achieving the arrest of terrorists? And, further, what will induce them to cooperate with the authorities in disclosing information about their comrades?

Among the various measures the democracies have employed to combat terrorism, a few have produced meaningful results in the arrest of terrorists. Those that provide the authorities with improved intelligence are especially meaningful. Measures directed at the general population through emergency legislation or increasing the size of security forces appear to be less effective than policies aimed specifically at terrorists. The high-technology means by which modern nations acquire intelligence about one another, e.g., spy satellites, seem inappropriate. Bribery or cash payments to members of terrorist groups or those familiar with their behavior are likely to have some effect. Recent American legislation authorizes the executive to pay up to $500,000 to any individual who provides information that leads to the arrest and conviction, in any country, of persons who committed terrorist acts.[79] This may be a step in the right direction. The fact that undercover American FBI agents recently were able to apprehend a wanted Shiite terrorist aboard a boat anchored off Nicosia, Cyprus, through the offer of a lucrative drug deal calls attention to the likelihood (see Chapter 4) that many terrorists are motivated by incentives other than the political goals of their organizations. If this is true, tangible incentives may be used by the authorities to combat the organizations.

The Italian and British policies of granting leniency to repentant and supergrass terrorists have had meaningful results. In both cases these policies, which offered defecting terrorists the possibility of a return to normal life, led to the arrest of hundreds of persons and in the Italian situation contributed to the destruction of the major terrorist organizations. The context in this latter instance was one in which the government had already raised the penalties associated with the commission of terrorist acts and, through improvements in the organization of its security forces, raised the probability that those involved would face arrest anyway. From this experience it is reasonable to believe that a policy that raises the likelihood of capture and punishment while simultaneously providing incentives for individuals to defect from terrorist bands before these sanctions are applied will prove the most effective means of dealing with the problem.

While these policies have had some impact in countering domestic terrorism, what of international terrorism, particularly its state-sponsored variety? What policies have the democracies employed in their efforts to reduce manifestations of such terrorism? Perhaps the best way to evaluate these measures is by distinguishing between those aimed at terrorist groups and those directed at the states that assist them.

In the case of foreign-based organizations whose members commit terrorist acts on the territory or within the jurisdiction of one or more of the democracies, approximately the same policies suitable for use against domestic terrorism seem appropriate. Improved intelligence-gathering techniques and the sharing of information on a bilateral basis or through the

Interpol and TREVI networks have had some payoff in recent years. International terrorists planning to shoot down civilian airliners in Rome and Nairobi were arrested before they could stage their attacks because of intelligence provided to the relevant authorities by concerned nations.[80] The same may be said about the arrest by Swiss and Italian police of individuals who had planned to bomb the U.S. Embassy in Rome. On other occasions alerts have been issued which permitted American diplomatic personnel to leave the sites of anticipated terrorist attacks before the attacks occurred. Also, most democracies have taken steps to prevent members of foreign terrorist groups from entering their countries.

Since U.S. citizens have been among the principal victims of international terrorism, close attention should be paid to the response of the United States. One legal reaction has been to expand the reach of American law. Congress has modified the law to allow U.S. agents operating outside the country to arrest foreign nationals suspected of committing acts of terrorist violence against Americans on foreign soil and return these individuals for prosecution in the United States.[81] Terrorists who have taken refuge in countries where the extradite or prosecute rule is meaningless, e.g., Lebanon, have now become subject to pursuit by U.S. law enforcement agencies. This law also permitted a lawyer representing American interests to participate in the successful 1987 prosecution before a French court of George Ibrahim Abdullah, a Lebanese national who had planned the murder of an American diplomat in Paris.

Recent U.S. legislation also requires the Department of Transportation to conduct periodic surveys of security procedures at airports outside the United States that are served by air carriers that also enjoy landing rights in this country. When these security procedures are found to be deficient, the law allows the president to prohibit all air service between the United States and the security-deficient airports.[82]

If the above represent some of the policies aimed at curtailing the activities of groups perpetrating acts of international terrorism, what measures have been used against those states that encourage or promote their operations? An assumption here is that this type of terrorism is a kind of surrogate warfare rather than a manifestation of criminality, and that policies directed against individuals or small groups will not be totally effective in deterring hostile actions that are actually undertaken by governments.

The most widely discussed response to state-sponsored terrorism concerns the use of force. The issue has stimulated debate among the Western allies and within the U.S. government itself during the Reagan administration. These discussions have focused on the overall desirability of using force, the circumstances under which the use of force is appropriate, and such particular concerns as the type of force to be used and which states are suitable targets for its use.

Among the democracies, Israel and the United States have emerged as the leading advocates as well as practitioners of the use of force.[83] Since these nations have been the principal targets, their attitudes hardly come as a surprise. In general, the advocates believe that states sponsoring terrorism will not be dissuaded unless and until force is applied and they are compelled to stop. Critics of this policy have argued that force inevitably leads to the loss of innocent lives and that, correlatively, it builds popular support for the regimes that are its targets. Given their vastly different situations in terms of strength, vulnerability, etc., the United States has tended to view force as a last resort while the Israelis see it, if not their first, pretty close to it.

Participants in the debate over the circumstances for using force have distinguished between retaliation and preemption.[84] In the former case, force is used only in response to an attack or series of attacks that are clearly traceable to a state initiative. The American air raid on Libya may serve as an example. Preemptive force would be employed when a state learns that such an attack or attacks are imminent before they are actually carried out. In addition to the adverse effect caused by the potential killing of innocents, the preemption alternative carries the burden of leaving the widespread impression that the state using force is the aggressor and its target the innocent victim.

If decisions are made to use force in circumstances thought appropriate, the remaining question involves the type of force to be used. Should the act involve conventional military units or ones designed for covert measures and special operations? Both the United States and Israel relied upon their air forces in striking at Libya and the PLO headquarters in Tunisia. From the point of view of the attacking states, these high-visibility measures had the advantage of minimizing the casualties they were compelled to absorb. On the other hand, air force bombing raids increase the likelihood of civilian casualties. The opposite may, but need not, be true with the use of special forces.

Despite the fact it may be an effective alternative, the conduct of covert operations against foreign political figures enjoys an especially unsavory reputation in the United States. At different times during the cold war, the CIA attempted to assassinate various political leaders, including Fidel Castro.[85] As a consequence, U.S. law now prohibits the use of violence against foreign political leaders. Furthermore, the conventions on internationally protected persons, the international law the United States is committed to upholding, make these covert measures doubly impermissible.[86]

Does the use of force work? Does it have any measurable effect on the incidence of terrorist attacks? Potentially, of course, it might produce an effect, but it may be the opposite of the one desired by its proponents: namely, an increase in the frequency of terrorism as leaders of the target states vent their wrath against the state that used force against them. In the case of the American raid on Tripoli and Benghazi, carried out in April 1986, there is some evidence that the impact, at least in the short run, was beneficial. According to U.S. State Department figures there was a radical decline in the number of terrorist attacks of Middle Eastern origin carried out in Western Europe in the five months following the air raids on these Libyan cities. Overall, comparing 1986 with 1985, there was a 50 percent reduction in the occurrence of attacks exhibiting this particular format.[87] So, a tentative answer to the question is that force does seem to have an impact in reducing the level of terrorism. But in the particular case under consideration, it should be noted that the American raid on Libya was one of several steps against that nation; others included the expulsion of approximately 500 Libyan diplomats and students from Western European countries.

The use of force against a state that sponsors terrorist groups carries with it a number of dangers, not least of which is the possibility that the wrong target will be selected. Libya was exceptional in that its leader openly boasted about his government's support for these groups. On many occasions the link between the supporting state and the terrorist group is not so visible.[88] In some cases the group may be the beneficiary of assistance from more than one donor. This was apparently the case with the 1983 bombing of the American Marine Corps barracks in Beirut. In this instance, both Iran and Syria were alleged to have played roles. There is also variation in the degree of control exercised by the state over the group. In some instances, direct planning and supervision are exercised by the state in carrying out specific missions, but in others the relationship is far more distant and deniable.

For these reasons, force is only one of a variety of measures democratic governments have developed in their effort to combat international terrorism. If some nations support terrorist activity in the pursuit of their national interests, they may reduce such support when their interests are harmed by terrorist activity. Public identification and the embarrassment that usually accompanies it may help. Syria has reduced its support for terrorist activity in Western Europe in part because of the adverse reaction to disclosures about its involvement with terrorist attacks in Great Britain and elsewhere.[89]

Sometimes democratic nations have things that terrorism-supporting states want. Currently, Iraq, a frequent haven for Abu Nidal's Fatah Revolutionary Council, is engaged in a war with Iran. The regime in

Baghdad has an interest in acquiring U.S. satellite pictures of Iranian troop deployments. Should these be forthcoming? The basis for an agreement may be at hand. The general point is that in addition or aɔ an alternative to force the democracies have a variety of sanctions—economic and political boycotts, denial of landing rights and diplomatic representation, the withdrawal of technical assistance—they have begun to apply in order to induce states to curtail their support for terrorism. If there is sufficient cooperation among the democracies, these measures may prove more effective in the long run.

The one form of terrorist activity that seems to arouse the greatest public concern is the seizure or kidnapping of hostages. It is obviously an act that cuts across the distinction between domestic and international terrorism. Furthermore, such an event, particularly when it involves victims chosen at random, creates a moral dilemma for democratic governments because of their sensitivity to the taking of human life and responsiveness to domestic public opinion. It should not be forgotten that the Iran-contra scandal in the United States was an outgrowth of the Reagan administration's concern about the fate of Americans taken captive by fundamentalist groups in Lebanon, ones with ties to the regime in Iran. The dilemma with which the democracies are confronted involves a decision between giving the terrorists what they want, thereby achieving freedom for their hostages, or resisting these demands and by so doing cause the hostages to be killed by their captors. If democratic governments concede to the terrorists, do they raise the likelihood that more individuals will be taken hostage in the future? If the tactic works, it will be repeated.

Over time, more and more democracies have reached the conclusion that a policy of concessions will not work and, as a consequence, have preferred to save the victims' lives by means other than acquiescence to the terrorists' demands. Accordingly, they have devised an array of tactics with which to deal with these situations.

The willingness to make concessions is not identical to a refusal to communicate with those holding hostages. Indeed, some of the democracies have trained individuals and groups skilled in this practice.[90] These individuals, in turn, have come away from their encounters with certain insights or rules of thumb they found to be useful. Among the approaches they have found to be helpful are ones that stress patience and sobriety. Negotiators should attempt to deglamorize the situation by, among other things, avoiding bringing high-ranking officials into the proceedings. It is also important for the government or sometimes governments concerned to speak with a single voice and that whatever messages are communicated to the captors be simple and straightforward ones which, if possible, both build trust and prevent mis-understanding.[91]

If, however, the terrorists cannot be convinced to free their hostages and if and when they begin to set deadlines for their execution, democratic governments are prepared to use force. As was discussed earlier, many democracies have created special units prepared for intervening rapidly in these situations in the hope of minimizing casualties. Nonetheless, such rescue operations are exceedingly risky undertakings.

CONCLUSION

Contemporary political terrorism has confronted the democracies with not one problem but many different types of problems. These problems have not been ones amenable to a single solution, be it organizational, legal, political, or military. But trial and error have led most democracies to a variety of policies that attempt to raise the costs and negative consequences for the perpetrators of terrorist attacks. A few of the democracies have added positive incentives for the terrorists to stop the violence and abandon the struggle. These measures appear to hold some promise. One lesson seems clear: doing nothing or reaching tacit understandings with terrorist organizations, as the French, Italian, and Greek governments have discovered, will not work. Contemporary terrorists will not depart the scene of their own volition. What, then, does the future hold? This question will be addressed in the final chapter.

KEY TERMS

Delta Force
Division for General Investigations
  and Special Operations (DIGOS)
European Community (EC)
"extradite or prosecute"
Federal Aviation Administration
  (FAA)
Grenschutz Gruppe 9 (GSG 9)
just-cause doctrine of war
justice-in-war concept
the Kommisar
low-intensity conflict
National Gendarmerie Intervention
  Team (GIGN)

North Atlantic Treaty Organization
  (NATO)
poisoned pawn
repentants
sea-air-land (SEAL) troops
SEAL Team 6
Special Air Services (SAS)
Special Operations Forces (SOF)
Special Weapons and Tactics
  (SWAT) Squad
Summit Seven
supergrasses
Task Force 160 (the Night Stalkers)
Terrorism, Radicalism, and Violence
  International (TREVI) group

NOTES

1 Paul Wilkinson, "The Laws of War and Terrorism," in David Rapoport and Yonah Alexander (eds.), *The Morality of Terrorism* (New York: Pergamon Press, 1982), pp. 308–324.
2 For a discussion, see Alfred Rubin, "International terrorism and International Law," in Yonah Alexander and Seymour Finger (eds.), *Terrorism: Interdisciplinary Perspectives* (New York: John Jay Press, 1977), pp. 121–127.
3 U.S. Department of State, *Iran's Use of International Terrorism,* Special Report 170 (Washington, D.C.: Bureau of Public Affairs, 1987).
4 See, for example, Brian Jenkins, *International Terrorism: The Other World War* (Santa Monica, Ca.: The Rand Corporation, 1985), pp. 19–20.
5 Michael Klare and Peter Kornbluh (eds.), "The New Interventionism: Low Intensity Warfare in the 1980s and Beyond," in *Low Intensity Warfare* (New York: Pantheon Books, 1988), pp. 3–20.
6 See, for example, *Report of the Ad Hoc Committee on International Terrorism,* United Nations General Assembly, Official Records, 28th Sess., suppl. 28 (A/9028), reprinted in Robert Friedlander (ed.), *Terrorism: Documents of International and Local Control,* vol. 1 (Dobbs Ferry, N.Y.: Oceana Publications, 1979), pp. 340–341.
7 Adeed Dawisha, *The Arab Radicals* (New York: Council on Foreign Relations, 1986), pp. 121–122.
8 Walter Laqueur, "Reflections on Terrorism," *Foreign Affairs* (Fall 1986), p. 94.
9 Paul Wilkinson, *Terrorism and the Liberal State,* 2d rev. ed. (New York: New York University Press, 1986), pp. 125–142.
10 Ibid., p. 128.
11 Michael Walzer, *Just and Unjust Wars* (New York: Basic Books, 1977), pp. 21–33; see also John Duggard, "International Terrorism and the Just War," in Rapoport and Alexander (eds.), op. cit., pp. 77–98.
12 Duggard, Ibid., p. 79.
13 For a discussion, see James Burtchael, "Moral Responses to Terrorism," in Neil Livingstone and Terrell Arnold (eds.), *Fighting Back: Winning the War against Terrorism* (Lexington, Mass.: Lexington Books, 1986), pp. 191–211; see also Victoria Toensing, "The Legal Case for Using Force," pp. 145–156.
14 J. Bowyer Bell, *A Time of Terror* (New York: Basic Books, 1978), pp. 87–89; Christopher Dobson and Donald Payne, *Counterattack* (New York: Facts on File, 1982), pp. 77–93.
15 William Farrell, *The U.S. Government Response to Terrorism* (Boulder, Col.: Westview Press, 1982), pp. 32–33; see also Marc Celmer, *Terrorism, U.S. Strategy and Reagan Policies* (New York: Greenwood Press, 1987), pp. 17–19.
16 Ernest Evans, "American Policy Response to International Terrorism," in Alexander and Finger (eds.), op. cit., pp. 106–117.
17 Bell, op. cit., p. 113.
18 Ibid., p. 86.
19 See, for example, Piero Luigi Vigna, "Italian Responses," in Benjamin Netanyahu (ed.), *International Terrorism: Challenge and Response* (Jerusalem: The Jonathan Institute, 1980), p. 198.

20 *Counterterrorism: Role of INTERPOL and the U.S. National Central Bureau,* GAO/GGP-87-93BR (Washington, D.C.: General Accounting Office, June 1987), p. 14.

21 For a discussion, see Irving Louis Horowitz, "Can Democracy Cope with Terrorism?" *The Civil Liberties Review* (May/June 1977), pp. 29–37.

22 Parker Borg, *International Terrorism: Breaking the Cycle of Violence,* Occasional Paper No. 8 (Washington, D.C.: Center for the Study of Foreign Affairs, 1987), pp. 16–18.

23 Ibid., pp. 18–19.

24 Dobson and Payne, op. cit., p. 10.

25 Juliet Lodge, "The European Community and Terrorism: From Principles to Concerted Action," in Juliet Lodge (ed.), *The Threat of Terrorism* (Boulder, Col.: Westview Press, 1988), pp. 229–264.

26 *Counterterrorism: The Role of INTERPOL and the U.S. National Central Bureau,* op. cit., pp. 33–42.

27 See Grant Wardlaw, *Political Terrorism* (Cambridge: Cambridge University Press, 1982), pp. 97–102; and Dobson and Payne, op. cit., pp. 19–50, 94–109, 133–146.

28 *Public Report of the Vice President's Task Force on Combatting Terrorism* (Washington, D.C.: U.S. Government Printing Office, 1986), pp. 31–33.

29 For accounts, see David Martin and John Walcott, *Best Laid Plans* (New York: Harper & Row, Publishers, Inc., 1988).

30 Stephen Googe, "Low Intensity Warfare: The Warriors and Their Weapons," in Klare and Kornbluh (eds.), op. cit. (see note 5), pp. 80–111.

31 Thomas Adams, "Organizing for Counterterrorism," *Syracuse Scholar,* 8:1 (1987), pp. 91–106.

32 Celmer, op. cit., p. 66.

33 Ariel Merari, "Soviet Attitudes towards Middle Eastern Terrorism," in Steven Spiegel, Mark Heller, and Jacob Goldberg (eds.), *The Soviet-American Competition in the Middle East* (Lexington, Mass.: D. C. Heath and Company, 1988), pp. 197–199.

34 Wardlaw, op. cit., pp. 97–100.

35 Dobson and Payne, op. cit., pp. 103–104.

36 On the general theme, see Murray Edelman, *The Symbolic Uses of Politics* (Urbana, Ill.: University of Illinois Press, 1967).

37 Copies of the documents are reprinted in Yonah Alexander, Marjorie Browne, and Allan Nanes (eds.), *Control of Terrorism: International Documents* (New York: Crane Russak, 1979), pp. 31–42.

38 Friedlander, op.cit., p. 74.

39 See, for example, Abraham Sofaer, "Terrorism and the Law," *Foreign Affairs* (Fall 1986), pp. 919–920; and Victoria Toensing, "The Legal Case for Using Force," in Livingstone and Arnold (eds.), op. cit., pp. 145–156.

40 Wardlaw, op. cit., p. 116; Borg, op. cit., p. 13.

41 For the texts, see Alexander, Browne, and Nanes (eds.), op. cit., pp. 72–75, 87–109.

42 For discussions see Wilkinson, *Terrorism and the Liberal State*, op. cit., pp. 260–261; and Wardlaw, op. cit., p. 113.

43 See Juliet Lodge (ed.), "The European Community and Terrorism: Establishing the Principle of 'Extradite or Try,'" in *Terrorism: a Challenge to the State* (New York: St. Martin's Press, 1981), p. 113.

44 For the texts, see Friedlander (ed.), op. cit., vol. 2, pp. 102–112.

45 Wilkinson, *Terrorism and the Liberal State*, op. cit., pp. 227, 245.

46 Friedlander (ed.), op. cit., vol. 1, pp. 94–95.

47 For the text, see Alexander, Browne, and Nanes (eds.), op. cit., pp. 77–85.

48 Wardlaw, op. cit., pp. 112–113.

49 Sofaer, op. cit., p. 911.

50 For the text, see Herbert Briggs (ed.), *The Law of Nations,* 2d ed. (New York: Appleton-Century-Crofts, 1952), pp. 1008–1012.

51 Douglas Feith, "Law in the Service of Terror—The Strange Case of the Additional Protocol," *The National Interest* (Fall 1985), p. 43.

52 See Harry Almond, "Using the Law to Combat Terrorism," in Livingstone and Arnold (eds.), op. cit. (see note 13), p. 170; and Sofaer, op. cit., pp. 913–917.

53 See Joseph Bishop, "Legal Measures to Control Terrorism in Democracies," in Netanyahu (ed.), op. cit., pp. 294–306.

54 Frank Clusky, "The Irish Response," in Netanyahu (ed.), op. cit., pp. 180–186.

55 For the texts, see Yonah Alexander and Allan Nunes (eds.), *Legislative Responses to Terrorism* (Boston: Martin Nijhoff Publishers, 1986), pp. 261–277; for a commentary, see Wardlaw, op. cit., pp. 126–130.

56 For a general discussion, see Thomas Emerson, *The System of Free Expression* (New York: Vintage Books, 1970).

57 Alexander and Nanes (eds.), op. cit., pp. 308–312.

58 *Public Report of the Vice President's Task Force*, op. cit., p. 15.

59 Allan Nanes, "Congressional Developments: Terrorism," *Terrorism,* 9:2 (1987), pp. 207–213; Marc Pearl, "Terrorism—Historical Perspectives on U.S. Congressional Action," *Terrorism,* 10:2 (1987), pp. 139–140.

60 Geoffrey Pridham, "Terrorism and the State in West Germany during the 1970s: A Threat to the State or a Case of Political Over-Reaction?" in Lodge (ed.), op. cit., pp. 46–50; Wardlaw, op. cit., pp. 121–126.

61 Leonard Weinberg and William Eubank, *The Rise and Fall of Italian Terrorism* (Boulder, Col.: Westview Press, 1987), pp. 127–128; Paul Furlong, "Political Terrorism in Italy: Responses, Reactions and Immobilism," in Lodge (ed.), op. cit., pp. 80–85.

62 *Public Report of the Vice President's Task Force*, op. cit., p. 15.

63 Kevin Boyle, Tom Hadden, and Paddy Hilyard, "The Facts on Internment in Northern Ireland," in Ronald D. Crelinstein, Danielle Laberge-Altmejd, and Denis Szabo (eds.), *Terrorism and Criminal Justice* (Lexington, Mass.: Lexington Books, 1979), pp. 103–115; John Finn, "Public Support for Emergency (Anti-Terrorist) Legislation in Northern Ireland," *Terrorism,* 10:2 (1987), pp. 113–124; Paul Wilkinson, "British Policy on Terrorism," in Lodge (ed.), *The Threat of Terrorism,* op. cit., pp. 29–55.

64 Frederic Spotts and Theodore Wieser, *Italy: A Difficult Democracy* (New York: Cambridge University Press, 1986), pp. 164–165; John Finn, "Public

Support for Emergency Legislation in Northern Ireland: A Preliminary Analysis," *Terrorism,* 10:2 (1987), pp. 113–124.

65 S. C. Greer, "The Supergrass System in Northern Ireland," in Paul Wilkinson and Alisdair Stewart (eds.), *Contemporary Research on Terrorism* (Aberdeen: Aberdeen University Press, 1987), pp. 510–535.

66 Franco Ferracuti, "Repentant Terrorist Legislation: A Preliminary Analysis of Problems and Results in Italy" (a paper presented at the World Congress of the International Political Science Association, Paris, July 1985).

67 "The World's Wars," *The Economist* (March 12–18, 1988), p. 19.

68 Christopher Hewitt, *The Effectiveness of Anti-Terrorist Policies* (New York: University Press of America, 1984), p. 91.

69 Ibid., pp. 35–42.

70 Robert Kupperman and Darrell Trent, *Terrorism: Threat, Reality, Response* (Stanford, Ca.: The Hoover Institution, 1979), pp. 75–112.

71 Jenkins, op. cit. (see note 4), p. 12.

72 Ibid., p. 12.

73 Valentine Herman and Rob Van der Laaw Bouma, "Nationalists without a Nation: South Moluccan Terrorism in the Netherlands," in Lodge (ed.), op. cit., pp. 138–141.

74 Hewitt, op. cit., pp. 43–47.

75 Weinberg and Eubank, op. cit., pp. 113–112.

76 Hewitt, op. cit., p. 88.

77 Alex Schmid, "Politically Motivated Violent Activists in the Netherlands in the 1980s," in Lodge (ed.), *The Threat of Terrorism*, op. cit., pp. 145–178.

78 Hewitt, op. cit., pp. 96–97.

79 Pearl, op. cit. (see note 59), p. 141.

80 Livingstone and Arnold (eds.), op. cit. (see note 13), pp. 231–232.

81 Borg, op. cit., p. 13.

82 Pearl, op. cit., p. 142.

83 See, for example, George Shultz, "The Challenge to the Democracies," in Benjamin Netanyahu (ed.), *Terrorism: How the West Can Win* (New York: Farrar, Strauss, Giroux, 1986), pp. 16–24, 199–226.

84 See, for example, Neil Livingstone, "Proactive Responses to Terrorism: Reprisals, Preemption and Retribution," in Livingstone and Arnold (eds.), op. cit., pp. 109–131.

85 Jeffrey Richelson, *The U.S. Intelligence Community* (Cambridge, Mass.: Ballinger Books, 1985), pp. 227–236.

86 Guy Roberts, "Covert Responses: The Moral Dilemma," in Livingstone and Arnold (eds.), op. cit., pp. 133–144.

87 Robert Oakley, "International Terrorism," *Foreign Affairs,* 65:3 (1987), p. 620; *Patterns of Global Terrorism 1986* (Washington, D.C.: U.S. Department of State, 1988), p. 2; David Shipler, "One Year after U.S. Raid, A Lower Libyan Profile," *The New York Times* (Apr. 12, 1987), p. 14.

88 See, for example, Judith Miller, "The Istanbul Synagogue Massacre," *The New York Times Magazine* (Apr. 14, 1987), pp. 14–52.

89 James Markham, "Europe's Anti-Terrorism Tied to U.S. Libya Raids," *The New York Times* (Apr. 14, 1987), p. 8.

90 See, for example, Richard Clutterbuck, "Managing the Episode," in Brian Jenkins (ed.), *Terrorism and Personal Protection* (Boston: Butterworth Publishers, 1985), pp. 232–248.

91 Brian Jenkins, "Effective Communications in a Hostage Crisis," in Martin Herz (ed.), *Diplomats and Terrorists: What Works, What Doesn't* (Washington D.C.: Institute for the Study of Diplomacy, 1982), pp. 48–54.

CHAPTER 7

FUTURE POSSIBILITIES

Is the age of terrorism coming to an end? Or is it likely to continue for the foreseeable future? If it does persist, will terrorism take on new characteristics—new causes, new weapons, and new groups?

It seems clear that important aspects of the international environment which helped to stimulate the growth of terrorism in the late 1960s have changed. The U.S. involvement in the Vietnam war ended more than a decade ago. The various urban guerrilla groups in North America and Western Europe that emerged in the wake of popular protests against American intervention have faded. The new post-1976 leadership in China does not provide a plausible model for Maoist-based revolutionary terrorism. In Latin America the Montoneros and the Tupamaros along with the right-wing death squads that sought to destroy them are no longer present.[1] Whatever role the Soviet Union played in seeking to destabilize the Western democracies during the 1970s seems less likely to continue under the direction of leaders concerned with domestic economic reform and limiting the arms race. Perhaps symptomatically, after their own diplomats were kidnapped in Lebanon in 1985, the Soviets joined the United States in supporting UN Security Council motions condemning all forms of terrorism as criminal acts, irrespective of their perpetrators' political views.[2] In most of the Third World, colonialism is becoming a distant memory. To the extent that Third World liberation movements offered inspiration to terrorist groups in the industrialized democracies, this element now seems less meaningful than it once did. The conflict between Israel and the Palestinians has not been resolved. But Palestinian efforts now appear (1988) to involve mass agitation and protest on the West Bank and Gaza Strip more than terrorist operations in Western Europe and elsewhere.

If terrorism is to end, what will or does the process look like? There are a few studies available that answer this question as it relates to individual groups in different countries.[3] According to these analyses, terrorist groups may come to one of several ends. The first and most obvious is *defeat,* an outcome brought on by their destruction at the hands of governmental authorities. In the United States this is the fate that befell the Symbionese Liberation Army, the Puerto Rican National Liberation Front, and the Black Panthers, among others. In Italy the Nuclei of Armed Proletarians, the Front Line, the New Order, and a host of other revolutionary and neo-Fascist organizations were brought to the point of collapse by the government's antiterrorist policies. As was discussed earlier, Turkey, Iran, Argentina, and Uruguay were able to eliminate their terrorist adversaries. The list of defeats could be extended even among the democracies.

In a peculiar way the defeat of some terrorist groups has not infrequently been tied to their successes: not in the sense of achieving their ultimate political aims but in their ability to expand their memberships. The larger the group, the more visible it becomes to the authorities and the more likely the latter are to plant or create informers. "Success" of this type may then prove the basis for later defeat.

But defeat is not the only or even the most frequent way in which terrorist groups have come to an end. Another is through a process of *backlash.* In some cases, as with Armenian communities in exile and French-speaking Canadians in Quebec, the ethnic groups whose causes the terrorists have sought to lead have displayed revulsion at the atrocities that were committed in their name. The process of delegitimizing the terrorists among their ostensible constituency has also been at work in Italy. There the labor unions and the Communist party brought thousands of workers into the streets of the major cities to demonstrate the proletariat's public opposition to the violence committed in its name by the Red Brigades and other revolutionary groups. Exhibitions such as these have proved to be demoralizing and have led to factional divisiveness within the groups over the value of their terrorist operations.

This process calls attention to a third way in which terrorist groups have ceased to function. Sometimes they are subject to *burnout* or disintegration for reasons that are largely internal to the organization. Many young people may be attracted to clandestine terrorist organizations because they promise to provide action and an opportunity to put their political ideals into practice. But the reality of life in the underground can prove disillusioning. Instead of action and excitement it often involves long periods of inaction and boredom. While it is true that leaders of the Italian Front Line were able to vacation aboard a cabin cruiser in the Mediterranean, this example is more the exception than the rule. Instead, a decline in the members' commitment to a terrorist group may occur as the result of factional disagreements, heightened demands for discipline, and the sort of endless ideological debate they sought to escape through their adherence. When these factors are coupled with external pressures—arrests, diminished prospects for success, public indifference or hostility, opportunities to repent and resume a normal life—the process of disintegration may become irreversible. The experience of the Vietnam-era Weather Underground in the United States is illustrative.

Finally, and to repeat an alternative discussed in Chapter 4, there have been some occasions when terrorist groups have undergone a *strategic shift* away from terrorism and toward other means for achieving their objectives. Sometimes this has involved the formation of or a return to a party or some other legitimate form of political activity. This happened with the Menachem Begin–led Irgun after the achievement of Israeli national independence. A similar process may now be at work in Colombia and Uruguay. A problem with this outcome is that terrorist groups, despite claims of vast support among the masses, usually turn out to be exceedingly unpopular when the ballots are counted. But, of course, there is always the long run for their leaders to contemplate. Other ways of attracting the public and mass media's attention may become available. In the democracies campaigns of civil disobedience likely will win more sympathy than acts of terrorist violence. Political leaders may prove more responsive to mass protests than to airliner hijacking and assassination attempts.

The end of individual members of the species, however, does not mean the extinction of the species itself. As some groups disappear, others emerge to take their place. The right-wing death squads in Argentina and Brazil have passed from the scene, but by one account over 100 of such organizations now exist in strife-ridden Colombia.[4]

There are certain conditions which facilitated the growth of terrorism in the late 1960s that still exist today, and some of these actually make it easier for terrorists to operate now than earlier. The international arms market now makes available an abundance of weapons that terrorists find useful. And the weapons themselves have gotten better. Some improvements have been made in television technology, for example, minicameras and direct satellite hookups, that assist the display of terrorist events. And despite obvious precautions, modern societies continue to be dependent upon technologies vulnerable to terrorist attack. "Political circumstances may change but these technological developments have permanently altered the environment."[5]

Furthermore, some of the political circumstances in the late 1980s promote the use of terrorism now and in the future. For one, there is the earlier experience itself for new groups to draw upon. Because of all the publicity, terrorist methods have become part of the repertoire of devices known to individuals and groups which come to their minds when they contemplate alternative means for manifesting their political views. Approximately the same observation applies to state sponsorship. Compared with conventional warfare, terrorism continues to be, within limits, a low-cost tool for the achievement of foreign policy goals.

If some of the old causes of terrorism have been overtaken by events, such as the end of the Vietnam war, new ones have arisen. Religious fundamentalism was not a major source of terrorism in the late 1960s, while it clearly is today. Ethnic separatism and/or nationalism was a major cause for the initial outbreak of terrorist activity, but it was confined to a comparative handful of groups. There are thousands of such ethnic groups around the world, several of which may provide likely causes for terrorist groups to champion. Also, the world abounds with multiethnic, multiracial societies, many of which are hardly models of social and political contentment. The restoration of democracy in a number of Latin American countries has not brought an end to the sorts of economic inequalities and injustices that prompted urban guerrillas to wage terrorist campaigns in the earlier years. And, more generally, the very openness of democratic societies seems to facilitate terrorist operations.

Projecting present trends into the future may not be the most effective means for forecasting the future. Nevertheless, there is some value in examining the direction events are taking at the present time.

There are data available concerning the characteristics of international terrorist events. One long-term trend that emerges from an examination of this information is the gradual geographic dispersion of terrorist activity. In the late 1960s these incidents occurred, on the average, in or affected the citizens of twenty-nine countries each year. During the early 1970s it grew to thirty-nine, and by the latter years of that decade the number rose to forty-three. By the mid-1980s (1985–1986), the average had reached eighty-one.[6] Thus, about half of the world's independent nation-states have been affected by terrorist events in recent years. In this connection, it is interesting to speculate about the consequences that the present Soviet policy of liberalization may have in the emergence of interethnic conflict in that nation and the potential reactions to it by members of the affected communities living abroad. Will such reactions come to encompass terrorist campaigns on behalf of the U.S.S.R.'s various Muslim groups, or could new terrorist activity come from Ukrainian and Baltic communities of émigrés living in the West?

There is some fluctuation in the year-to-year volume of international terrorist incidents (although the long-term trend is upward), but there is a clear pattern observable in the intensity of the attacks. At the beginning of the contemporary period terrorists tended to concentrate their attacks on property, public buildings, and other largely symbolic targets. Few people were killed. By the late 1970s and into the 1980s, however, the number of terrorist incidents in which fatalities occurred increased substantially as a proportion of such events. And within this general pattern, the average number of deaths incurred for each fatal attack had also increased. The most devastating of these events were the destruction of an Air India flight over the Atlantic in 1985, allegedly carried out by members of a Sikh separatist group (329 deaths); the suicide bombing of the Marine Corps barracks in Beirut in 1983 (241 deaths); and the fire bombing of a crowded movie theater in the Iranian city of Abadan in 1979 (430 deaths). There is some dispute over responsibility for this last incident. But it occurred in the midst of a religious campaign against what was perceived to be Western contamination of Iranian life.[7]

There are a number of proposed explanations to account for the increased destructiveness of terrorist attacks. One has it that the longer terrorism persists, the more dramatic any one event must be to attract the attention of the mass media. Over time audiences become less attentive to what have become near routine episodes. Another explanation suggests that the longer its perpetrators engage in terrorism, the less sensitive they become to the taking of human life. The political outlook of a group may make some difference in its willingness to kill. In Italy, the leftist revolutionaries were relatively precise in selecting their targets, while the neo-Fascists often were responsible for the anonymous bombings of public places, such as the August 1980 destruction of the railroad station in Bologna that caused the deaths of eighty-four vacation-bound passengers. The contention is that neo-Fascist and other right-wing groups have a fundamental contempt for human life which makes it easier for them to carry out attacks involving multiple fatalities.[8] A similar case can be made for terrorist groups of ethnic inspiration whose targets are members of some other religious, racial, or ethnic community they regard as less than fully human.

If this political explanation makes sense, it is logical to believe that the more terrorist activity in the future is dominated by rightist or ethnic-separatist organizations, the more likely their attacks will involve the sort of intercommunal atrocities and massacres presently under way in Sri Lanka.

The issue of fatalities is related to the question of targets. As the more obvious targets—embassies, airports, corporate headquarters, leading officials—become better protected, the less inhibited terrorist groups face a number of possibilities. First, they may use standoff weapons such as mortars and hand-held rocket launchers to defeat the types of physical barriers that now protect public buildings. Second, since it is impossible to protect everything and everybody, they may increasingly turn their attention to members of the general public. In London and Paris, department stores, particularly during peak shopping hours, have proved to be especially inviting targets.

There is also the possibility of terrorist groups making use of weapons of mass destruction as a way to defeat the better protected targets and cause widespread panic among the general public. Among the various devices that terrorists might employ to threaten or kill large numbers of people, none has caused greater concern than nuclear weapons. This possibility has served to inspire several works of fiction, including novels and films. How likely is it that terrorists will enter the nuclear age?

In a sense they already have, although a bit more slowly than claimed by the authors of the fictional accounts. The members of the Italian Red Brigades unit that kidnapped General Dozier questioned him about the location of American nuclear weapons in Europe.[9] And in an interview he granted to a French reporter, the West German terrorist Bommi Baumann observed that "we live in the age of the nuclear bomb and power stations" and that the use of these devices was "in the spirit of the times...also in the spirit of the group."[10]

In some cases the terrorists have done more than simply raise questions and engage in speculation. In Spain, the ETA has staged several attacks on nuclear power plants while they were under construction in the Basque region. In 1984 the Communist Combatant Cells in Belgium bombed the offices of a business firm that builds transporters for the Pershing II missiles.[11] For the most part these incidents, and others like them, seem to represent attempts by terrorists to win support among followers of such popular causes as environmental protection and opposition to the deployment of American intermediate-range nuclear missiles in Europe. They are not the types of events that have aroused the greatest concern. The latter involve not terrorist efforts to prevent the deployment of nuclear missiles or the use of nuclear-powered generators, but the use of such mechanisms to threaten mass destruction.

There are several ways by which terrorists could "go nuclear." Among the most obvious, they could steal a bomb or build one themselves through the theft of the materials necessary for its construction. They could sabotage a nuclear generating plant or take control of such a facility and threaten a nuclear accident unless their demands were met.[12]

Most discussions concerning these possibilities have focused on their technical feasibility and political likelihood. So far as the former is concerned, the superpowers alone now possess over 50,000 nuclear weapons. Also, there are presently more than 260 civilian nuclear power plants located around the world. By the year 2000 about eighty to ninety metric tons of plutonium will be discharged each year just by those installations used in the Western world.[13] In addition, nuclear weapons and material must be stored and fabricated at different locations and transported by special means, sometimes over long distances. In other words, the chain is exceedingly long with many links in it for terrorists to attack.

Some of the links, though, are stronger than others. For example, most nuclear weapons are equipped with safety devices, for example, permissive action links (PALs), that prevent their detonation by unauthorized individuals. Terrorists may steal nuclear material, but do they have the ability to make a bomb with it without the assistance of physicists and engineers? Terrorists are rarely trained in these sciences. Those responsible for the protection of nuclear facilities are not unaware of the dangers involved, and such organizations as the International Atomic Energy Agency (IAEA) and various national bodies have taken steps to reduce the dangers by providing better monitoring and improved security. However, assuming that the current arrangements are not foolproof or failsafe and that it is possible for terrorists to acquire the means, will they choose to do so?

Terrorist groups possessing the greatest capacity to make use of the nuclear option are ones that receive support from states. Unlike members of the group, states are immovable, with names and permanent addresses. If states were to aid their "clients" in this area, they would then become vulnerable to retaliation by other governments whose citizens were threatened by the blackmail. For this reason, the patrons have a strong incentive—their own destruction—to avoid providing this type of assistance. But there are also constraints working against the use of nuclear means by groups that lack state sponsors. The short-term advantage a group might gain has to be balanced against the long-term effects. Even the constitutional democracies, if they were confronted by such a terrorist threat, would likely use all the coercive means at their disposal to bring an end to whichever group caused the threat. Furthermore, by using or threatening to use nuclear weapons or disperse nuclear material in the atmosphere, terrorist groups are not likely to win many friends for whatever cause on behalf of which the action was undertaken. To use a corporate, nonterrorism-related analogy, the Bhopal chemical disaster in

India has not improved Union Carbide's corporate image around the world. Unfortunately, all this is mere speculation, and given sufficient sense of desperation the leaders of terrorist groups might not apply the same reasoning employed here.

On the other hand, terrorists have not as yet chosen to take advantage of other and easier means of mass destruction, ones that are more readily available to them than nuclear ones. Many chemical or biological agents that can be used to poison the atmosphere and contaminate the water supply are easier to make or steal than nuclear weapons. And the Iran-Iraq war has shown that at least one state has been willing to use poison gas against civilians as well as enemy forces. There have been cases when poison has been used, though on a highly selective basis and for a limited purpose. A Palestinian group managed to inject mercury into or-anges shipped from Israel to Western Europe as a way of harming the former's export industry. And members of a religious cult, in their effort to take over an Oregon township, injected bacteria into a town's water supply to prevent voters from going to the polls. Whether or not these developments will culminate in a sustained terrorist campaign remains to be seen. It seems reasonable to believe, though, that before terrorists go nuclear they will experiment with this less earth-shaking type of option.

Finally, whatever means are used, it seems unlikely that terrorism will come to a complete stop in the foreseeable future. There are few societ-ies in the world that have been successful in eliminating violent crimes, ones committed for purely private motives. Recent defeats suffered by the Mafia in Sicily and the United States have been matched by victories achieved by criminal gangs from Colombia and elsewhere. Political ter-rorism may be viewed in a similar light. In a world of conflicting political objectives, it may be inevitable. The tasks are to prevent its escalation and limit its effects.

KEY TERMS

backlash	International Atomic Energy
burnout	Agency (IAEA)
disillusionment	permissive action links (PALs)
	strategic shift

NOTES

1 For a summary, see Brian Jenkins, *Future Trends in International Terrorism* (Santa Monica, Ca.: The Rand Corporation, 1985), pp. 1–2.
2 Ariel Merari, "Soviet Attitudes toward Middle Eastern Terrorism," in Steven Spiegel, Mark Heller, and Jacob Goldberg (eds.), *The Soviet-American Com-*

petition in the Middle East (Lexington, Mass.: D. C. Heath and Company, 1988), pp. 198–199.

3 Martha Crenshaw, "How Terrorism Ends" (a paper presented at the 1987 annual meeting of the American Political Science Association, Chicago, September 1987); Jeffrey Ross and Tedd Gurr, "Why Terrorism Subsides: A Comparative Study of Trends and Groups in Terrorism in Canada and the United States" (a paper presented at the 1987 annual meeting of the American Political Science Association, Chicago, September 1987).

4 "The World's Wars," *The Economist* (March 12–18, 1988), p. 19.

5 Brian Jenkins, *The Future Course of International Terrorism* (Santa Monica, Ca.: The Rand Corporation, 1985), p. 2.

6 Jenkins, *Future Trends in International Terrorism*, op. cit., p. 9; *Patterns of Global Terrorism: 1986* (Washington, D.C.: U.S. Department of State, 1988), p. 2.

7 Gary Sick, *All Fall Down* (New York: Random House, 1985), p. 47.

8 On the question of rightist groups, see Konrad Kellen, "The Potential for Nuclear Terrorism: A Discussion," in Paul Leventhal and Yonah Alexander (eds.), *Preventing Nuclear Terrorism* (Lexington, Mass.: D. C. Heath and Company, 1987), pp. 119–120.

9 Thomas Davies, "What Nuclear Weapons Means and Targets Might Terrorists Find Attractive?" in Paul Leventhal and Yonah Alexander (eds.), *Nuclear Terrorism: Defining the Threat* (Washington, D.C.: Pergamon-Brassey's, 1986), p. 57.

10 Quoted in Kellen, op. cit., p. 111.

11 Ibid., pp. 131–132.

12 See, for example, International Task Force on the Prevention of Nuclear Terrorism, "The Task Force Report," in Leventhal and Alexander (eds.), *Preventing Nuclear Terrorism*, op. cit., p. 7; see also Louis Rene Beres, *Terrorism and Global Security* (Boulder, Col.: Westview Press, 1979), pp. 15–29.

13 David Albright, "World Inventories of Plutonium," in Leventhal and Alexander (eds.), *Nuclear Terrorism: Defining the Threat,* op. cit., p. 159.

GLOSSARY

Abbas, Abu Left-wing Palestinian and leader of the Palestine Liberation Front (PLF), accused by the U.S. government of planning the *Achille Lauro* hijacking in October 1985.

Action Front of National Socialists Extreme right-wing neo-Nazi terrorist organization based in West Germany.

adaptation The responses and strategies a hostage may make or use to reduce stress and maximize chances of survival.

African National Congress (ANC) The most important of the black South African organizations opposing the South African government; it has become increasingly militant and revolutionary.

Agca, Mehmet Ali Right-wing Turkish gunman and convicted murderer who tried to assassinate Pope John Paul II in St. Peter's Square in Rome on May 13, 1981. Agca claimed that he was a member of a right-wing Turkish terror group called the Grey Wolves. He later claimed he had been working on behalf of the Bulgarian Secret Service and the KGB. Agca was sentenced to life in prison.

Al Dawa (the Call) An organization intent on establishing a political order in Iraq in alignment with the Iranian fundamentalists. Now operating from exile in Iran, it has staged terrorist operations against Iraqi targets located in various Middle Eastern and Western European nations.

Amal The militia of the minority Shiite Muslims of Lebanon led by Nabih Berri. It is drawn from the poorest part of Lebanon's Muslim population.

anarchism A political doctrine which maintains that all government authority is undesirable. Anarchists have advocated the abolition of governments by violent means, if necessary.

Angry Brigade British left-wing anarchist-terrorist group active during the early 1970s.

Apostolic Anti-Communist Alliance Right-wing terrorist group located in Spain that emerged as a reaction to threats of left-wing groups to bring a Marxist-Leninist regime to power.

April 19 Movement (M19) *See* Armed Revolutionary Forces of Colombia (FARC).

Arab and Jew: Wounded Spirits in a Promised Land David Shipler's Pulitzer prize–winning book dealing with the problems of social interactions between these two groups of people.

Arafat, Yasser Chairman of the Palestine Liberation Organization since 1969 and head of the Fatah since the early 1960s; he has become one of the most important leaders of the Arab world.

Argentina Anticommunist Alliance (AAA) Extreme right-wing terrorist organization founded in 1974 with some official support; it included police officers and soldiers in its ranks and killed anyone suspected of supporting left-wing groups.

Armed Forces of National Liberation (FALN) Far-left terrorist group, an organization of American-based Puerto Rican separatists, which emerged in 1974.

Armed Revolutionary Forces of Colombia (FARC) An organization which, along with the April 19 Movement (M19) and the National Liberation Army (FLN), has attempted to establish liberated zones in the countryside with terrorist activities in Bogotá, Colombia, and other cities.

Aryan Brotherhood Extreme right-wing terrorist group which practices white supremacist violence in the United States and Canada.

Aryan Nations movement A right-wing American umbrella organization threatening white supremacist violence that established links with most of the right-wing extremist groups in Canada and the United States.

Assassins A sect from the Shiite tradition which waged a terrorist campaign at the purification of Islam for almost two centuries (1090–1275 A.D.).

Ayatollah Khomeini Spiritual and political leader of the Shiite nation of Iran.

backlash A strong adverse reaction to terrorist atrocities by the groups the terrorists hope to lead.

Basques A people of unknown origin inhabiting the western Pyrenees region in France and Spain who have fought throughout their history to establish an independent country.

Beirutization The division of a city into numerous armed militant groups each of which has total control over its individual area.

Black Liberation Army A small nationalistic terrorist organization, based on the east coast of the United States, that was formed in the 1970s and reemerged in the early 1980s; it indiscriminately attacked uniformed police officers.

Black Panther Party (BPP) (the Black Panthers) Highly militant U.S. black-power organization founded in 1966 by Huey Newton and Bobby Seale. They hoped to politicize the violence which was then erupting in the black ghettos of many American cities.

Black September Palestinian terrorist organization named after the bloody events in Jordan in September 1970 when King Hussein of Jordan turned his army against the Palestinian organizations, driving them into exile.

Brigate Rosse (the Red Brigades) Italian left-wing terrorist organization and one of the largest of the European left-wing groups which began in the late 1960s.

burnout A condition whereby a terrorist group may simply disintegrate for reasons that are largely internal to the organization.

Carter, Jimmy U.S. president whose administration was severely shaken stemming from its unsuccessful efforts to win the release of American captives in the U.S. embassey in Teheran, Iran.

Charles Martell Club Extreme neo-Nazi French terrorist group.

Chiaie delle Stefano Leader of an Italian neo-Fascist terrorist group who refers to his members as an "elite of heroes."

Christian Patriots' Defense League Extreme right-wing group which preaches white supremacist violence in the United States and Canada.

Communist Hunting Command (CCC) Extreme right-wing terrorist group in Brazil aimed at all Brazilian leftists.

Communist Patriotic Fund Left-wing terrorist group operating in Chile that attempted the assassination of General Augusto Pinochet in 1986.

contagion effect The belief that the reporting of terrorist acts arouses individuals or groups in the audience to commit similar deeds by virtue of observation of the initial act or acts.

Continuous Struggle (LC) Italian New Left movement that believed in revolution through mass mobilization and political struggle.

conventional warfare Combat governed, ideally, by a specific code of conduct that prohibits the killing of innocent civilians or the taking of hostages.

coping The conscious, often innovative strategies people devise in order to adjust to a difficult situation, such as being held hostage.

Council of Europe A regional organization that encourages political, economic, and social cooperation and seeks to develop a sense of European unity among its members.

counterterrorism Active defense against terrorism which involves intelligence gathering, police work, and military force.

Covenant, Sword and the Arm of the Lord Extreme right-wing terrorist group which preaches white supremacist violence in the U.S. and Canada.

creative elaboration The use of fantasy to deal with a difficult situation.

Curcio, Renato The founding member and one-time leader of the Red Brigades, the Italian left-wing terrorist group. One of the most dangerous of the European terrorist organizers, he is now serving a life sentence in an Italian jail.

death squads Right-wing terrorist groups formed in nations where violent leftist insurgencies have been mounted.

Decline of the West A historical account by German writer Oswald Spengler on why the influence and power of the Western world has diminished. Utilized by Nazis and neo-Nazis in justification of their philosophy.

defense mechanisms The largely unconscious or almost automatic adjustments the individual makes to a stressful, anxiety-producing situation.

Delta Force Special United States Army unit under the special operations forces assigned to counterterrorism activities.

denial A refusal to believe that a given event is actually taking place.

diffuse terrorism Acts of violence and terrorism committed by members of groups who seek to lead normal lives most of the time.

Direct Action (AD) The extreme left-wing terrorist group thought to be a major participant in the wave of attacks in Paris in the winter of 1981–1982 and spring of 1982.

disillusionment The condition whereby members of a terrorist group become disenchanted with the organization for various reasons.

Division for General Investigations and Special Operations (DIGOS) Unit formed by the National Police of Italy to combat terrorist groups and organized crime.

dolce vita The "good life" that members of certain terrorist groups have become engaged in, a life that had disgusted them as exhibited in bourgeois society.

domestic terrorism Terrorist campaigns intended to bring about a fundamental change in the distribution of wealth, power, and status in society.

enosis A goal of many Greeks and Greek Cypriots to forge a union of the island of Cyprus with the nation of Greece.

EOKA (Ethniki Organosis Kyprion Agoniston) Greek nationalist organization founded in 1954 that employed terrorism in a successful attempt to dislodge the British from Greece.

Erikson, Erik Psychologist who expounded the human development theories to explain why some young adults have become terrorists.

European Community (EC) A regional organization, the governing body of the European Economic Community (EEC), a group of nations which has developed a common market among its members.

European National Fascists (FNE) Violently anti-Semitic neo-Nazi French terrorist group.

Euzkadi Ta Askatasuna (ETA) A guerrilla and terrorist organization of the Basques of northern Spain and southern France attempting to establish an independent Basque homeland.

"extradite or prosecute" By international law, states are obligated either to extradite individuals accused of certain terrorist acts to the nation in which they were committed or to prosecute the offenders themselves.

Fatah The largest single component of the Palestine Liberation Organization.

Fatah Revolutionary Council (FRC) The Syrian-backed umbrella organization of the terrorist network run by Abu Nidal.

Federal Aviation Administration (FAA) Government agency responsible for involvement with antiskyjacking activities in the United States.

Federal Bureau of Investigation (FBI) Government body responsible for countering domestic terrorism in the United States.

Fighters against Jewish Occupation Extreme neo-Nazi French terrorist group.

Fighting Communist Cells (CCC) Left-wing terrorist group based in Belgium which is working to eliminate the American military and economic presence from the European continent.

Fighting Popular Forces Left-wing terrorist group fighting in Portugal (in conjunction with the CCC in Belgium) to eliminate the American presence from the European continent.

French National Liberation Front   Extreme neo-Nazi French terrorist group.

Front du Liberation de Quebec (FLQ)   Militant, mainly left-wing French-Canadian group that wants to separate Quebec from the rest of English-speaking Canada.

Front Line   An Italian left-wing terrorist group that emerged in 1976; it was particularly active in Milan, Turin, and Naples.

Gandhi, Indira   Former prime minister of India, she was assassinated by Sikh members of her bodyguard in October 1984 in revenge for the Indian Army's attack on the Golden Temple of Amritsar in June 1984.

Gemayel, Bashir   Christian militia leader and president-elect of Lebanon who was killed by a car bomb in September 1982 before he could take office. Gemayel's death inflamed the Christian forces in the country and led directly to the Sabra and Shatilla massacres of October 1982.

German Red Cells   Left-wing terrorist organization composed of "after-hours" terrorists who commit occasional acts of violence while leading normal lives most of the time.

Ghaddafi, Muammar   President of Libya since 1969, and widely regarded in the West and particularly in the United States as one of the main instigators and supporters of international terrorism.

Grenschutz Gruppe 9 (GSG 9)   West Germany's antiterrorist regiment.

Grey Wolves   Neo-fascist Turkish terrorist group active in Turkey and Western Europe in the 1970s.

guerrilla warfare   Irregular warfare fought by small bands against an invading army or in rebellion against an established government.

Guevara, Ernesto "Che"   Latin American guerrilla leader and revolutionary theorist who helped Fidel Castro to power in Cuba.

Hanafi Muslim sect   A black nationalist group that split off from the Nation of Islam organization, which had murdered some of their leaders and family members. Responsible for the takeover of three buildings in Washington, D.C., in March 1977.

hijacking   The taking over of public service vehicles for political reasons.

Hizbollah (Party of God)   A militant Shiite Muslim political and religious sect which utilizes terrorist operations through its military.

Holy War Organization   Extreme Muslim fundamentalist group in Egypt, a splinter group of the Muslim Brotherhood. It assassinated President Anwar Sadat while he was reviewing a military parade in Cairo.

homofighter   Member of a terrorist group whose violence is directed at its own compatriots.

hostage taking   An act in which the victim is held at the place he or she was at the time the captors took control of the situation.

In Re Castioni (1890)   Case in which the British court ruled that to constitute a political offense the act in question had to occur during a general political revolt and to have been related to this uprising.

In Re Meunier (1894)   Case in which the British court ruled that anarchists who committed isolated acts of politically motivated violence were not to be covered by the political exclusion rule.

insurgent terrorism (terrorism from below)   Acts of terror perpetrated by individuals and/or groups wishing to usurp and replace the authority of the government.

intellectualization Stress-reducing mechanism which operates by draining a situation of its emotional content and making it more a puzzle to be solved or a problem whose resolution warrants speculation.

International Atomic Energy Agency (IAEA) An agency of the United Nations established in 1957 to foster cooperation among nations developing atomic energy for peaceful purposes.

International Civil Aviation Organization (ICAO) A specialized agency of the United Nations established in 1947 to develop and to regulate international air transportation.

International Maritime Organization (IMO) Organization whose member governments are involved in promoting the safety of international merchant shipping.

international terrorism Terrorism involving citizens or territory of more than one country.

Interpol International police agency headquartered in France.

Irgun A Jewish guerrilla and terrorist unit established in the 1930s to protect Jewish settlers in Palestine against Arab attacks; it waged a terror campaign against the British in the later years of World War II.

Iron Guard A fascist terrorist group which developed in Romania in the 1920s and which emerged into one of the most feared organizations in Eastern Europe.

Islamic Jihad (Islamic Holy War) Shadowy pro-Iranian Lebanese fundamentalist group that became known when it accepted responsibility for the attacks in October 1983 on the American Marine and French Army headquarters in Beirut.

Islamic Liberation Extreme Muslim fundamentalist group in Egypt which used terrorism to topple the government of Sadat; a splinter group of the Muslim Brotherhood.

Islamic Tendency Movement (MII) Extreme Muslim fundamentalist group in Tunisia which has employed terrorism in an attempt to topple the existing regime.

just-cause doctrine The belief that wars can be fought for just reasons as well as for unjust reasons.

justice-in-war concept Concept referring to the way wars are conducted—how the weapons or implements are used and what treatment is given participants and nonparticipants in the conflict.

kidnapping An act in which a person or persons are forcefully removed from one setting and taken to another, usually secret location.

kneecapping The shooting of kneecaps, a tactic utilized by the Red Brigades and the Provisional Irish Republican Army to intimidate opponents and informers.

Kommisar An elaborate computer-based data file developed by West Germany which contains an enormous volume of information on terrorists and terrorist groups.

Ku Klux Klan A right-wing American white supremacist organization dedicated to defending white America against blacks and what it perceives as inferior races; it has a long history of violence through terrorist activity.

left-wing terrorism Terrorist activities used by groups in an attempt to overthrow a society they see as unjust and repressive.

Liberation Tigers of Tamil Eelam (the Tamil Tigers) The largest and most violent of the Tamil (Hindu) guerrilla-terrorist groups fighting for an independent Tamil state at the northern end of the overwhelmingly Buddhist island of Sri Lanka.

low-intensity conflict Conflict arising from the belief that terrorism should be opposed by military units prepared to carry out special operations and by intelligence agencies skilled in the use of covert measures.

Marighella, Carlos Brazilian terrorist, revolutionary theorist, and author of the terrorist handbook *Minimanual of the Urban Guerrilla*.

Matthers, Robert Jay The founder, in 1983 at age 31, of the American neo-Nazi, white supremacist organization called the Order; he was later killed in a shootout with the police in December 1984 in the state of Washington.

Mau Mau African terrorist organization which operated in Kenya against the British colonial regime in the struggle for independence between 1953 and 1960.

Meinhof, Ulrike West German terrorist leader and one of the founding members of the Baader-Meinhof gang. After a short but well-known career as a terrorist leader, Meinhof hanged herself in her cell in a German top-security prison in 1976.

Military Sports Group Hoffman Extreme right-wing neo-Nazi terrorist organization based in West Germany.

Minimanual of the Urban Guerrilla A notorious guerrilla-terrorist handbook written in the late 1960s by Carlos Marighella. It was an influential document among Latin American and West European terrorist groups in the early 1970s.

minimum force necessary Terrorist tactic which calls for violence no more brutal than needed to attract attention under the assumption that acts considered too savage may damage popular support.

Montoneros Left-wing Argentine terrorist organization active between 1970 and 1976. It evolved from the left wing of the Perónist movement.

Moro, Aldo Italian politician, president of the Christian Democratic party, and six times prime minister of Italy who was kidnapped and then killed by members of the Brigate Rosse in 1978.

Movement of October 8 (MR-8) A left-wing terrorist organization operating in Brazil in the late 1960s and early 1970s.

Mozambique National Resistance A nationalist resistance movement with support from South Africa, it has subsequently carried out a number of terrorist attacks against helpless civilians.

Muslim Brotherhood Fundamentalist Islamic organization with a long tradition of political and sectarian violence, it remains today a potent ideological and religious force in the Islamic world.

National Democratic party (NPD) Extreme right-wing political party in West Germany made up of a number of terrorist groups such as Viking Youth, Military Sports Group Hoffman, and Action Front of National Socialists.

National Front (FN) Along with the National Vanguard (AN) and New Order (ON), an Italian neo-Fascist terrorist group operating during the 1970s in the hope of bringing about the collapse of Italian democracy by means of a coup d'état.

National Front party of Jean Marie Le Pen A major force on the French political scene, it is an extreme right-wing party that came into some strength after a wave of violence perpetrated by small neo-Nazi French terrorist groups.

National Gendarmerie Intervention Team (GIGN) Unit formed by the national police of France to combat terrorist groups and organized crime.

National Liberation Action (ALN) Founded by Carlos Marighella in 1968, one of several guerrilla groups to pursue an armed struggle against the Brazilian military government.

National Liberation Army (FLN) *See* Armed Revolutionary Forces of Colombia (FARC).

National Liberation Front A nationalist group in the 1950s which carried out indiscriminate attacks against the French population in Algeria for the purpose of achieving independence from France.

National Vanguard (AN) Right-wing terrorist group located in Italy that has emerged as a reaction to the threat by left-wing groups to bring Marxist-Leninist regimes to power.

nationalist-separatist terrorism Acts of terror utilized by groups to wrest an independent homeland from a larger power.

NATO (North Atlantic Treaty Organization) The major defense alliance of the Western powers.

New Order *See* National Front (FN).

Nidal, Abu A major Palestinian terrorist organizer thought to be behind many important terrorist incidents; he is also a dedicated enemy of PLO chairman Yasser Arafat.

Nuclei of Armed Proletarians (NAP) Far-left terrorist group founded in the 1970s, confined largely to Naples and Rome.

Nuclei of Armed Revolutionaries Right-wing terrorist group located in Italy that has emerged as a reaction to the threat by left-wing groups to bring Marxist-Leninist regimes to power.

Odessa Extreme neo-Nazi French terrorist group.

Okamoto, Kozo One of the members of the Japanese United Red Army who machine-gunned two dozen Puerto Rican pilgrims at the Tel Aviv Airport in 1972.

Order, the American neo-Nazi white supremacist organization founded in 1983; it has evolved into a paramilitary group with sophisticated weapons and has staged a number of armed robberies.

Palestine Liberation Organization (PLO) The main political and diplomatic vehicle of the Palestinian cause, and effectively the government-in-exile of the Palestinian people.

Palme, Olof Socialist prime minister of Sweden and world statesman who was shot dead in a Stockholm street in 1986. The assassin was never found.

Partisan Action Groups (GAP) Far-left terrorist group founded in the 1970s in Italy.

Patriotic Union A leftist political party in Colombia which has had over 450 members killed by death squads since 1986.

People's Revolutionary Army (ERP) A Marxist-Leninist terrorist group, based in Argentina, dedicated to the overthrow of the capitalist system in Argentina and other South American countries.

People's Will, the   The first terrorist organization in Russia, it launched a terror campaign against czarist officials in 1878, culminating in the assassination of Alexander II in 1881.

permissive action links (PALs)   The various types of safety devices on nuclear weapons that prevent their detonation by unauthorized individuals.

piracy   Illegal act or acts of violence, detention, or depredation against a ship for private ends.

poisoned pawn   A captured terrorist held in prison serving as an invitation to additional attacks, ones committed by groups out to liberate their imprisoned comrades in exchange for new captives.

Popular Democratic Front for the Liberation of Palestine (PDFLP)   A factional offspring of the PFLP. A militant left-wing terrorist group.

Popular Front for the Liberation of Palestine (PFLP)   Led by George Habash, one of the most militant of the Palestinian groups associated with the Palestine Liberation Organization.

Popular Front for the Liberation of Palestine–General Command (PFLP-GC)   An offshoot of the PFLP which emerged in October 1968, shortly after the PFLP had been formed.

Popular Revolutionary Vanguard (VPR)   A left-wing terrorist organization operating against Brazil in the late 1960s and headed by Carlos Lamarca.

Posse Comitatus   Extreme right-wing terrorist group which preaches white supremacist violence in North America.

Princip, Gavrilo   A Serbian student who assassinated Archduke Ferdinand, which led to the outbreak of World War I. He was a member of an illegal nationalist organization called Young Bosnia that wanted to separate Bosnia-Herzegovina from the Austro-Hungarian Empire.

propaganda by deed   A belief advocated by some anarchists that terrorism should be utilized in order to send a message.

Provisional Irish Republican Army (PIRA)   Terrorist organization trying to bring about an end to British rule in Northern Ireland. Claiming affiliation with the Roman Catholic minority, the IRA's provisional wing has carried out bombings and political murders throughout Great Britain.

Purple Rose   Extreme right-wing terrorist group located in Guatemala which has executed thousands of people suspected of leftist sympathies.

reactionary terrorism   Use of terrorism in an effort not to change the social or political status quo but to preserve it.

Reagan, Ronald   American president whose administration was severely shaken by its unsuccessful efforts to win the release of American captives in Lebanon by providing weapons to the revolutionary Iranian regime.

Red Army Faction   *See* Rote Armee Fraktion.

Red Brigades   *See* Brigate Rosse.

Reign of Terror   A period during the French Revolution in which suspected opponents of the revolution were hunted down and executed.

repentants   In Italy, imprisoned members of the terrorist groups willing to provide authorities with information and testimony who have been rewarded by reduced sentences or complete freedom and a new identity.

Revolutionary Catechism   Written in 1869 by Serge Nechayev, it was an attempt to create a secret society among young Russian university students that would spark the revolution by assassinating all those who supported the czarist regime.

Revolutionary Cells (RZ) Left-wing West German terror group which was formed in the 1970s and which specialized in attacking American multinational companies.

Revolutionary Left (Dev Sol) Extreme militant left-wing terrorist organization in Turkey.

Revolutionary Road (Dev Yol) Extreme militant left-wing terrorist organization in Turkey.

revolutionary terrorism Terrorist campaigns intended to bring about a fundamental change in the distribution of wealth, power, and status in society.

right-wing terrorism Terrorist activities launched by groups in defense of an established order or in reaction to the success of left-wing groups.

Rote Armee Fraktion (Red Army Faction) Left-wing German terrorist organization regarded as the most violent and effective of the West German terrorist groups. Evolved from the Baader-Meinhof Gang founded in 1967.

Sabra and Shatilla massacres Occurring in Beirut (September 16–18, 1982), the massacre of Palestinian and other Arab men, women, and children in two refugee camps in Beirut by the Lebanese Christian militia in revenge for the assassination of president-elect Bashir Gemayel.

Sadat, Anwar President of Egypt who was assassinated by fundamentalist Muslims in October 1981 while taking the salute at a military parade in Cairo.

Sanchez, Illich Ramirez (Carlos the Jackal) Venezuelan-born terrorist organizer responsible for numerous major terrorist incidents around the globe; he is believed to have contacts with many of the Arab and European terrorist groups around the world. Some commentators believe that he is, in fact, an officer of the Soviet KGB.

SEAL Team 6 United States Navy special team trained for counterterrorism.

SEALs United States Navy special sea-air-land troops intended for special warfare missions.

Second of June Movement Left-wing West German terrorist group closely aligned with the Red Army Faction.

Secret Anti-Communist Army Extreme right-wing terrorist group located in Guatemala which has executed thousands of people suspected of leftist sympathies.

Shining Path (Sendero Luminoso) Maoist guerrillas and terrorists who have been waging war against the government of Peru since 1980.

social reinsertion A policy undertaken by the Spanish government to allow former members of terrorist groups to participate in democratic politics.

Socialist Revolutionaries Political party in czarist Russia which assassinated a number of czarist officials between 1902 and 1908 in an attempt to bring down the czarist regime.

Spear of the Nation Military branch of the African National Congress (ANC).

Special Air Services (SAS) The British government's antiterrorist regiment.

Special Operations Forces (SOF) United States military units prepared for use in low-intensity conflicts likely to occur in the Third World.

Special Weapons and Tactics (SWAT) squads Special units set up by the FBI to combat domestic crime and terrorism in the United States.

state-sponsored terrorism Support of quasi-independent terrorist groups by sympathetic governments.

state terrorism (terrorism from above) Acts of terror perpetrated by governments using their own military or police forces.

Stockholm syndrome Refers to the propensity of some victims to develop friendly feelings toward or even, in some cases, an identification with their captors.

strategic shift A process in which a terrorist group may decide to move away from the use of terrorism and toward other means for achieving their objectives.

Summit Seven Great Britain, France, Canada, Japan, Italy, West Germany, and the United States—democracies with the strongest economies whose leaders meet on an annual basis.

supergrasses In Britain, imprisoned members of terrorist groups who are willing to provide the authorities with information and testimony and who have been rewarded by reduced sentences or complete freedom and a new identity.

Symbionese Liberation Army (SLA) Left-wing California-based terrorist group active during the early 1970s. The kidnapping of Patricia Hearst eventually led to their destruction after a spectacular shootout with police.

Task Force 160 (the Night Stalkers) Specially trained United States helicopter pilots dealing with counterterrorism tasks.

terrorism A politically motivated crime intended to modify the reaction of an audience.

Third Position Right-wing terrorist group located in Italy that has emerged as a reaction to the threat of left-wing groups to bring Marxist-Leninist regimes to power.

TREVI A group made up of EC members and other interested nations (Switzerland, Israel) to study terrorism, radicalism, and violence internationally.

Tupamaro Hunting Command Extreme right-wing terrorist unit formed in Uruguay to help repress revolutionary activity.

Tupamaros Left-wing revolutionary terror group founded in 1965 in Uruguay, and suppressed by the Uruguayan security forces in the early 1970s.

Turkish People's Liberation Army (IPLA) Extreme militant left-wing terrorist organization founded in 1968.

Turkish People's Liberation Front (TPLF) Extreme militant left-wing terrorist organization in Turkey.

Turner Diaries, The Written by William Pierce, an American neo-Nazi activist, it describes the efforts of a small band of patriots to overthrow the Jewish-controlled federal government and rescue the United States from racial contamination.

Ulster Defense Association (UDA) The largest and most powerful of the many Protestant paramilitary groups which have been operating in Northern Ireland since the troubles began.

United Red Army of Japan (Japanese Red Army) Small, brutal, and especially fanatical left-wing Japanese group very active in the early 1970s.

Ustasha A right-wing Croatian independence movement which acquired a reputation for extreme ruthlessness and terrorist activities. Its aim is an independent state of Croatia to be carved out of Yugoslavia.

Viet Cong   The Communist-led guerrillas of South Vietnam who were active between 1956 and 1975.

Viet Minh   Communist-led coalition made up of Vietnamese nationalist groups which employed terrorism and guerrilla warfare in driving the French colonial regime out of Indochina.

Viking Group   Extreme right-wing neo-Nazi terrorist organization based in West Germany.

Weather Underground   Left-wing American terrorist group which emerged in the late 1960s out of the Students for a Democratic Society (SDS).

White Hand   Extreme right-wing terrorist group located in Guatemala which has executed thousands of people suspected of leftist sympathies.

"white terror"   *See* right-wing terrorism.

Worker Collective Autonomy   Italian left-wing organization composed of "after-hours" terrorists who commit occasional acts of violence while leading normal lives most of the time.

Worker Power (POTOP)   Italian New Left movement that believed in revolution through mass mobilization and political struggle.

Wrath of God, the   A special military unit established by Israel in the aftermath of the Munich massacre, it proceeds to wage a campaign of assassination against PLO figures in Western Europe and Lebanon.

xenofighter   Member of a terrorist group whose violence is directed at a foreign target.

Zealots   Extreme terrorist group instrumental in provoking the Jewish revolt against Rome. Conducted terrorist attacks against moderate Jews, Greeks, and their Roman rulers.

Zionist Occupation Government (ZOG)   Name given to the ruling order in America that is believed by some extreme right-wing terrorist groups to be totally controlled by Jews.

BIBLIOGRAPHY

Adams, James, *Secret Armies*. New York: Atlantic Monthly Press, 1987.
———, *The Financing of Terror*. New York: Simon and Schuster, 1986.
Adams, Thomas, "Organizing for Counterterrorism," *Syracuse Scholar*, 8:1 (1987), pp. 91–106.
Alexander, Yonah, and John Gleason (eds.), *Behavioral and Quantitative Perspectives on Terrorism*. New York: Pergamon Press, 1981; *Legislative Responses to Terrorism*. Boston: Martin Nijhoff Publishers, 1986.
——— and Kenneth Myers (eds.), *Terrorism in Europe*. London: Croom Helm, 1982.
——— and Seymour Finger (eds.), *Terrorism: Interdisciplinary Perspectives*. New York: John Jay Press, 1977.
———, Marjorie Browne, and Allan Nanes (eds.), *Control of Terrorism: International Documents*. New York: Crane Russak, 1979.
Amnesty International, *Torture in the Eighties*. London: Amnesty International Publications, 1984.
Aron, Raymond, *The Opium of the Intellectuals*. New York: W. W. Norton & Company, Inc., 1957.
Arthur, Paul, *Government and Politics in Northern Ireland*. 2d ed. Essex: Longman Group, 1984.
Barnes, Samuel, and Max Kaase, *Political Action*. Beverly Hills, Ca.: Sage Publications, 1979.
Barnet, Richard, and Ronald Muller, *Global Reach: The Power of the Multinational Corporations*. New York: Simon and Schuster, 1974.
Becker, Jillian, *Hitler's Children*. Philadelphia: J. B. Lippincott Company, 1977.
———, *The PLO*. New York: St. Martin's Press, 1984.

Bell, J. Bowyer, *A Time of Terror*. New York: Basic Books, 1978.

———, *Terror Out of Zion*. New York: Avon Books, 1977.

Beres, Louis Rene, *Terrorism and Global Security*. Boulder, Col.: Westview Press, 1979.

Billington, James H., *Fire in the Minds of Men*. New York: Basic Books, 1980.

Blackmer, Donald, and Sidney Tarrow (eds.), *Communism in Italy and France*. Princeton: Princeton University Press, 1975.

Boer, Connie, "The Polls: Terrorism and Hijacking," *Public Opinion Quarterly*, 43 (1979), p. 412.

Bonner, Raymond, "Peru's War," *The New Yorker* (Jan. 4, 1988), pp. 31–58.

Borg, Parker, *International Terrorism: Breaking the Cycle of Violence*. Occasional Paper No. 8. Washington, D.C.: Center for the Study of Foreign Affairs, 1987.

Briggs, Herbert (ed.), *The Law of Nations*. 2d ed. New York: Appleton-Century-Crofts, 1952.

Brown, Carl, "The Middle East: Patterns of Change," *The Middle East Journal*, 41:1 (1987), pp. 26–39.

Burton, Anthony, *Urban Terrorism*. New York: Free Press, 1975.

Butt, Gerald, *The Arab World*. Chicago: Dorsey Press, 1987.

Caprini, Michael Delli, and Bruce Williams, "Television and Terrorism: Patterns of Presentation and Occurrence," *The Western Political Quarterly*, 40:1 (1987), pp. 45–64.

Carsten, F. L., *The Rise of Fascism*. Berkeley: University of California Press, 1969.

Celmer, Marc, *Terrorism, U.S. Strategy and Reagan Policies*. New York: Greenwood Press, 1987.

Chafets, Ze'ev, *Double Vision*. New York: William Morrow, 1985.

Chalmers, David M., *Hooded Americanism*. Chicago: Quadrangle Books, 1965.

Christopher, Maura, "Terrorism's Brutal Impact—In Dollars and Cents," *Scholastic Update* (May 16, 1986), p. 23.

Clark, Robert, and Michael Haltzel (eds.), *Spain in the 1980s*. Cambridge, Mass.: Ballinger Books, 1987.

Clark, Robert P., *The Basque Insurgents*. Madison: University of Wisconsin Press, 1984.

———, *The Basques: The Franco Years and Beyond*. Reno, Nev.: University of Nevada Press, 1979.

Cline, Ray, and Yonah Alexander, *Terrorism: The Soviet Connection*. New York: Crane, Russak, 1984.

Cobban, Helena, *The Palestinian Liberation Organization*. Cambridge: Cambridge University Press, 1984.

Cohn, Norman, *The Pursuit of the Millennium*. New York: Oxford University Press, 1970.

Corbett, Michael, *Political Tolerance in America*. New York: Longmann, 1982.

Cordes, Bonnie, et al., *A Conceptual Framework for the Analysis of Terrorist Groups*. Rand/R-3151-SL. Santa Monica, Ca.: The Rand Corporation, 1985.

——— et al., *Trends in International Terrorism*. Rand/R-3183-SL. Santa Monica, Ca.: The Rand Corporation, 1984.

Coser, Lewis, *The Function of Social Conflict*. New York: The Free Press, 1956.

Crelinstein, Ronald D., and Denis Szabo, *Hostage Taking.* Lexington, Mass.: Lexington Books, 1979.

Crelinstein, Ronald D., Danielle Laberge-Altmejd, and Denis Szabo (eds.), *Terrorism and Criminal Justice.* Lexington, Mass.: Lexington Books, 1978.

Crenshaw, Martha, "An Organizational Approach to the Analysis of Political Terrorism." A paper presented at the World Congress of the International Political Science Association, Paris, July 1985.

——, "How Terrorism Ends." A paper presented at the annual meeting of the American Political Science Association, Chicago, September 1987.

—— (ed.), *Terrorism, Legitimacy and Power.* Middletown, Conn.: Wesleyan University Press, 1983.

——, "The Causes of Terrorism," *Comparative Politics,* 13:4 (1981), pp. 379–397.

——, "The Strategic Development of Terrorism." A paper presented at the 1985 annual meeting of the American Political Science Association, New Orleans, August 29–September 1, 1985, p. 9.

Crozier, Brian, *The Rebels.* Boston: Beacon Press, 1960.

Dahl, Robert, *Modern Political Analysis.* 3d ed. Englewood Cliffs, N.J.: Prentice-Hall, Inc., 1976.

Davis, L. J., "Ballad of an American Terrorist," *Harper's* (July 1986), pp. 53–62.

Dawisha, Adeed, *The Arab Radicals.* New York: Council on Foreign Relations, 1986.

Day, Arthur, *East Bank/West Bank.* New York: Council on Foreign Relations, 1986.

Dobson, Christopher, and Ronald Payne, *Counterattack.* New York: Facts on File, 1982.

—— and ——, *The Never Ending War.* New York: Facts on File, 1987.

—— and ——, *The Terrorists.* rev. ed. New York: Facts on File, 1982.

Downs, Anthony, *Inside Bureaucracy.* Boston: Little, Brown and Company, 1966.

Eckstein, Harry (ed.), *Internal War.* New York: The Free Press, 1964.

Edelman, Murray, *The Symbolic Uses of Politics.* Urbana, Ill.: University of Illinois Press, 1967.

Emerson, Thomas, *The System of Free Expression.* New York: Vintage Books, 1970.

Erikson, Erik, *Identity: Youth and Crisis.* New York: W. W. Norton & Company, 1968.

Farrell, William, *The U.S. Government Response to Terrorism.* Boulder, Col.: Westview Press, 1982.

Fauriol, Georges (ed.), *Latin American Insurgencies.* Washington, D.C.: NDU Press, 1985.

Feith, Douglas, "Law in the Service of Terror—The Strange Case of the Additional Protocol," *The National Interest* (Fall 1985), p. 43.

Ferracuti, Franco, "Repentant Terrorist Legislation: A Preliminary Analysis of Problems and Results in Italy." A paper presented at the World Congress of the International Political Science Association, Paris, July 1985.

Feuer, G. Lewis, *The Conflict of Generations.* New York: Basic Books, 1969.

Finn, John, "Public Support for Emergency (Anti-Terrorist) Legislation in Northern Ireland," *Terrorism,* 10:2 (1978), pp. 113–124.

Freedman, Lawrence, and Yonah Alexander (eds.), *Perspectives on Terrorism.* Wilmington, Del.: Scholarly Resources, 1983.

Friedlander, Robert (ed.), *Terrorism: Documents of International and Local Control,* vol. 1. Dobbs Ferry, N.Y.: Oceana Publications, 1979.

Friedman, Thomas, "Poll in West Bank Finds Palestinians Favor Arafat," *The New York Times,* Sept. 9, 1986, sec. 1, p. 6.

Gal-Or, Noemi, *International Cooperation to Suppress Terrorism.* New York: St. Martin's Press, 1985.

Gallo, Max, *Spain Under Franco.* New York: E. P. Dutton and Co., Inc., 1974.

Gallup, George (ed.), *The Gallup International Public Opinions Polls: Great Britain,* vol. 2. New York: Random House, 1975.

Gallup Report, The, 204 (September 1982), p. 28.

Gallup Report, The, 247 (April 1986), p. 12.

Gillespie, Richard, *Soldiers of Perón.* Oxford: Clarendon Press, 1982.

Goren, Roberta, *The Soviet Union and Terrorism.* London: George Allen & Unwin, Ltd., 1984.

Graber, Doris, *Mass Media and American Politics.* 2d ed. Washington, D.C.: Congressional Quarterly, 1984.

—— (ed.), *Media Power in Politics.* 2d ed. Washington, D.C.: Congressional Quarterly, 1984.

Graham, Hugh, and Ted Robert Gurr (eds.), *Violence in America.* New York: New American Library, 1969.

Greene, Thomas H., *Comparative Revolutionary Movements*. Englewood Cliffs, N.J.: Prentice-Hall, Inc., 1974.

Gurr, Ted, "The Role of the State in Political Violence." A paper prepared for presentation at the World Congress of the International Political Science Association, Paris, July 1986.

Hacker, Frederick, *Crusaders, Criminals, Crazies*. New York: W. W. Norton & Company, 1976.

Halperin, Ernest, *Terrorism in Latin America.* Beverly Hills, Ca.: Sage Publications, 1976.

Hans, Rogger, and Eugen Weber (eds.), *The European Right.* Berkeley: University of California Press, 1966.

Harkabi, Yehoshafat, *The Bar Kokhba Syndrome.* Chappaqua, N.Y.: Russel Books, 1983.

Hastings, Elizabeth, and Philip Hastings (eds.), *Index to International Public Opinions 1978–1979.* Westport, Conn.: Greenwood Press, 1980.

—— and —— (eds.), *Index to International Public Opinions 1979–1980.* Westport, Conn.: Greenwood Press, 1980.

Hermann, Margaret (ed.), *Political Psychology.* San Francisco: Jossey-Bass, 1986.

Hersh, Seymour, "Target Quaddafi," *The New York Times Magazine* (Feb. 22, 1987), pp. 16–26.

Herz, Martin (ed.), *Diplomats and Terrorists: What Works, What Doesn't.* Washington, D.C.: Institute for the Study of Diplomacy, 1982.

Hewitt, Christopher, *The Effectiveness of Anti-Terrorist Policies.* New York: University Press of America, 1984.

Hill, Christopher, *The World Turned Upside Down.* New York: Viking Press, 1972.

Hoffman, Bruce, *Right-Wing Terrorism in Europe.* Rand/N-1856-AF. Santa Monica, Ca.: The Rand Corporation, 1982.

Horowitz, Irving Louis, "Can Democracy Cope with Terrorism?" *The Civil Liberties Review* (May/June 1977), pp. 29–37.

Hoskin, Gary, "Colombia's Political Crisis," *Current History* (January 1988), pp. 9–12, 38–39.

Huff, C. R., and I. L. Barak (eds.), *The Mad, the Bad and the Different.* Lexington, Mass.: Lexington Books, 1981.

Hutchinson, Martha Crenshaw, *Revolutionary Terrorism.* Stanford, Ca.: Hoover Institution, 1978.

Janis, Irving, *Victims of Groupthink.* Boston: Houghton Mifflin Company, 1972.

Janke, Peter, and Richard Sim, *Guerrilla and Terrorist Organizations: A World Directory and Bibliography.* New York: The Macmillan Company, 1983.

Jenkins, Brian, *Future Course of International Terrorism.* Rand/P-7139. Santa Monica, Ca.: The Rand Corporation, 1985.

———, *Future Trends in International Terrorism.* Rand/P-7176. Santa Monica, Ca.: The Rand Corporation, 1985.

———, *International Terrorism: The Other World War.* Rand/R-3302-AF. Santa Monica, Ca.: The Rand Corporation, 1985.

——— (ed.), *Terrorism and Personal Protection.* Boston: Butterworth Publishers, 1985.

Joll, James, *The Anarchists.* Cambridge: Harvard University Press, 1980.

Kellen, Konrad, *Terrorists—What Are They Like?* Rand/N-1300-SL. Santa Monica, Ca.: The Rand Corporation, 1979.

Kidder, Rushworth, "State-Sponsored Terrorism," *Christian Science Monitor* (May 14, 1986), pp. 11–24.

Klare, Michael, and Peter Kornbluh (eds.), *Low Intensity Warfare.* New York: Pergamon Press, 1982.

Kohl, James, and John Litt, *Urban Guerrilla Warfare in Latin America.* Cambridge: MIT Press, 1974.

Kupperman, Robert, and Darrell Trent (eds.), *Terrorism: Threat, Reality, Response.* Stanford, Ca.: Hoover Institution Press, 1979.

Laqueur, Walter, *The Age of Terrorism.* rev. ed. Boston: Little, Brown and Company, 1987.

———, *Guerrilla: A Historical and Critical Study.* Boston: Little, Brown and Company, 1976.

———, "Reflections on Terrorism," *Foreign Affairs* (Fall 1986), pp. 86–100.

———, *Terrorism.* Boston: Little, Brown and Company, 1977.

———, *The Terrorism Reader.* New York: New American Library, 1978.

Lee, Alfred McClung, *Terrorism in Northern Ireland.* New York: General Hall, 1983.

Lee, Martin, and Kevin Coogan, "Killers on the Right," *Mother Jones,* 13:4 (1987), pp. 45–54.

Lenczowski, George, *The Middle East in World Affairs.* 4th ed. Ithaca, N.Y.: Cornell University Press, 1982.

Leventhal, Paul, and Yonah Alexander (eds.), *Nuclear Terrorism: Defining the Threat.* Washington, D.C.: Pergamon-Brassey's, 1986.

—— and —— (eds.), *Preventing Nuclear Terrorism.* Washington, D.C.: Pergamon-Brassey's, 1987.

Lewis, Bernard, *The Assassins: A Radical Sect in Islam.* New York: Oxford University Press, 1967.

Lipset, Seymour, and Philip Altbach (eds.), *Students in Revolt.* Boston: Beacon Press, 1969.

Livingstone, Neil, and Terrell Arnold (eds.), *Fighting Back: Winning the War against Terrorism.* Lexington: Lexington Books, 1986.

Lodge, Juliet (ed.), *Terrorism: A Challenge to the State.* New York: St. Martin's Press, 1981.

—— (ed.), *The Threat of Terrorism.* Boulder, Col.: Westview Press, 1988.

Lord, Franklin, *Political Murder.* Cambridge, Mass.: Harvard University Press, 1985.

Markham, James, "Europe's Anti-Terrorism Tied to U.S. Libya Raids," *The New York Times,* Apr. 14, 1987, sec. 1, p. 8.

Martin, David, and John Walcott, *Best Laid Plans.* New York: Harper & Row, Publishers, Inc., 1958.

Maurois, Andre, *A History of France.* New York: Minerva Press, 1968.

Melman, Yossi, *The Master Terrorist: The True Story of Abu Nidal.* New York: Avon Books, 1987.

Merari, Ariel, "Classification of Terrorist Groups," *Terrorism,* 1 (1978), pp. 331–346.

—— (ed.), *On Terrorism and Combating Terrorism.* Frederick, Md.: University Publications of America, 1985.

Merkl, Peter (ed.), *Political Violence and Terror.* Berkeley: University of California Press, 1986.

Metz, Steven, "The Ideology of Terrorist Foreign Policies in Libya and South Africa," *Conflict,* 7:4 (1987), pp. 379–402.

Mickolus, Edward, *Transnational Terrorism: A Chronology of Events 1968–1979.* Westport, Conn.: Greenwood Press, 1980.

Milburn, Michael, Brian Cistuli, and Marjorie Garr, "Survey and Experimental Studies of the Effect of Television News on Individuals' Attributions about Terrorism." A paper presented at the Annual Scientific Meeting of the International Society of Political Psychology, New York, July 1–5, 1988.

Miller, Abraham (ed.), *Terrorism, the Media and the Law.* Dobbs Ferry, N.Y.: Transnational Publishers, 1982.

——, *Terrorist and Hostage Negotiations.* Boulder, Col.: Westview Press, 1980.

Miller, Judith, "The Istanbul Synagogue Massacre," *The New York Times Magazine* (Apr. 14, 1987), pp. 14–52.

Mommsen, Wolfgang, and Gerhard Hirschfeld (eds.), *Social Protest, Violence and Terror in Nineteenth and Twentieth Century Europe.* New York: St. Martin's Press, 1982.

Moore, John Norton (ed.), *The Arab-Israeli Conflict.* Princeton, N.J.: Princeton University Press, 1977.

Muhlberger, Detlef (ed.), *The Social Basis of European Fascist Movements.* London: Croom Helm, 1987.

Nanes, Allan, "Congressional Developments," *Terrorism,* 9:2 (1987), pp. 207–213.

National Foreign Assessment Center, *Patterns of International Terrorism: 1980.* PA81-10163U. Washington, D.C.: U.S. Government Printing Office, 1981.

Netanyahu, Benjamin (ed.), *International Terrorism: Challenge and Response.* Jerusalem: The Jonathan Institute, 1980.

—— (ed.), *Terrorism: How the West Can Win.* New York: Farrar, Straus, Giroux, 1986.

Nimmo, Dan, and Charles Bonjean (eds.), *Political Attitudes and Public Opinion.* New York: David McKay, 1972.

"Northern Ireland: Brotherly Hate," *The Economist* (June 25, 1988), pp. 19–22.

Oakley, Robert, "International Terrorism," *Foreign Affairs,* 65:3 (1987), pp. 611–629.

O'Brien, Connor Cruise, "Bloody Business," *The New Republic* (Dec. 2, 1985), p. 36.

——, *The Siege.* New York: Simon and Schuster, 1986.

Ochberg, Frank, and David Soskis (eds.), *Victims of Terrorism.* Boulder, Col.: Westview Press, 1982.

Oots, Kent Lane, *A Political Organization Approach to Transnational Terrorism.* New York: Greenwood Press, 1986.

O'Toole, Kathleen, "Talking Terrorism," *Campus Report* (Feb. 10, 1988), p. 11.

Pacifici, Robin Erica Wagner, *The Moro Morality Play.* Chicago: University of Chicago Press, 1986.

Parry, Albert, *Terrorism from Robespierre to Arafat.* New York: Vanguard Press, 1976.

Pearl, Marc, "Terrorism—Historical Perspectives on U.S. Congressional Action," *Terrorism,* 10:2 (1987), pp. 139–140.

Porzecanski, Arturo, *Uruguay Tupamaros.* New York: Praeger Publishers, 1973.

Possony, Stefan, "Giangiacomo Feltrinelli: The Millionaire Dinamitero," *Terrorism,* 2:3 (1979), pp. 213–230.

Post, Jerrold, "Group and Organizational Dynamics of Political Terrorism." A paper presented at the Annual Scientific Meeting of the International Society of Political Psychology, Amsterdam, July 1986.

Public Report of the Vice President's Task Force on Combating Terrorism. Washington, D.C.: U.S. Government Printing Office, February 1986.

Pushkarev, Sergei, *The Emergence of Modern Russia.* New York: Holt, Rinehart and Winston, 1963.

Quandt, William, et al., *The Politics of Palestinian Nationalism.* Berkeley: University of California Press, 1973.

Rapoport, David C., "Fear and Trembling: Terrorism in Three Religious Traditions." *The American Political Science Review,* 3:78 (1984), pp. 658–677.

—— and Yonah Alexander (eds.), *The Morality of Terrorism: Religious and Secular Justifications.* New York: Pergamon Press, 1983.

"Revolution, Reform and Subversion in West European Countries," *World Opinion Update,* 2:5 (1978), pp. 114–117.

Richelson, Jeffrey, *The U.S. Intelligence Community.* Cambridge, Mass.: Ballinger Books, 1985.

Ross, Jeffrey Ian, and Ted Gurr, "Why Terrorism Subsides: A Comparative Study of Trends in Terrorism in Canada and the United States." A paper presented at the annual meeting of the American Political Science Association, Chicago, September 1987.

Rubenstein, Richard E., *Alchemists of Revolution.* New York: Basic Books, 1987.

Rustow, Dankwart, *Turkey: America's Forgotten Ally.* New York: Council on Foreign Relations, 1987.

Safran, Nadav, *Israel: The Embattled Ally.* Cambridge, Mass.: Harvard University Press, 1978.

Sanford, Nevitt, and Craig Comstock (eds.), *Sanctions for Evil.* San Francisco: Jossey-Bass, 1971.

Sayari, Sabri, *Generational Changes in Terrorist Movements: The Turkish Case.* Rand/P.7124. Santa Monica, Ca.: The Rand Corporation, 1985.

Schmid, Alex, *Political Terrorism: A Research Guide to Concepts, Theories, Data Bases and Literature.* New Brunswick, N.J.: Transaction Books, 1983.

——— and Janny de Graaf, *Violence as Communication.* Beverly Hills, Ca.: Sage Publications, 1982.

Seidel, Gill, *The Holocaust Denial.* Leeds: Beyond the Pale Collective, 1986.

Sheehan, Thomas, "Italy: Terror on the Right," *The New York Review of Books,* 27:21 (1981), pp. 23–26.

Shipler, David, *Arab and Jew: Wounded Spirits in a Promised Land.* New York: Penguin Books, 1986.

———, "One Year after U.S. Raid, A Lower Libyan Profile," *The New York Times,* Apr. 12, 1987, sec. 1, p. 14.

Silj, Allesandro, *Never Again without a Rifle.* New York: Karz Publishers, 1979.

Singular, Stephen, *Talked to Death.* New York: Simon and Schuster, 1987.

Slann, Martin, and Bernard Schechterman (eds.), *Multidimensional Terrorism.* Boulder, Col.: Lynne Rienner, 1987.

Smith, Colin, *Carlos: Portrait of a Terrorist.* New York: Holt, Rinehart and Winston, 1976.

Sofaer, Abraham, "Terrorism and the Law," *Foreign Affairs* (Fall 1986), pp. 919–920.

Spiegel, Steven, Mark Heller, and Jacob Goldberg (eds.), *The Soviet-American Competition in the Middle East.* Lexington, Mass.: D. C. Heath and Company, 1988.

Spotts, Frederick, and Theodore Wieser, *Italy: A Difficult Democracy.* New York: Cambridge University Press, 1986.

Sterling, Claire, *The Terror Network.* New York: Holt, Rinehart and Winston, 1981.

———, *The Time of the Assassins.* New York: Holt, Rinehart and Winston, 1983.

Stohl, Michael (ed.), *The Politics of Terrorism.* New York: Marcel Dekker, 1983.

Stohl, Michael, and George Lopez (eds.), *The State as Terrorist.* Westport, Conn.: Greenwood Press, 1984.

Sugar, Peter (ed.), *Native Fascism in the Successor States, 1918–1945.* Santa Barbara, Ca.: ABC-Clio, 1971.

Taleghani, Ayatollah, *Society and Economics in Islam.* Tehran: n.d.

Talmon, J. L., *The Origins of Totalitarian Democracy.* New York: Frederick A. Praeger, 1960.

Thackrah, John, *Encyclopedia of Terrorism and Political Violence.* New York: Routledge and Kegan Paul, 1987.

United States Department of State, *Iran's Use of International Terrorism.* Special Report 170. Washington, D.C.: U.S. Government Printing Office, 1987.

——, *Patterns of Global Terrorism: 1984.* Washington, D.C.: U.S. Government Printing Office, 1985.

——, *Patterns of Global Terrorism: 1985.* Washington, D.C.: U.S. Government Printing Office, 1986.

——, *Patterns of Global Terrorism: 1986.* Washington, D.C.: U.S. Government Printing Office, 1988.

Verba, Sidney, *Small Groups and Political Behavior.* Princeton, N.J.: Princeton University Press, 1961.

Walzer, Michael, *Just and Unjust Wars.* New York: Basic Books, 1977.

——, *The Revolution of the Saints.* Cambridge, Mass.: Harvard University Press, 1965.

Wasmund, Klaus, "The Political Socialization of Terrorist Groups in West Germany," *Journal of Political and Military Sociology,* 2:2 (1983), p. 227.

Weinberg, Leonard, "The Radical Right and Varieties of Right-Wing Politics in the United States." A paper presented at the Annual Scientific Meeting of the International Society of Political Psychology, San Francisco, July 1987.

—— and William Eubank, "Italian Women Terrorists," *Terrorism,* 9:3 (1987), pp. 241–262.

—— and ——, "Neo-Fascist and Far Left Terrorists in Italy," *The British Journal of Political Science* (October 1988).

—— and ——, *The Rise and Fall of Italian Terrorism.* Boulder, Col.: Westview Press, 1987.

Wilkinson, Paul, *Terrorism and the Liberal State.* New York: New York University Press, 1979.

—— and Alisdair Stewart (eds.), *Contemporary Research on Terrorism.* Aberdeen: Aberdeen University Press, 1987.

Wilson, James Q., *Political Organizations.* New York: Basic Books, 1973.

"The World's Wars," *The Economist* (Mar. 12–18 1983), p. 19.

Wright, Robin, *Sacred Rage: The Wrath of Militant Islam.* New York: Simon and Schuster, 1986.

Zimmermann, Ekkart, "Terrorist Violence in West Germany: Some Reflections on the Recent Literature." A paper presented at the World Congress of the International Political Science Association, Paris, July 1985.

Index